D1201856

Contents

Introduction

The intention of *The A–Z of Art* is to provide a popular survey of artists and their work from medieval times to the present day. The book takes a familiarly linear approach to the history of art, apart from a few individuals whose work has been generally incorporated into the cultural mainstream. Many of the names that have been included will be recognizable; others will not. Limiting the number to 386 was at times a frustrating task and inevitably we had to exclude some skilled practitioners. While acknowledging the contribution made by artists in previous centuries, and without attempting to deliver a definitive selection, we have included as many living artists as possible. *The A–Z of Art* is therefore an indispensable guide to the visual arts, containing an unparalleled range of work. Art appreciation is by nature compromising and subjective. Rather than be dictated to by the conventions of art history, in many cases we have been guided by personal taste.

In the text we have sought to combine the essential biographical details of each artist with a selective account of their work. The entries are concise and informative, providing the reader with essential knowledge to access the work with sympathy and appreciation. Our aim throughout has been to provide a new approach to art and a point of departure – to excite and inspire those with a limited understanding of art history as well as being a useful reference work for art enthusiasts. The sequential structure promotes an extraordinary juxtaposition of movements, periods, styles and techniques, enabling surprising comparisons between artists and their works.

Choosing one piece to represent each artist was challenging. Each image was chosen either because it is typically representative of a particular artist or because it is a supreme example of the artist's work. The selection is devised to highlight artists working across a broad range of media, from the more traditional means of representation such as painting, drawing, printing and sculpture, to multimedia and installation. Some of the pieces are not easily reproduced and the work is best appreciated in situ, wherever possible. An "Other Masterpieces " category provides two supplementary examples of each artist's work, complemented by a gallery guide and an extensive subject index.

Nicola Hodge and Libby Anson

Agar Eileen

Born Buenos Aires, Argentina 1899; died London, England 1991

The Autobiography of an Embryo *1933–1934; oil on board; 90 x 213.5 cm; Tate Gallery, London, England*

Eileen Agar came to England from Argentina when she was five years old. An independent spirit, she rebelled against her prosperous Victorian upbringing, deciding at an early age that she wanted to be an artist. She was the first woman to join the Surrealist movement and her work featured in the International Surrealist Exhibition, London, 1936. Despite forming long and lasting friendships with her fellow Surrealists, Agar retained a certain distance from them. She used forms of nature to symbolize workings of the unconscious in her paintings and rejected the masculine notion of woman as muse. Her singular imagination was also developed through sculptures and assemblages. After painting **The Autobiography of an Embryo**, Agar was asked how she, who had never had a child, could know anything about it. The artist replied that the girl having the child does not know what is happening inside her, but what was important was to record such extraordinary metamorphosis. The four panels of this large narrative painting are intended to be read from left to right. The circles divide like cells in the process of creation.

OTHER MASTERPIECES Angel of Anarchy; *1936–1940; Tate Collection, London, England*
The Reaper; *1936; Tate Gallery, London, England*

Aitchison Craigie

Born Edinburgh, Scotland 1926

Crucifixion *1987, oil on canvas, 216 x 183 cm, Tate Gallery, London, England*

Craigie Aitchison is a curious phenomenon among painters. He held his first one man show in 1958 and his themes and inimitable style have barely altered since. He seems to have avoided forming an allegiance with any of the major art movements that have gripped Britain since 1945. **Crucifixion** exemplifies the lifelong theme that has informed much of his work. It is a surprisingly large canvas, dark and reverent. Aitchinson's Christ is strangely armless but forms a motif that was logical for the painter: "Everybody knows who he is. He doesn't need arms". The childlike simplicity of this rendition of a potent Christian symbol belies the primitive power of Aitchison's subtlety. Mournfully coloured bands made the minimalist landscape background and infer a depth of field. The hill, like a Calvary, is Goat Fell, a childhood holiday place on the Isle of Arran. The mystical sense of light illuminating the figure, the faithful pose of the dog, the attendant birds and the sparkling star at the centre of the cross are incongruous but appropriate elements contributing to the picture's soul. They form ideas, meanings and associations that strike at the heart of the spectator – whatever his religious beliefs.

OTHER MASTERPIECES Model and Dog, *1974–1975, Tate Collection, London, England*
Nandi Bull in Front of Temple III *1999–2000, Private Collection*

Albers Josef

Born Bottrup, Germany 1888; died New Haven, USA 1976

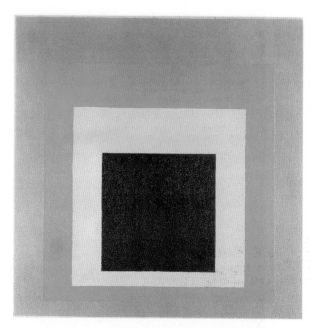

Homage to the Square: Blue Climate *c.1964; oil on board; 76.2 x 76.2 cm; Tate Collection, London, England*

Josef Albers' early academic training in Berlin, Essen and Munich encouraged a formal approach which he later combined with a sense of experimentation developed while studying, and later teaching, at the Bauhaus. During his time in Weimar, Albers worked as a designer of furniture as well as an abstract painter. He refined his abstract style after moving to the USA in 1933, where he also became seduced by colour. In the United States he continued to study and to teach, publishing an influential book on colour theory in 1963. He was regarded as one of the great geometric abstract painters at a time when abstract painting in general had been monopolized by Abstract Expressionists such as Pollock and Rothko. His **Homage to the Square** series of paintings exemplify his cool detached approach to pictorial composition. In **Homage to the Square: Blue Climate** each square hovers on top of the other – there is no chaotic competition between colours, rather a gentle and peaceful receptivity. Through the application of successive different layers of pure colour, Albers manages to create the optical illusion of depth in his work.

OTHER MASTERPIECES Homage to the Square: Apparition; *1959 Guggenheim Museum, New York City, USA* **Skyscrapers**; *1927; Mr and Mrs James H Clark, Dallas, Texas, USA*

Alma-Tadema Sir Lawrence

Born Drontyp, Netherlands 1836; died Wiesbaden, Germany 1912

A Favourite Custom
*1909; oil on wood; 66 x
45.1 cm; Tate Collection,
London, England*

After training at the
Antwerp Academy,
Lawrence Alma-Tadema
became a pupil of Baron
Hendryk Leys, a historical
genre painter. From Leys,
Alma-Tadema absorbed a
feeling for the realistic
rendering of surfaces. In
1863 Alma-Tadema
visited Italy where the
ruins of Pompeii made a
particularly lasting
impression. Another
civilization was opened to
him through a visit to
Egypt in 1902. In 1870,
he settled in England
where his Neoclassical
paintings of ancient
civilizations were very
popular in Victorian
society. He built up a
large collection of personal sketches and photographs of archaeological items, jewellery and
ornaments to aid his re-creation of the domestic genre of the ancient world. A meticulous
worker, he took great care in the application of his paint and eschewed the use of glaze and
varnish. He also reversed the customary method by working from lighter to darker colours on a
white ground. This resulted in a remarkable freshness and intensity of colour, which can be
seen in **A Favourite Custom**. The painting also displays Alma-Tadema's extraordinary skill at
depicting substances, in particular water and marble.

OTHER MASTERPIECES The Roses of Heliogabalus; *1888; Private Collection*
The Finding of Moses; *1904; Private Collection*

Altdorfer Albrecht

Born Regensburg, Germany c.1480; died Regensburg, Germany c.1538

Landscape at Regensburg
*c.1520—1530; painting on
wood; 30.5 x 22.2 cm;
Alte Pinakothek, Munich,
Germany*

Albrecht Altdorfer held
important social positions
as architect and councillor
in his native city of
Regensburg, Bavaria. As a
painter he developed a
series of works in which
landscape predominated.
Almost unheard of in its
time, he painted scenes that rarely contained human figures. His earliest paintings show the
influence of Cranach and Dürer. A trip to the Danube and the Austrian Alps in 1511 produced
oil paintings as well as drawings and etchings in which the dramatic possibilities of the
landscape were acutely observed by the artist. **Landscape at Regensburg** is a typical work,
with its sweeping vista swamped by a mass of forest foliage. A luminous sky with gathering
clouds helps to create an atmosphere of unease. This is not the tamed and domesticated
landscape scene observed by most artists prior to the fifteenth century. Altdorfer has given us a
glimpse of the wilder side of nature, and as the critic Kenneth Clark observed, in some of
Altdorfer's landscapes we have the feeling "that the world has been newly created".

OTHER MASTERPIECES St George; *1511; Alte Pinakothek, Munich, Germany*
Battle of Arbela; *1529; Alte Pinakothek, Munich, Germany*

André Carl

Born Quincy, USA 1935

144 Magnesium 119, 1969 *1969; metal; 365.8 x 365.8 cm; Tate Collection, London, England*

Carl André is the sculptor of the notorious floorpiece, **Equivalent VIII**, popularly known as **The Bricks**, in the Tate collection in London, England. Epitomizing the reductive Minimalist art movement, the work gave prominence to André among the American Minimalists working during the 1960s and 1970s. André attended the Phillips Academy in Andover (1951–1953)). On his subsequent visit to Europe, his interest in neolithic sites compounded his admiration for the sculpture of Constantin Brancusi. In the late 1950s, André was introduced to artist Frank Stella who became a close friend, André using his studio to make his work. In keeping with the minimal aesthetic, André explored the notion of negative space by cutting into his sculpture. **Last Ladder**, 1959, was a response to Brancusi's **Endless Column**. He began exhibiting in 1964, and in 1965 he formulated the integration of modular units into a grid structure when, according to writer David Bourdon, "He realized his sculpture had to be as level as water". **144 Magnesium 119, 1969**, one of six versions made in different metals, conforms to this criterion. It becomes part of the environment over which we can walk. It negates any anthropomorphic associations, common in the consideration of "conventional" sculpture.

OTHER MASTERPIECES Last Ladder, *1959, Tate Collection, London, England*
Equivalent VIII, *1966, Tate Collection, London, England*

Andrea del Sarto

Born Florence, Italy 1486; died Florence, Italy 1530

Madonna delle Arpie
*c.1515; tempera on wood;
208 x 178 cm; Galleria degli
Uffizi, Florence, Italy*

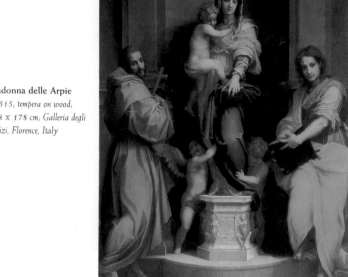

A pupil of Piero di Cosimo, Andrea del Sarto's feeling for tone and colour was more characteristic of the Venetian than the Florentine school. Known because of his excellent draughtsmanship skills as "the faultless painter", Andrea's carefully composed work, mainly fresco paintings, was much admired and studied. At first sight, **Madonna delle Arpie** is typical of the High Renaissance in its balanced composition and grand manner. Closer inspection, however, reveals an underlying tension due to the precariousness of the Madonna's position. She just manages to hold on to the climbing child, the painter's rendition of which is a startlingly naturalistic observation for the time. A soft light pervades this and many other works by the artist, helping to model and sculpt the human forms. Andrea was invited by the French king, Francis I to Paris in 1518 but broke his contract to return to Florence the following year. Never quite living up to his earlier promise, Andrea del Sarto's work was nonetheless of great importance to the development of Florentine painting. His life and work were celebrated in the nineteenth century by the English poet Robert Browning.

OTHER MASTERPIECES Assumption of the Virgin; *1526; Palazzo Pitti, Florence, Italy*
Maddona del Sacco; *1525; San Annunziata Church, Florence, Italy*

Andrews Michael

Born Norwich, England 1922; died London, England 1995

The Deer Park *1962, oil on canvas; 214 x 244.5 cm; Tate Collection, London, England*

Michael Andrews studied at the Slade School of Art in London under Sir William Coldstream from 1949 until 1953 when he received the Rome Scholarship in painting. After graduating, Andrews taught in a number of key art schools in the capital and has been categorized within a group of artists, termed by R.B. Kitaj in 1976 as the School of London. The connection between them was their "dedication to the human form". From 1975, Andrews made regular trips to Scotland. The rough, Glenartney landscape and grounds of Drummond Castle provided his subjects and the backdrop to his ideas. He left London for Norfolk in 1977, not returning to living in London until 1992. A second major landscape series resulted from his experience of Ayers Rock, Australia in 1983. Andrews's association with other London artists, such as Bacon, Freud, Auerbach and Kossoff, is reinforced by his paintings of The Colony Room, a club in Soho that was frequented by these artists and their acquaintances. In a similar spirit, **The Deer Park** recalls the revellers featured in Norman Mailer's novel of the same name. It is a dream-like, disjointed image that Andrews produced at a pace. His later work is less painterly, mimicking screenprinted, photographic and collaged imagery.

OTHER MASTERPIECES Good and Bad at Games (Tripitych); *1964–1968; Australian National Gallery, Canberra, Australia* **The Blue and Yellow of the Yacht Club**; *1969; Whitworth Art Gallery, Manchester, England*

Angelico Fra

Born Vicchio di Mugelio, Italy, c.1387–1400; died Rome, Italy 1455

Noli Me Tangere
c.1442; fresco; 177 x 139 cm; Museo di San Marco dell' Angelico, Florence, Italy

Fra Angelico was a Dominican friar in the monastery at Fiesole. The convent of San Marco was taken over by his Order in 1436, and he was commissioned to decorate the friars' cells with frescoes painted directly on to wet plaster walls. These were intended to stimulate prayer and meditation rather than to be a factual record of the Biblical story. He wanted to represent the sacredness of Christ in all its glory and simplicity; although he understood the principles of perspective, as seen here in the rendition of the tomb door, these were often sacrificed for a simple style. In the nineteenth century Angelico's paintings captured the imagination of the Pre-Raphaelites, who saw in them the charm of a pure faith. In this fresco, Christ appears to Mary Magdalene. She has been weeping after discovering that his tomb is empty. A figure appears. At first she mistakes him for a gardener as he is carrying a hoe. Suddenly realizing who it is, she goes to embrace him. But he moves away, telling her not to touch him – literally "**Noli Me Tangere**".

OTHER MASTERPIECES Linaiuoli Madonna; *commissioned 1433; Museo di San Marco, Florence, Italy* Christ Glorified in the Court of Heaven; *c.1435, National Gallery, London, England*

Anguissola Sofonisba

Born Cremona, Italy c.1527; died Palermo, Italy c.1625

Three Sisters Playing Chess *1555; oil on canvas; 70 x 94 cm; Museum Narodowe, Poznan, Poland*

The best-known female artist of the sixteenth century, Sofonisba Anguissola was born into a noble Italian family. Her mother died young, leaving her wealthy husband with five talented daughters. Unusually, this liberal father gave his daughters a full classical education, which included learning to paint. It was this enlightened attitude that enable Anguissola to earn her own living as a portrait painter in the Spanish court and helped her to transcend the constraints of her class and gender. In **Three Sisters Playing Chess** Anguissola breaks with tradition by concentrating on those scenes or models available to her. Placing her sisters in a domestic setting gives the portrait an immediacy, which allowed the contemporary Italian art historian Vasari to attribute to her the development of the conversational portrait, as opposed to the formal frontal or profile portrait. Although there are undoubtedly technical faults with the composition, particularly the perspective, each of the sisters comes across as a well-realized individual. Their relationship to each other is rendered with a tenderness and informality.

OTHER MASTERPIECES Self-Portrait; *1561; Collection of Earl Spencer, Althorp, England*
Portrait of a Young Nobleman; *early 1560s; Walters Art Gallery, Baltimore, USA*

Antonello da Messina

Born Messina, Italy, c.1430; died Messina, Italy c.1479

Portrait of a Young Man
c.1475; oil on canvas;
35.6 x 25.4 cm; National
Gallery, London, England

Antonello da Messina was a Sicilian, the only major southern Italian painter of the fifteenth century. He was greatly influenced by various aspects of the work of the Flemish painters, particularly their attention to detail and the play of light on surfaces. Although there is no evidence to suggest that he actually visited Flanders, he probably came across the work of artists from the Netherlands while working in Naples. In 1475 he went to Venice, where he passed on to Giovanni Bellini the oil painting technique that he had learnt from masters such as van Eyck. This knowledge was communicated in turn to many other contemporary painters, significantly influencing the future development of the Venetian school. Generally, the figures in Antonello's work are bathed in strong light, highlighting their features and every tuck and fold of their robes. **Portrait of a Young Man** displays this virtuoso technique, giving the painting its intense realism. Other works, such as **St Jerome in his Study**, with its sweeping perspective on to a far distant landscape, show his ability to render a complex architectural construction.

OTHER MASTERPIECES St Sebastian; *c.1475; Gemäldegalerie, Dresden, Germany*
St Jerome in his Study; *c.1445–1446; National Gallery, London, England*

Atkinson Terry

Born Thurnscoe, England 1939

Bunker in Armagh. 17 *1985; pastel on black paper; 120.5 x 151 cm; Collection of the Artist*

Terry Atkinson has an established reputation as a painter, lecturer, writer and activist whose radical artistic methods and theoretical views have made him a prominent figure in the Conceptual Art movement in Britain. He studied in 1959 at Barnsley School of Art and at the Slade School of Art in London from 1960–64. Atkinson's art is most clearly identified by his involvement from 1968 with Art & Language, of which he was a founding member with Michael Baldwin, Harold Hurrell and David Bainbridge. Based on Marxist theory and Wittgensteinian philosophy and working as a corporate identity, their strategies for production were textually based examinations of art's role in society and the critical arena. Their work, encouraged and influenced by American artist Joseph Kosuth, aimed to make clear "that art is didactic as opposed to transcendental". Atkinson left the group in 1975 and has since concentrated on writing and series of paintings that incorporate personal, political and historical elements. **Daughter having returned from an armed mission being greeted by her mother near a Christmas wreath**, the full title of **Bunker in Armagh. 17**, is one of a number of works based on British attitudes to Northern Ireland. "The whole idea of the bunker," he said, "was a metaphor for my own fixed positions."

OTHER MASTERPIECES The Stone-Touchers 1; *1984–1985; Gimpel Fils Gallery, London, England* Distemper Yellow Axe-Head Enola Gay Mute; *1990; Norwich Gallery, Norwich, England*

Auerbach Frank

Born Berlin, Germany 1931

Euston Steps – study *1980–1981; oil on hardboard; 122.6 x 152.7 cm; Arts Council Collection, London, England*

Frank Auerbach was sent to England from Germany in 1939, never to see his immediate family again. In 1947, he became a British citizen and moved to London. From 1948–1952 he studied at St Martin's School of Art in London and at the Borough Polytechnic under David Bomberg whose teaching, he recalled, instilled, "an atmosphere of research and of radicalism that was extremely stimulating". Auerbach trained at the Royal College of Art in London from 1952–1955. Since 1954, Auerbach has worked in the same studio in Primrose Hill, London. He includes in his subjects his immediate environment, **Euston Steps**, for example, and the people close to him. In spite, or because of, this narrow range, his work has an intensity that is the result of numerous reworkings and the application of successive layers of charcoal or impasto, each a fresh attempt at perception. Sculpting the souls rather than the visual realities of his subjects, the raw physicality of the paint is like clay under his direction. Somewhere within the thick, sensual pigment, the material substance of the original subject, and the painting as an object, is obscured; a presence becomes tangible above all.

OTHER MASTERPIECES Head of E.O.W.V.; *1961; Private Collection, on loan to Tate Collection, London, England* **Park Village East–Winter**; *1998–99; National Museum & Gallery, Cardiff, Wales*

Avercamp Hendrick

Born Amsterdam, Netherlands 1585; died Amsterdam, Netherlands 1634

Winter Landscape with a Frozen River and Figures *c. 1620; oil on canvas; 103 x 164 cm; Harold Samuel Collection, Corporation of London, England*

Hendrick Avercamp was a Dutch landscape painter who worked in Kampen. He concentrated on minutely rendering the details of wintry landscapes animated by crowds of tiny figures and played a significant part in the development of realistic landscape tones and colours. He lent naturalism to scenes with deep recession, hitherto divided into fantasy colours by the late sixteenth-century Flemish school. His work is often compared with contemporary Jan Bruegel because of the similarity of subject matter. His paintings, such as **Winter Landscape with a Frozen River and Figures**, provide a fascinating insight into the social activities of the seventeenth century in the Netherlands. Avercamp brings to life a whole town or community by showing them engaged in a range of pursuits in the wintry conditions. Some are enjoying themselves tobogganing, or skating on the frozen river, others work, conveying their goods by sledge or horse. Many simply stand around and chat. The light in this work is typically carefully observed. His nephew, Barent Avercamp was his pupil and imitator.

OTHER MASTERPIECES Frozen River; *c. 1625; Boymans-Van Beuningen Museum, Rotterdam, Netherlands* **A Scene of the Ice near a Town**; *c. 1615; National Gallery, London, England*

Ayres Gillian

Born London, England 1930

Woodbines of Sweet Honey *1984; oil on canvas; 600 x 120 cm; Collection of the Artist*

At the age of fourteen, Gillian Ayres made the decision to become a painter. She studied at London's Camberwell School of Art from 1946–1950 and exhibited her work the following year in the Young Contemporaries exhibition. Her strength, from her years as a student, has been her determination to resist the teaching she received, emphasizing a systematic approach to figuration. Instead, she has consistently followed her intuitive and freely expressed method of working in an abstract style. Her interest in artistic developments of the post-war period in Europe were personified via her contact with the painter Roger Hilton. The exciting explorations and working methods of the American Abstract Expressionists, most notably Jackson Pollock, inspired her to reject the conventional techniques of easel painting. An influential teacher and example to younger artists, Ayres has worked on both large-scale and small-scale works, changing from acrylic to oil paint in 1978. **Woodbines of Sweet Honey** reveals Ayres's skill for managing her medium and adapting her compositional structure to the unusual shape of the support. Her colours remain clear and gestural brushwork distinct, despite the range of pigment and depth of impasto.

OTHER MASTERPIECES Break-Off; *1961; Tate Collection, London, England* **At This Stage**; *2001; UK Government Art Collection, London, England*

Bacon Francis

Born Dublin, Ireland 1909; died Madrid, Spain 1992

Triptych *1972; oil on canvas; 198 x 147 cm (each panel); Tate Collection, London, England*

Born of English parents, Francis Bacon came to London from Dublin in 1925. He established himself as a furniture designer and interior decorator. In 1929, on his return to London – after travelling to Berlin and Paris from 1927–1928 – he began painting. He was declared unfit for military service in 1943 and in 1944, after destroying his earlier works, produced the painting with which he declared his career as an artist began. The painting, a triptych, **Three Studies for Figures at the Base of a Crucifixion**, provided a format and subject that was to recur in Bacon's oeuvre, as shown by **Triptych**, completed nearly thirty years later. He settled in London in 1950. Despite having no formal art training, Bacon exploited the artistic achievements of the past, particularly those of Velasquez and Rembrandt, to formulate his art. The innovation of Eadweard Muybridge's photographs of figures in motion also had a profound effect on his work and the human cry was an emotive subject he investigated to startling effect. Bacon's technical abilities have produced some of the most powerfully disturbing and controversial images of twentieth-century European painting.

OTHER MASTERPIECES Study from the Human Body – Figure in Movement; *1982; Marlborough Fine Art, London, England* **Pope II**; *1951; Kunsthalle, Mannheim, Germany*

Balla Giacomo

Born Turin, Italy 1871; died Rome, Italy 1958

Girl Running on the Balcony *1912; oil on canvas; 125 x 125 cm; Collection Galleria Civica d'Arte Moderna, Milan, Italy*

Italian painter Giacomo Balla was one of the founders of Futurism, signing the Futurist manifesto which was published in 1910. In this document Balla, along with artists including Umberto Boccioni and Carlo Carrá, outlined their primary objective to depict movement, which they saw as symbolic of their commitment to the dynamic forward thrust of the twentieth century. Futurism celebrated the machine – the racing car was heralded as the triumph of the age – and early Futurist paintings were concerned with capturing figures and objects in motion. In **Girl Running on the Balcony**, Balla attempts to realize movement by showing the girl's running legs in repeated sequence. Other paintings, such as **Dog on a Leash**, got to grips with the problem of recreating speed and flight by superimposing several images on top of each other. Inevitably, the advances that were made by this short-lived movement were eventually to be overtaken by the art of cinematography. Futurism was finished soon after the start of the First World War, after which Futurist ideals became increasingly associated with Fascism. Balla began to plough an independent path in his work, at first toward abstraction and, after 1931, toward figuration.

OTHER MASTERPIECES Automobile and Noise; *1912; Collection Peggy Guggenheim, Venice, Italy* **Dog on a Leash**; *1912; Museum of Modern Art, New York City, USA*

26

Balthus Balthazar Klossowski de Rola

Born Paris, France 1908; died Switzerland, 1997

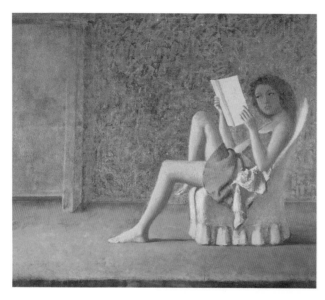

Katia Reading *1968–1976; oil on canvas; 179 x 211 cm; Private Collection*

Balthus looked to the Austro-German poet Rainer Maria Rilke, a friend of his mother's, for paternal and cultural influence. Balthus's lover of children's literature and illustrations persisted into his adult life. He was a precocious artistic talent and his lifelong interest in the art of the Orient was also initiated at an early age. He came into contact with Japanese and Chinese prints via the interest shown in him by the painter Bonnard after Balthus moved to Paris in 1924. He favoured working in an impressionistic manner copying from old masters, in particular Poussin, Masaccio and Piero della Francesca, rather than receive direct tuition. Images of sexuality and intimacy, particularly of adolescent girls, recur. **The Guitar Lesson**, 1934, set the tone for the preoccupations with developed in his art. Undertones of the erotic and of violence pervade curiously theatrical, contrived settings. In 1943 Balthus moved to Switzerland. Living privately and in seclusion Balthus re-invented his technique many times. **Katie Reading** seems to have been produced in an age quite distant from our own. It reveals the strangely naive, chalky quality of his work which, during the 1970s, showed an increased interest in light and decoration.

OTHER MASTERPIECES The Living Room; *1941–3; Minneapolis Institute of Arts, Minneapolis, USA* Le Lever; *1955; Scottish National Gallery of Modern Art, Edinburgh, Scotland*

Bartolommeo Fra

Born Florence, Italy c.1472; died Florence, Italy, c.1517

Madonna and Child
*c.1540; fresco; Museo di
San Marco dell'Angelico,
Florence, Italy*

Fra Bartolommeo studied to be a painter in Florence before his interest in mysticism allowed
him to become influenced by the charismatic and fiery Dominican priest Savonarola. In 1500,
after Savonarola was burnt as a heretic, Bartolommeo became a monk, entering the monastery
of San Marco where he resumed painting in 1504. Bartolommeo's friendship with Raphael and
visits to Rome and Venice helped strengthen his careful compositions and enrich his palette. In
Madonna and Child the circular composition focuses the attention on the relationship
between mother and son. Bartolommeo eliminates unnecessary details – the Madonna is
wearing a plain cloak – and this simplification helps give the work its note of religious intimacy.
It is for this particular contribution that Bartolommeo is so well regarded. He was painting at a
time when Raphael, Michelangelo and Leonardo had already made their presence felt. This was
hardly an auspicious time for any artist and, in his early forties, Bartolommeo was so
overwhelmed when he saw Michelangelo and Raphael's work in the Vatican that he refused to
take part in any artistic creation there himself.

OTHER MASTERPIECES Pieta; *c.1511–1512; Palazzo Pitti, Florence, Italy*
The Virgin Adoring the Child with St Joseph; *c.1500; National Gallery, London, England*

Bastien-Lepage Jules

Born Damvillers, France 1848; died Paris, France 1884

The Haymakers *1877; 180 x 195 cm; Musée du Louvre, Paris, France*

The sentimentality of Bastien-Lepage's most famous works such as **The Haymakers** made him popular with his contemporaries and the public, and it is thought he may have influenced artistic styles in England and France during his lifetime. He is best remembered for his scenes of rural life and the portraits – among his sitters was Sarah Bernhardt – that he exhibited during the 1870s, and although he died young he made enough of an impact on the art world to be compared with Millet and have the French writer Emile Zola write about the measure of influence and popularity of his work. His paintings are now exhibited in many of the major art institutions around the world and are still very much in evidence throughout his native land. **The Haymakers** is generally regarded as his masterpiece, and the craft of his painting is beautifully executed in this wonderfully observed rural scene. The influence of the Barbizon school may be detected, but this realism was a perfect deflection to the Impressionist revolution, which was to part with tradition after Bastien-Lepage's death.

OTHER MASTERPIECES Sarah Bernhardt, *1879; Musée Fabre, Montpellier, France*
Joan of Arc, *1879; Metropolitan Museum of Art, New York City, USA*

Beardsley Aubrey Vincent

Born Brighton, England 1872; died Menton, France 1898

ISOLDE

Isolde *1895; pen, ink and watercolour; 28 x 17.7 cm; Fogg Art Museum, Harvard University, Massachusetts, USA*

In the 1890s the decorative style of Art Nouveau was identified as the new expression for design and experimentation with materials, not only in the fine and applied arts but in architecture too. Aubrey Beardsley was a prodigious talent whose striking black and white illustrations owe their sophistication and economy of means to the impression made on him by Japanese art and by Whistler. Working as an insurance clerk he was originally encouraged to draw by Pre-Raphaelite artist Burne-Jones in 1891, but he did not achieve fame with his inimitable style until 1894, exemplified by **Isolde**. The publications of his controversial illustrations for Oscar Wilde's *Salome* and the first volume of *The Yellow Book* confirmed his skill for originality in mustering the grotesque and the ornamental with refined and economic draughtsmanship. The suggestion of depravity that pervades these deceptively elegant works echoes the decadence and fin-de-siècle atmosphere of the time and Beardsley has long been recognized as a leading figure in the Aesthetic movement of this period.

OTHER MASTERPIECES The Eyes of Herod; *1893; Fogg Art Museum, Harvard University, Massachusetts, USA* **Self-Portrait**; *c.1892; British Museum, London, England*

Beckmann Max

Born Leipzig, Germany 1884; died New York City, USA 1950

Quappi with Parrot *1936; oil on canvas; 110.5 x 65.5 cm; Stadtisches Museum, Mülheim an der Ruhr, Germany*

An outsider who never subscribed to any particular school, Max Beckmann is nevertheless regarded as one of this century's greatest figurative painters. During his service in the First World War, Beckmann suffered a nervous breakdown. After being dismissed as a "degenerate artist" by the Nazis from a teaching post, Beckmann left Germany in 1937 to settle in Amsterdam. From this point on he resolved to put what he saw as the individual's tragic fight against evil at the centre his work. Initially he concen᾽ ᷈ed on graphics, producing a la number of prints and woo ᷈ts, before reverting to paint ᷈e artist's hard-edged, exp᷈ ᷈ionistic still lifes, portraits, lar ᷈apes and figure compositions ᷈ w upon everyday life as we᷈ mythical scenes for inspiration. Beckmann's metaphorical paintings with their claustropho᷈ ᷈nteriors, mutilated figures, monstrous birds and fish are a critique of modern urban s᷈ ᷈y and an attempt to find some spiritual meaning within it. **Quappi with Parrot**, a portr᷈ ᷈of his second wife, Mathilde, was painted in the 1930s, and shows characteristic᷈ ᷈ong modelling of form. In 1947 Beckmann moved to the United States where for the last ᷈e years of his life he experienced a new vitality and optimism.

OTHER᷈ ᷈STERPIECES Portrait of Heinrich George and his Family; *1935; Nationalg᷈ e, Berlin, Germany* **The Theatre Box**; *1928; Staatsgalerie Stuttgart, Germany*

Bell Vanessa

Born London, England 1879; died Charleston, England 1961

The Tub *1917; oil on canvas; 180.3 x 164.4 cm; Tate Collection, London, England*

Vanessa Bell was a student at the Royal Academy between 1901 and 1904, where she was taught by John Singer Sargent. She became part of the intellectual circle known as the Bloomsbury Group, which included her sister, the writer Virginia Woolf, her husband Clive Bell and fellow artist Duncan Grant. Bell left her husband for Grant and the pair then settled at Charleston in East Sussex. This old country house is full of paintings and decorations by the couple. Both artists were called upon by Roger Fry to design and decorate furniture, fabric and pottery for the Omega Workshops. Vanessa Bell was overwhelmed by the seminal Post-Impressionist exhibition of 1910, remarking that it was as if, "one might say things one had always felt instead of trying to say things that other people told one to feel". Her work developed a Post-Impressionist style between 1912 and 1918, making for a new informality in her portraits and using arbitrary configurations as the basis for her large paintings. **The Tub** is a simplified, unusual and striking composition which has a monumentality due to the use of an upright, near life-size figure.

OTHER MASTERPIECES A Conversation; *1913–1916 Courtauld Institute, London, England*
Mrs St John Hutchinson; *1915; Tate Collection, London, England*

Bellany John

Born Port Seton, Scotland 1942

The Bride, the Oyster and the Singing Red Fish
*1985; oil on canvas;
122 x 122 cm;
Beaux-Arts Collection,
London, England*

John Bellany attended Edinburgh College of Art, moving to London in 1965 to study at the Royal College of Art. The underlying themes of his painting have remained consistent throughout his artistic career. From his earliest work he has portrayed the environment of his youth in potent images of fishermen, the sea and the myths and characters populating the tight-knit community of the harbour. His Calvanistic upbringing imbues his art with a reverence for religious belief, which is narrated via compositions that speak of mortality and of good and evil. Following years of self-destruction in the 1970s, revealed in paintings full of angst, Bellany survived a liver transplant operation in 1988. Subsequent work reveals a renewed zest and vitality. It celebrates a spiritual, physical and artistic rebirth in vibrant watercolours, glowing canvases and lyrical etchings and drawings. Allegorical diptychs and triptychs recur in Bellany's more recent work, which reflects the artist's voyage through life. These visual metaphors are "odysseys" conveyed in rich, poetic, visual language. **The Bride, the Oyster and the Singing Red Fish** typifies Bellany's subject matter, skilled painterly techniques and the debt he owes to the stylistic influence of Max Beckmann.

OTHER MASTERPIECES Celtic Feast; *1974; Sheffield City Art Galleries, Sheffield, England*
Lovers by the Sea; *1993; Flowers East Gallery, London, England*

Bellini Gentile

Born Venice, Italy c. 1429; died Venice, Italy c. 1507

Procession in Piazza San Marco *1496; oil on canvas; 367 x 745 cm; Galleria dell'Accademia, Venice, Italy*

Gentile Bellini was highly honoured during his lifetime in Venice. He enjoyed the position of the town's official painter, was made a Knight of the Empire in 1469 and was the court painter to the Turkish ruler Sultan Mahomet II in Constantinople. He is now probably best known for his large-scale narrative paintings, commissioned as decorations for the Scuole – powerful charitable clubs of the time. These pictures are a minutely detailed record of the building, costumes, decoration and personalities of fifteenth-century Venice. Indeed, his reputation for accuracy is such that the depiction of the Byzantine mosaics on the front of San Marco church in this painting is used as the basis for most discussion of the originals, which were subsequently destroyed. In **Procession in Piazza San Marco**, members of the Scuole of San Giovanni Evangelista are represented in the foreground, in their white habits. They are participating in the procession of the Holy Cross in St Mark's Square, Venice, on April 25, 1444, while the women watch from the windows. During the procession, a merchant threw himself to the ground in front of the Cross to pray for his dying son; miraculously, the boy recovered from his illness immediately afterward.

OTHER MASTERPIECES The Miracle of the Cross; *c. 1500; Galleria dell'Accademia, Venice, Italy* The Healing of Pietro Dei Ludovici; *c. 1501; Galleria dell'Accademia, Venice, Italy*

Bellini Giovanni

Born Venice, Italy c.1430; died Venice, Italy 1516

Doge Leonardo Loredan
*c.1501–1504; tempera on
wood; 61 x 44.5 cm;
National Gallery, London,
England*

Brother of Gentile and
son of Jacopo, Giovanni
was probably the greatest
of the Bellini dynasty. He
was the pre-eminent
teacher of his generation,
with a sizeable workshop
staffed by pupils and
assistants, among whom
were Giorgione and
Titian. Like his brother,
he became chief painter
to the State, although
Titian tried desperately to
usurp him. In 1506, when
Giovanni was 76, Dürer
wrote that he was "very
old but still the best in
painting". Here Bellini
portrays the elected ruler of Venice, the **Doge Leonardo Loredan**. In this style of portraiture
Bellini was strongly influenced by a characteristic Flemish attention to detail and texture, and
especially the play of light on the surface of the subject. The Doge is exquisitely portrayed in
his ceremonial robes, made in an old-fashioned style but from a newly imported material –
damask – which has gold thread running through it. Instead of using gold leaf for the thread,
Bellini paints the surface roughly so as to catch the light and give a metallic finish – a
revolutionary technique at the time.

OTHER MASTERPIECES The Madonna of the Meadow; *c.1500–1505; National Gallery,
London, England* **The Agony in the Garden**; *c.1465; National Gallery, London, England*

Bernini Gianlorenzo

Born Naples, Italy 1598; died Rome, Italy 1680

Ecstasy of Saint Theresa *c. 1650;*
white marble; lifesize; Santa Maria
della Vittoria, Rome, Italy

Bernini was a sculptor,
painter and architect
and a formative influence as an
outstanding exponent of the Italian
Baroque. He was an exceptional portrait
artist and owes to his father his
accomplished techniques in the handling
of marble and also an impressive list of
patrons that included the Borghese and the
Barbarini families. Bernini originally worked in the late Mannerist tradition but rejected the
contrived tendencies of this style. By 1624 he had adopted an expression that was passionate
and full of emotional and psychological energy. His figures are caught in a transient moment
from a single viewpoint, bursting into the spectator's space. In 1644 such interpretation reached
maturity in his rendition of the vision and **Ecstasy of Saint Theresa**. The Spanish nun swoons
in heavenly rapture at the point of an angel's arrow. The work is a prime example of Bernini's
vision of a decorative whole combining different materials and colours within an architectural
space. A succession of powerful patrons in Rome and in Paris assured his reputation as an
entrepreneurial artist who captured the spirit of the Counter-Reformation. His extreme and
intense characterizations have fallen in and out of favour but his Baroque legacy remains intact.

OTHER MASTERPIECES Bronze Bust of Pope Gregory XV; *1622; Museo Civioco, Bologna,*
Italy **Neptune and Triton**; *1620; Victoria and Albert Museum, London, England*

Beuys Joseph

Born Krefeld, Germany 1921; died Düsseldorf, Germany 1986

The End of the Twentieth Century 1983–1985; basalt, clay and felt; Tate Collection, London, England

Joseph Beuys is credited with being one of the most influential figures in twentieth-century European art. He was certainly the first significant artist to come out of post-war Germany. Not a sculptor in the conventional sense, he strove to communicate an "expanded theory of sculpture". In 1943, he was saved from death by Tartars when, as a pilot, he was shot down over the Crimea. They wrapped him in felt and fat and revived him with honey and horse's milk. This now mythical story underlies many of Beuys's conceptual strategies. Materials and objects of symbolic significance are juxtaposed, or a performance is created to present artifice as a metaphor for life and survival. **The End of the Twentieth Century**, one of Beuys's last, large-scale installations, comprises thirty-one blocks of basalt rock, each one bearing a deliberately inflicted "wound" re-filled with rock, clay and felt. Beuys revolutionized artistic thinking with his oft-quoted axioms, "Everybody is an artist", being the most familiar. Beuys meant that humans are creative beings, in art, science or procreation. His work is sophisticated, if somewhat obscure. However, his enigmatic persona and philosophies, at once personal and universal, made him a charismatic mentor.

OTHER MASTERPIECES Fat Battery; *1963; Tate Collection, London, England*
Felt Suit; *1970; Tate Collection, London, England*

Bingham George Caleb

Born Virginia, USA 1811; died Kansas City, Missouri, USA 1879

Raftsmen Playing Cards *1847; oil on canvas; 71 x 96.5 cm; St Louis Art Museum, Missouri, USA*

George Caleb Bingham had a technical facility for painting that he developed over a remarkably short space of time. After only a few months training at the Pennsylvania Academy of Fine Arts, he travelled to Europe and around the United States before settling in Missouri. In the 1830s Bingham was producing rather wooden portraits but, by 1845, his style had developed to such an extent that his work was unrecognizable. **Raftsmen Playing Cards** is typical of the dreamy lyricism of Bingham's mature work. With these paintings of North American frontier life, often of views of the Missouri river, Bingham focuses on everyday scenes. In an age when the camera was not widely available, Bingham provides an interesting insight into his fellow citizens in Missouri and their way of life. In 1856 he followed in the footsteps of a number of other American artists, choosing Düsseldorf as a place to study. Unfortunately, on returning home, his style deteriorated due to an adoption of a dry academic technique. Eventually, Bingham moved into politics.

OTHER MASTERPIECES Fur Traders Descending the Missouri; *1845; Metropolitan Museum of Art, New York City, USA* The County Election; *c.1851; St Louis Art Museum, Missouri, USA*

Blake Sir Peter

Born Dartford, Kent, England 1932

Self-Portrait with Badges
1961; oil on hardboard;
172.7 x 120.6 cm; Tate
Collection, London, England

Peter Blake received a first-class diploma from the Royal College of Art, London in 1956. He is considered one of the leading Pop Artists of his generation. Blake's appropriation of popular culture within his oeuvre extends to his incorporation of real ephemera in his painted constructions. He is known for focusing on popular icons – The Beatles, Marilyn Monroe and Elvis Presley – and wrestling heroes with names such as Irish Lord X, and Masked Zebra Kid. The pin-up girl was also a recurring subject, sometimes disguised as Tarzan's Jane, Ophelia or Titania. In these, using photographic sources, Blake exploits his technical dexterity, relishing his ability to mimic the translucency of young skin and moist lips with paint. The results make covetable items. Blake's work centres on nostalgia and the structure of his assemblages, collages and paintings suggests the kaleidoscopic nature of recollections jumbled in the mind, heightened by fantasy, clarified by sensuous detail. In the early to mid-1970s, Blake produced a collection of souvenir pieces for friends, real and imagined. His skill at portraiture is shown in **Self-Portrait with Badges**, a tentative interpretation of himself as a forlorn figure, covered in symbols of his interests. He was knighted in 2002.

OTHER MASTERPIECES The Toy Shop; *1962; Tate Collection, London, England*
Tarzan, Jane, Boy and Cheetah; *1966; Galerie Meyer-Ellinger, Frankfurt, Germany*

Blake William

Born London, England 1757; died London, England 1827

The River of Life *c. 1805; pen and watercolour on paper; 305 x 336 cm; Tate Collection, London, England*

William Blake was a poet, illustrator, engraver, draughtsman, writer and painter whose efforts, due to their idiosyncratic and unorthodox nature, were largely unappreciated in his own lifetime. The knowledge Blake gained from working as an engraver enabled him to produce his own work in which he surrounded one of his poems with his own hand-coloured illustration. A powerful imagination is evident in every aspect of Blake's work. Among his most important works are the **Illustrations of the Book of Job** (1825), and the hundred or so watercolours for Dante's *Divine Comedy*. **The River of Life** is a clear, bright watercolour in which Blake imagines the stream described in the Revelation of St John winding its way through paradise. A deeply mystical man, Blake claimed he had visionary experiences that prompted him to invent his own belief system in which the creator of the universe, whom he renamed Urizen, wrought vengeance on mankind through Jesus, renamed Orc. His social and political conscience railed against the prevailing academic painting of the eighteenth century. He saw it as representing all that he came to despise about the rational, materialistic age in which he found himself.

OTHER MASTERPIECES The Ancient of Days; *1794; British Museum, London, England*
Pity; *1795; Tate Collection, London, England*

Böcklin Arnold

Born Basel, Switzerland 1827; died San Domenico, Italy 1901

Island of the Dead *1886; oil on wood; 80 x 50 cm; Museum of Art, Leipzig, Germany*

With Ferdinand Hodler, Arnold Böcklin was a leading Swiss painter during the nineteenth century. He trained extensively in Germany, Paris and Flanders, spending a period in Rome between 1850 and 1857. Apart from being in Munich from 1871 to 1874, he remained in Italy until his death. Böcklin's emphatic idealism, heightened with romantic and symbolic overtones, was to prove influential to a number of artists, including Max Klinger and Franz von Stuck. Stylistically, the Modernist camp opposed the near naturalistic interpretation of landscape, nymphs and satyrs. Böcklin's treatment of his subject matter was critically received by the German Impressionists. In 1905, their principal supporter, Meier-Graefe, declared that in relation to reality, Böcklin's paintings were irrelevant, fanciful and technically, "wrong". Böcklin made several versions of **Island of the Dead**. It has a monumentality and grandeur reminiscent of German painter Caspar David Friedrich's sublime landscapes. The enigmatic, morbid theatricality of the scene and the mysterious shrouded figure that, by implication, could represent the viewer's future, would have appealed to the European fin-de-siecle decadents.

OTHER MASTERPIECES Pan in the Reeds; *1857 Neue Pinakothek, Munich, Germany*
Triton and Nereid; *1873–1874; Kunstmuseum, Basel, Switzerland*

Boltanski Christian

Born Paris, France 1944

Reserve of the Dead Swiss *1990; tin boxes and newsprint; Centre Julio Gonzalez, Valencia, Spain*

The resonant, emotional power of Christian Boltanski's work is largely based on the association that the viewer brings to his installations. Our propensity to keep traces – clothes, documents and memorabilia – of the people who have affected our lives, long after their death, forms the investigative basis of Boltanski's work. The poverty of Boltanski's materials is linked to Arte Povera: notions of survival and social experience that stem from concepts explored by Joseph Beuys. Autobiographical connotations, indicative of the artist's Jewish-Catholic upbringing, often emerge. **Reserve of the Dead Swiss** typically uses numerous photographic portraits of people whom the spectator knows to be dead. Mounted on stacks of rusted tin containers, the wall they create appears like a mass memorial at a crematorium. The nature of the images, often taken from the Second World War period, instils a fear that here are archival pictures from the Holocaust. This fantasy is heightened by the sense of interrogation implied by the intensity of the lights directed from above. These obscure, rather than clarify, individual faces. What we cannot know about the lives of those displayed we fabricate in our imagination, as if the whole history of each were contained in the boxes we witness.

OTHER MASTERPIECES Invitation to Image Model (**Model Image**); *1976; Galerie Sonnabend, Paris, France* **Hotel Chase (Altar to the Chase High School**); *1987; Museum of Contemporary Art, Los Angeles, USA*

Bomberg David

Born Birmingham, England 1890; died London, England 1957

Trees in Sun, Cyprus *1948; oil on canvas; 63.9 x 76.5 cm; Tate Collection, London, England*

During the first phase of his career, David Bomberg produced large canvases typical of the geometric and angular compositions prevalent at the beginning of the twentieth century. The Cubist paintings of Braque and Picasso were clearly influential, as well as the ideals of dynamism promoted by the Futurist movement. After a brief flirtation with Vorticism, a British art movement founded by Wyndham Lewis and developed in reaction to Cubism and Futurism, Bomberg went on to form the London Group in 1913. A group dedicated solely to mounting exhibitions, it nevertheless became identified in the 1950s with a new school of English painting known as the social realists, or "Kitchen Sink" painters. In the 1920s Bomberg started to make representational paintings, such as the Palestine paintings (1923–1927) and these, with other later works, including **Trees in Sun, Cyprus,** moved toward a more expressionistic style, with their loose, lively brushwork and strong colours. Toward the end of his career and after having sealed his reputation as an important artist, though it was to soar after his death, David Bomberg taught for eight years in London.

OTHER MASTERPIECES In the Hold; *1913–1914; Tate Collection, London, England*
The Mud Bath; *1914; Tate Collection, London, England*

Bonheur Rosa Frances

Born Bordeaux, France 1822; died near Fontainebleau, France 1899

Ploughing in the Nivernais *1849; oil on canvas; 173 x 260 cm; Musé Nationale du Chateau de Fontainebleau, France*

Despite painting in a genre completely dominated by male artists, Rosa Bonheur developed into an extremely successful and well regarded landscape and animal painter. Bonheur's mother died young. Left to her own devices in a household where her father was also a painter, she had space and time to realize her artistic potential. Important also to the development of her practice was a radical political outlook – a utopian socialism which legitimised her activities as a woman and as an artist. Close anatomical studies of animals, whether on the dissecting table or at work in the fields, inspired her strong drawing. Conventional ideas of decency and decorum dictated that her visits to the Paris horse market, for example, were generally made in disguise. However, Rosa Bonheur enjoyed dressing as a man and spent most of her time in men's clothes. A prototype feminist, she once declared that the only males who attracted her were the bulls she painted. Her energetic and unsentimental painting **Ploughing in the Nivernais** was her first major success; a later work, **The Horse Fair** was the largest animal painting ever to have been produced.

OTHER MASTERPIECES The Horse Fair; *1853; Metropolitan Museum of Art, New York City, USA* Gathering for the Hunt; *1856; Pioneer Museum, Stockton, USA*

Bonnard Pierre

Born Fontenay-aux-Roses, France 1867; died Le Cannet, France 1947

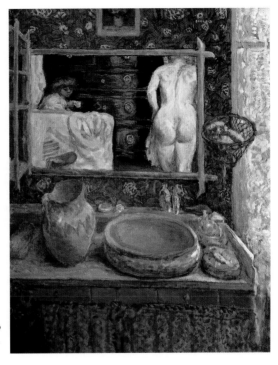

Mirror on the Washstand 1908; oil on canvas, 120 x 97 cm; Pushkin Museum, Moscow, Russia

Pierre Bonnard came to Paris in 1888 where he studied at the Academie Julien and the Ecole des Beaux-Arts. He met Denis, Vuillard and others who, influenced by Gauguin's expressive use of colour and pattern, formed a group called the *Nabis*, from a Hebrew word meaning prophets. He exhibited and was associated with the group until 1899. Representational modelling and perspective were rejected in favour of decoration and flat, rhythmical description of form. This was inspired by Art Nouveau and the current vogue for Japanese prints. He admired the exuberance and passion in the work of van Gogh and in 1903, in support of artistic developments of similar intensity, he co-founded the Salon d'Automne, organized by the Fauves. What he learnt from these artists he subtly absorbed within his own refined, intimate paintings of interiors. **Mirror on the Washstand** reveals Bonnard contemplating a typical domestic subject. Bathed in the southern light of Le Cannet, where he worked from 1926, stands Marthe, his wife, whom he often used as his model. Although the spirit of the work is cognisant of the achievements of Impressionism he constructed a shimmering recollection rather than a direct record of his subject.

OTHER MASTERPIECES The Table; 1925; Tate Collection, London, England
Nude in a Bathroom; 1932; Collection of Mrs Wolfgang Schoenborn, New York City, USA

Bosch Hieronymous

Born Hertogenbosch, Netherlands c.1450; died Hertogenbosch 1516

The Garden of Earthly Delights
c.1504; oil on panel 220 x 195 cm; Museo del Prado, Madrid, Spain

Heironymous Bosch produced some of the most inventive fantasy paintings that have ever existed. His obsessive and nightmarish vision has its antecedents in the Gothic twilight world of the late Middle Ages and, although the allegorical medieval world view is now lost, there have been many recent attempts to "read" his pictures, not least by those who have attempted to interpret Bosch by dream analysis. **The Garden of Earthly Delights** demonstrates Bosch's dazzling ability to build up a hugely detailed landscape through a series of bizarre exaggerations and distortions. The complete work consists of four paintings on a series of folding panels; the outer panel reveals the **Third Day of Creation** when closed. Inside, **The Garden of Earthly Delights** is flanked on the left by the **Garden of Eden** and on the right by **Hell**. A wild sexual orgy features in the central panel, where lust is shown to be the cause of man's downfall. There are over a thousand figures in this work altogether. Standing alone in its lifetime, Bosch's work has a timeless and modern quality that greatly endeared him to Surrealists in the twentieth century.

OTHER MASTERPIECES Hell *(Right Wing Of A Triptych): c.1510; Museo del Prado, Madrid, Spain* **Last Judgement**, *1504; Akademie der Bildenden Kunste, Vienna, Austria*

Botticelli Sandro

Born Florence, Italy, c.1445; died Florence, Italy 1510

Venus and Mars *1483; oil on canvas; 69 x 173.5 cm; National Gallery, London, England*

Botticelli initially trained as a goldsmith and then probably became a pupil of Filippo Lippi. When he was aged about 30 he began to enjoy the patronage of the Medici family, for whom he painted his best-known mythological works, **Primavera** and the **Birth of Venus**. In **Venus and Mars**, Botticelli playfully portrays Mars, the God of War, utterly vanquished by Venus, the Goddess of Love and Beauty. At the time of painting there was much ribald entertainment in poetry about men's exhaustion after sexual activity. The canvas could have formed the back of a chest or bench that was put in the bedroom on the occasion of a wedding – this may account for its unusual shape. Botticelli paints his subjects with marble-like skin and harsh lines, which correspond with the Florentine obsession with sculpture, but he softens this with curly hair and delicate material. He combines archaic figures with contemporary artefacts – modern armour and costume – and alludes to his patrons, the Vespucci family, with the wasps (*vespe* in Italian) buzzing around Mars' head.

OTHER MASTERPIECES The Birth of Venus; *1485; Galleria degli Uffizi, Florence, Italy*
Mystic Nativity; *1500; National Gallery, London, England*

Boucher François

Born Paris, France 1703; died Paris, France 1770

Woman at her Toilet *1769; oil on canvas; 102 x 80 cm; Agnew & Sons, London, England*

The son of a Parisian painter and lace designer, François Boucher began his career engraving the pictures of Antoine Watteau. After winning the Prix de Rome of the Academy, Boucher spent four years in Italy where he could indulge his love of Italian Rococo painting, in particular the work of Tiepolo. In 1765, restored to Paris, he obtained the patronage of Louis XV's mistress Madame de Pompadour and through her influence became the king's official court painter. In work that unashamedly pandered to the frivolous and hedonistic excesses of the Parisian aristocracy, Boucher's highly decorative paintings delight in revealing the luxuriousness of the costumes and the elegance of the surroundings. **Woman at her Toilet** is one of his more intimate portraits, in which the artist's concern is with capturing the delicate surface details. In his many variations of pastoral and mythological themes, Boucher focuses on the female body. Much in demand in their time, these erotic paintings uncover fleshy and voluptuous women in a variety of provocative poses. Boucher was also highly regarded as a decorator and designed interiors, tapestries, theatrical productions, porcelain and even slippers.

OTHER MASTERPIECES Madame de Pompadour *1759; Wallace Collection, London, England*
Reclining Girl; *1752; Alte Pinakothek, Munich, Germany*

Boudin Eugène

Born Hornfleur, France 1824; died Deauville, France 1898

The Beach *1867; oil on canvas, 41 x 64 cm; Christie's, London, England*

Born into a seafaring family, Eugène Boudin is mostly known for his paintings of sea and sky. Although often described as the "the painter of beaches", the beach itself in his painting **The Beach** only occupies the bottom third of the canvas and it is the large, luminous sky that predominates in the work. Boudin worked directly from nature on the Normandy coast and in particular at the fashionable resorts of Deauville and Trouville. His seascapes and beach scenes were painted at many different times of the year and in a variety of changing weather conditions. Boudin was responsible for introducing Claude Monet to this method of painting outdoors, Monet returning the compliment by painting the beach at Trouville several years later. Boudin's overriding concern was light, and in his dabs of pure colour and loose and delicate brushwork, he prefigured Impressionism, making the link between Corot and the Impressionists. Indicative of the esteem in which he was held by the Impressionists, Boudin was included in their first exhibition in 1874.

OTHER MASTERPIECES The Beach at Trouville; *1898; Musée d'Orsay, Paris, France*
The Beach at Trouville; *1863; Phillips Collection, Washington DC, USA*

Bourgeois Louise

Born Paris, France 1911

Cumul I *1969; white marble; 56.5 x 127 x 121.9 cm; Beaubourg Museum, France*

Louise Bourgeois completed two years' art training in Paris before moving to the USA in 1938. Her early work was two-dimensional; she began to make sculpture in the late 1940s. Since her early, painted wooden constructions, she has used a range of materials, including bronze, marble and latex, producing work that appears abstract but highly suggestive of the body and of its sexual implications. The idea for the **Cumul** series came to her when she flew over the Sahara desert and noticed, "little huts nestling together near water – a metaphor of loneliness and togetherness". Taking the name from cumulus clouds, Bourgeois worked on the series obsessively. **Cumul I** is a marble piece that, through its amorphous form and budding shapes, emphasises physicality and the human need to touch and be touched. Bourgeois experienced an unhappy childhood and her work often seeks to address primal notions of intimacy, loss and separation. She has also created installations known as **Red Rooms**, which correspond to the emotionally fraught spaces that she inhabited in her own childhood. Bourgeois's work was long neglected; it is only since the 1980s that she has received the attention she deserves as one of the most significant sculptors of her time.

OTHER MASTERPIECES One and Others; *1955; Whitney Museum of American Art, New York City, USA* **Spider**; *1997; Kemper Museum of Contemporary Art, Kansas City, Missouri, USA*

Bouts Dieric

Born Haarlem, Netherlands c.1415; died Louvain, Belgium 1475

The Last Supper
1464; triptych, tempera on wood; 88.5 x 71.5 cm (sides) 180 x 150 cm (middle); Saint Peters, Louvain, Belgium

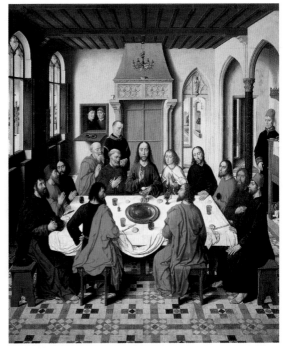

It is likely that Dieric Bouts trained in Brussels and Bruges and in both cities would have seen works by Jan van Eyck and Rogier van der Weyden. He was also friendly with Petrus Christus. Records show that he married into a prominent and wealthy family from Louvain, where he made his home. **The Last Supper** is a fine example of clearly delineated perspective, one of Bouts's defining characteristics; it has its focal point above Christ's head. Although this evinces a strong Italian influence, the style and setting are very much northern. The sober colours, gawky, bony figures and the dour faces could not be further from the classical ideal of beauty that was taking root in Italy at this time. It was a Flemish custom to have dinner guests seated round all sides of the table, and for them to use the tablecloth to wipe their mouths on, hence the swathes of material. The interior space is utterly plausible, an effect heightened by the landscape visible through the windows and the trompe l'oeil in the background; this could be a double-portrait on the far wall, or two figures peering through a hatch.

OTHER MASTERPIECES The Entombment; *c.1450–1460; National Gallery, London, England*
Portrait of a Young Man; *1462, National Gallery, London, England*

Boyce Sonia

Born London, England 1962

Missionary Position II *1985; watercolour, pastel and crayon on paper; 123 x 183 cm; Tate Collection, London, England*

Sonia Boyce's family comes from the Caribbean. Growing up in Britain, in a culture in which her family are immigrants, has been a formative influence on her art. Her work, as can be seen in **Missionary Position II** discusses the issues raised by life experienced from such a perspective. Boyce graduated from Stourbridge College in 1983. As a black woman artist operating in white, male-dominated, British society, gender, familial and racial relationships have overtly influenced her work. Using her art as a political activity, she and other women artists – such as Lubaina Himid, Sutapa Biswas and Claudette Johnson – have sought recognition not only for their own practice but for the work of all black artists working in Britain. To make her concerns about the "Disabling categories of race" more specific, she referenced her family and herself in large-scale drawings. These date from the mid 1980s and illustrate a particular narrative that belongs within her personal, cultural history. Experimentation with surface design and colour as conventional pictorial devices developed into work with collage, sculpture, photocopying, video and installations.

OTHER MASTERPIECES From Tarzan to Rambo...; *1987; Tate Collection, London, England*
Do You Want To Touch?; *1993; Centre 181 Gallery, London, England*

Boyd Arthur

Born Murrumbeena, Australia 1920; died Melbourne, Australia 1999

Shearers Playing for a Bride *1957–1958; oil on canvas; 149.9 x 175.3 cm; Gift of Tristan Buesst, National Gallery of Victoria, Melbourne, Australia*

Arthur Boyd described his childhood, although spent in poverty, as idyllic. He began painting at an early age, sketching at every opportunity. Seeing a van Gogh postcard and an early Kokoschka painting as a child proved of lasting influence, particularly to his expressive handling of paint and colour. In 1937, a meeting with painter Jo Bergner, a Polish immigrant, brought to Boyd's awareness a different culture beyond the insular society of his own. During Boyd's time in the army, beginning in 1940, his work became more politically oriented and some of it was confiscated by officials. After he left the army, Boyd embarked on religious paintings, finding inspiration in prints by Bosch and Bruegel and paintings by Stanley Spencer, combined with the imagery of South Melbourne. Between 1952–1955, he experimented with an abstract mode that provided a complete contrast to the series of paintings, of which **Shearers Playing for a Bride** is one, based on the Aborigines. Boyd signed the Antipodean Manifesto in 1959, declaring his support for a "National Realism". He moved to England in the same year, subsequently splitting his time between England and Australia. His later paintings included mythological themes, as well as reconsidering his past inside of landscape imagery.

OTHER MASTERPIECES The Mockers; *1945; Art Gallery of New South Wales, Australia*
Persecuted Lovers; *1957; Art Gallery of South Australia, Australia*

Brancusi Constantin

Born Hobitza, Romania 1876; died Paris, France 1957

Sleeping Muse I *1909; white marble; 17.8 x 27.9 x 20.3 cm; The Hirshhorn Museum and Sculpture Garden, Smithsonian Institution, Gift of Joseph H Hirshhorn, 1966, Washington DC, USA*

Constantin Brancusi was a Romanian sculptor who trained initially as a carpenter and stone mason. He settled in Paris in 1904 where his early influences included African as well as oriental art. Although Rodin was another early influence, Brancusi decided he wished to make much simpler work and began an evolutionary search for pure form. While never entirely rejecting the natural world, Brancusi undoubtedly succeeds in conveying a sense of gravity by reducing his work to a few basic elements. Paradoxically, this process also tends to highlight the complexity of thought that has gone into its making. Witness the studied serenity and distilled eroticism of **Sleeping Muse I**, for example. In contrast to his many polished works in marble and bronze are his roughly hewn works in wood. Brancusi did much to encourage a revival of carving and great respect for an artist's materials. During his later years, he polished the surface of his earlier works. Monumental, subtle and intimate, Brancusi's sculptures are rightly now considered to be the work of a modern master.

OTHER MASTERPIECES Adam and Eve; *1921; Solomon R Guggenheim Museum, New York City, USA* **Princesse X**; *1915–1916; Musée National d'Art Moderne, Paris, France*

Braque Georges

Born Argenteuil-sur-Seine, France 1882; died Paris, France 1963

Guitar and Jug *1927; oil on canvas; 81 x 116.5 cm; Tate Collection, London, England*

Georges Braque developed his painting skills while working for his father, a house decorator. He moved to Paris in 1900 to study where he was drawn to the work of the Fauve artists, including Matisse, Derain and Dufy, as well as to the late landscapes of Cézanne. Meeting Picasso marked a huge turning point in Braque's development and together they evolved as leaders of Cubism. After a brief interlude in which he was called up to fight in the First World War, Braque's style developed in the direction he was to follow for the rest of his life. In establishing the principle that a work of art would be autonomous and not merely imitate nature, Cubism redefined art in the twentieth century. Braque's large compositions incorporated the Cubist aim of representing the world as seen from a number of different viewpoints. He wanted to convey a feeling of being able to move around within the painting. The still life subject remained his chief preoccupation from 1927 to 1955. **Guitar and Jug** is an example of Braque's later introduction of objects derived from observation of the real world into his Cubist framework. Typically, Braque here deploys a narrow range of muted and earthy colours.

OTHER MASTERPIECES The Portuguese; *1911; Kunstmuseum, Basel, Switzerland*
Studio VI; *1952; Galerie Maeght, Paris, France*

Bratby John

Born London, England 1928; died London, England 1992

Still-Life with a Chip Frier
1954; oil on hardboard; 130 x 93 cm; Tate Collection, London, England

John Bratby has a mixed reputation but is popularly known as one of the so-called "Kitchen Sink" School of painters who came to prominence within the British art scene during the 1950s. Bratby trained at the Royal College where he quickly achieved notoriety for painting college dustbins rather than concentrating on traditionally academic subject matter. He achieved early success with his first exhibition in 1954. He won awards in 1956 and 1958 while representing Britain at the Venice Biennale. His work during the 1950s accords with the gritty realism that was prevalent in English literature at the time. In painterly terms this view of the world manifested itself in images of domestic life and tableaux created on table-tops and window ledges with everyday items. Bratby's thick paint, bright colours and apparent disregard for careful draughtsmanship is typified by **Still Life with a Chip Frier**. His style was considered shocking and led to accusations of vulgarity. This seems most appropriate with regard to his latest paintings featuring his second wife, Patti. However, his work has been widely collected and in the 1960s and 1970s he received a number of commissions for portraits of well-known figures.

OTHER MASTERPIECES Window, Self-Portrait, Jean and Hands; *1957; Tate Collection, London, England* **Gloria with Angst**; *1960; Laing Art Gallery, Newcastle-Upon-Tyne, England*

Bronzino Agnolo

Born Florence, Italy 1503; died Florence, Italy 1572

Eleanora Toledo and her Son *c.1550; oil on canvas; 114 x 94 cm; Galleria degli Uffizi, Florence, Italy*

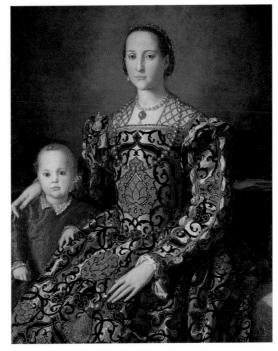

Agnolo Bronzino was the leading court painter of the Florentine school in the middle of the sixteenth century. A Mannerist, Bronzino was a pupil of Jacopo Pontormo, with whom he worked on frescoes. Continuing his master's interest in light, Bronzino developed a rich feeling for colour: his paintings are distinguished by a sudden burst of raspberry-red or icy-blue. His allegorical and religious works reveal an unprecedented interest in the female form. Unwilling to give his subjects any particular spiritual significance, Bronzino seemed especially drawn to the nude in seductive paintings that maintain a sense of critical detachment. In large allegorical works, such as **Venus, Cupid, Folly and Time**, his pale, elongated nudes pose against a backdrop of symbolic figures and luxurious fabric. As court painter to the first absolute ruler Cosimo de Medici, Bronzino undertook the portrait of his wife and son, **Eleanora Toledo and her Son**. In this work, Bronzino reveals his skills as a draughtsman, brilliantly conveying the rigid hauteur of his aristocratic sitters as well as capturing the detailed patterning of Eleanora's dress.

OTHER MASTERPIECES Venus, Cupid, Folly and Time; *c.1550; National Gallery, London, England* **Guidabaldo Della Rovere**; *1530; Palazzo Pitti, Florence, Italy*

Brown Ford Madox

Born Calais, France 1821; died London, England 1893

The Last of England *1855; oil on wood panel; 82.5 x 75 cm; Birmingham City Museums and Art Gallery, England*

Ford Madox Brown's considerable technical skills were acquired during his training in Antwerp, Paris and Rome. Settling in London in 1845, Brown came into contact with the Pre-Raphaelite Brotherhood but he never joined them. Although he shared the Brotherhood's desire to emulate the sincerity they found in early Renaissance art, Brown's deepening social conscience was a barrier to full acceptance by the group. **The Last of England** shows Brown's keen interest in social issues. Moved by the sight of emigrants leaving England and with Woolner, as the only sculptor to join the Brotherhood, about to depart for Australia, Brown keenly empathized with their plight. He used himself and his second wife as models for the circular composition. Attention is focused on the couple as they reflect upon the fate that they may have in store. The starkness of their situation is further emphasized by the realistic details, such as the ship's nets and rigging. Brown recreated the scene in the open air on dull days "to insure the peculiar look of light all round, which objects have on a dull day at sea".

OTHER MASTERPIECES Work; *1860–1863; City of Manchester Art Gallery, Manchester, England* **An English Autumn Afternoon**; *1825–1854; Birmingham City Museums and Art Gallery, Birmingham, England*

Bruegel Jan

Born Antwerp, Belgium 1568; died Antwerp, Belgium 1625

Still Life of Flowers *1524; oil on canvas; 37 x 27 cm; Museo del Prado, Madrid, Spain*

Jan Bruegel was the son of Pieter Bruegel. He made a prolonged visit to Italy in 1590 during which Cardinal Frederigo Borromeo became his patron. In 1595 he travelled with his patron to Milan where the Cardinal was appointed Archbishop. In 1596 Bruegel returned to Antwerp. He was a highly accomplished painter who drew inspiration from flower, landscape and Garden of Eden subjects. His landscapes were different from his father's, the younger man specializing in small wooded scenes, featuring an array of animals and mythological figures. His mature style reveals a painstaking attention to detail, which elicited the admiration of his contemporaries, including Rubens, with whom he collaborated. In **Still Life of Flowers** the blooms have been arranged with meticulous precision. Bruegel has carefully selected the flowers for their differing sizes and textures, reinforcing the balanced composition through his use of strong chiaroscuro. His ability to conjure the smooth surfaces of petals and the polished finish he applied to other subjects, led to his nickname, "Velvet" Bruegel. His son Jan the Younger (1601–1678) was also a painter.

OTHER MASTERPIECES The Garden of Eden; *c.1620; Victoria and Albert Museum, London, England* A Basket of Flowers with a Silver Gilt Tazza; *Fitzwilliam Museum, University of Cambridge, England*

Bruegel Pieter

Born Brögel, Netherlands, c.1525; died Brussels, Belgium 1569

Tower of Babel *1563; tempera on wood; 114 x 155 cm; Kunsthistorisches Museum, Vienna, Austria*

Pieter Bruegel the Elder was the most important member of a family of painters and the greatest of the early Netherlands artists. A late medieval, fantasy style revealing the influence of Bosch is typical of Bruegel's early work, of which the intriguing and ingenious **Tower of Babel** is an outstanding example. After joining the studio of Pieter Coecke who encouraged him to develop his landscapes, Bruegel travelled through France and Italy between 1552 and 1554. His drawings of mountain scenery, made while in the Alps, formed the basis for later compositions. In the late 1550s he started work on the genre scenes and huge landscapes for which he is best known. Given the nickname "Peasant Bruegel" because of his habit of adopting disguise to enter these rowdy celebrations of rural life, Bruegel's close-up observations are at once affectionate and satirical. In 1563, settled in Brussels and with patronage, Bruegel started work on a series which took the months of the year as his theme. In his evocation of atmosphere and feeling he showed a new sensitivity toward landscape.

OTHER MASTERPIECES Hunters in the Snow; *1569; Kunsthistorisches Museum, Vienna, Austria* **Peasant Wedding Feast**; *c.1566–1567; Kunsthistorisches Museum, Vienna, Austria*

62

Burne-Jones Edward

Born Birmingham, England 1833; died London, England 1898

King Cophetua and the Beggar Maid
1884; oil on canvas; 292 x 136 cm;
Tate Collection, London, England

Edward Burne-Jones's original intention was to enter the church but he changed his mind while studying at Oxford University with William Morris who became his friend. Both men were much influenced by their reading of Ruskin and the Pre-Raphaelite pictures they saw at the Royal Academy. After studying under his hero, Dante Gabriel Rossetti, Burne-Jones paid his first visit to Italy in 1859. In 1862 he went back to Italy with Ruskin, and the work he produced on his return showed the influence of Botticelli and Mantegna. Burne-Jones's dreamy, romantic style is strongly associated with the second phase of the Pre-Raphaelites. His highly decorative paintings draw upon mysticism and an imagined literary past and represent a retreat from nineteenth-century industrialism. His popularity was at its height in the 1880s and **King Cophetua and the Beggar Maid** dates from this period. The painting tells the story of a king who searches far and wide for a bride, only to fall in love with a woman disguised as a beggar. Burne-Jones designed stained glass windows and tapestries for William Morris, for whom he also illustrated books.

OTHER MASTERPIECES The Beguiling of Merlin; *1874; Lady Lever Art Gallery, Port Sunlight, England* **Perseus and the Graiae**; *1892; Staatsgalerie, Stuttgart, Germany*

Burra Edward

Born London, England 1905; died Rye, England 1976

Harlem *1934;*
watercolour; 55.2 x 42 cm,
Cecil Higgins Art Gallery,
Bedford, England

Edward Burra was a
sickly child and illness
plagued him throughout
his life. His formative
education was
undertaken at home.
From 1921–1923 he
studied at Chelsea
Polytechnic and for a
further two years at the
Royal College of Art,
London. He had a liking
for the quirky and the
absurd, which explains
why the work of the
Dadaists, Surrealists and
German artists,
particularly George
Grosz, proved
inspirational to him.

Due to his illness tempering his own experiences, he delighted in the vitality of the other, more
colourful lives he observed on his travels and on the cinema screen. The social scene and
licentiousness of the streets, bars and nightclubs were of particular and lasting fascination to
him. When he had the opportunity to visit America, in 1933, the watercolour paintings he
made in response, such as **Harlem**, satirize the characters and the local urban environment
without being critical or referencing political issues; a hint of menace pervades Burra's bright
tonality. Such lighthearted illustrations are contrasted by works produced after 1936 in response
to the Spanish Civil War and the Second World War. Burra's later paintings focus on landscape
and still life.

OTHER MASTERPIECES The Snack Bar; *1930; Tate Collection, London, England*
Medusa; *c.1938; Manchester City Art Galleries, Manchester, England*

Cahn Miriam

Born Basel, Switzerland 1949

City *1985; drawing; 272 x 379 cm; Tate Collection, London, England*

After training in Basel and Paris in the 1960s and 1970s, Miriam Cahn moved to West Berlin. It was there that she produced her best-known work in the 1980s. Primarily working on paper, using black chalk, Cahn relied on her physicality and intuition to create her drawings from the chalk dust. In describing the process that produced her work, Cahn referred to putting herself "as a whole person, as a whole woman, into certain moods" before settling down to work on the floor. The scraping of the chalk dust from a larger block was part of the ritualistic preparation, the results of which relied on the artist pushing her body into the piece. Cahn described her creative process as similar to reading tea leaves, initialling her works LIS, which stands for Lesen in Staub (reading in the dust). Panoramic landscape such as **City**, blurry female figures, children, animals and mask-like faces are common threads in her drawings. Cahn works in a series, no individual picture taking precedence – the direct emotional strength of her work is most evident when the work is viewed as a whole. She has also produced large watercolours referring to nuclear explosions. Most of her later works have been richly coloured paintings.

OTHER MASTERPIECES Wolken Series *1988; Haus Am Waldsee, Berlin, Germany*
Atom Bomb Series; *1988; Haus Am Waldsee, Berlin, Germany*

Calder Alexander

Born Philadelphia, USA 1898; died New York City, USA 1976

The Black Eye *1961; painted sheet metal and rod; 69 x 172.6 cm; Phillips, London, England*

Alexander Calder developed the mobile as a three-dimensional kinetic art form, having appropriated the idea from Russian Constructivist Alexander Rodchenko. Calder originally trained as an engineer before studying at the Art Students League in New York City, where he specialized in making sculpture from welded metal. He spent time in Europe from 1926, being impressed by the formal qualities and tonal implications of Mondrian's work and the art of Joan Miro. Their respective influences can be seen in Calder's subsequent work, which elegantly combines elements of Abstraction, Surrealism and Constructivism. He joined the Abstraction-Creation group in 1931 and held his first exhibition of "mobiles", a name suggested by Duchamp, in 1932. Calder was also producing static, sculptural constructions, or "stabiles", as entitled by Jean Arp. The mobiles that followed were wind-driven, an advance that Calder preferred to the earlier motorized or hand-driven pieces. **The Black Eye** is a classic piece, made during a period when Calder's stabiles had reached monumental proportions as public works of art.

OTHER MASTERPIECES Antennae with Red and Blue Dots; *1960; Tate Collection, London, England* **Performing Seal**; *1950; Museum of Contemporary Art, Chicago, USA*

Campin Robert

Born Tournai, Belgium c.1375; died Tournai, Belgium 1444

Joseph in his Workshop *c.1425; oil on wood; 64.5 x 27.3 cm; Metropolitan Museum of Art, Cloisters Collection, New York City, USA*

Art historians have argued for centuries over whether Campin was the same man as the Master of Flémalle, whose contribution to artistic styles was as revolutionary as van Eyck's. Known to be active from 1406, Campin was based in Tournai, a prosperous manufacturing and trading city. He used the city and its bourgeois citizens as a source for much of his painting. **Joseph in his Workshop** is the right wing of a triptych of **The Annunciation** and aptly illustrates the sometimes convoluted symbolism of northern European art. The mousetrap on the windowsill of St Joseph's workshop is thought by some to be an allusion to a well-known doctrine of the time, according to which the Devil was tricked by the marriage of the Virgin Mary rather as mice are fooled by cheese in a mousetrap. St Joseph is located with a thoroughly domestic setting, in a style resolutely naturalistic. Having made the two mousetraps, it appears he is making a cover for a footstool, into which would be placed a hot pan to warm the feet. The minutely detailed townscape that can be seen in the background is almost like a picture hanging on the brick wall.

OTHER MASTERPIECES Werl Altar; *1438; Museo del Prado, Madrid, Spain.*
The Virgin and Child Before a Firescreen; *c.1400–1425; National Gallery, London, England.*

Canaletto Antonio

Born Venice, Italy 1697; died Venice, Italy 1768

A Regatta on the Grand Canal *c.1747–1750; oil on canvas; 85 x 134.5 cm; Fine Arts Gallery of San Diego, San Diego, USA*

Antonio Canaletto originally worked as a theatrical scene painter for his father. In 1719, he visited Rome where he was influenced by Panini, the leading exponent of view paintings. Tiepolo, the supreme Rococo painter, and Piazetta also made strong impressions upon him. At this time Venetian artists were courted by the whole of Europe; by the age of thirty, Canaletto had established a lucrative market in Britain for his views of the canals and buildings of his native city. He based himself in London for ten years from 1746. The topographical tradition in which he worked date back to the narrative cycles of the Venetian Scuole painters who, like Canaletto, celebrated the public life of the city. To ensure an accurate representation, Canaletto used a camera obscura. This reflects an image on to paper from which the draughtsman can then trace round the edges. **A Regatta on the Grand Canal** records the pageantry and splendour of a Venetian festive occasion. This atmospheric composition demonstrates his skill in rendering light and shade, and his seemingly effortless ability to suggest a mass of people.

OTHER MASTERPIECES The Stonemason's Yard; *1726–1730; National Gallery, London, England*
Venice: The Basin of St Mark's on Ascension Day; *c.1740; National Gallery, London, England*

Canova Antonio

Born Treviso, Italy 1757; died Venice, Italy 1822

Three Graces *1817; white marble; 173 x 97.2 x 75 cm; National Gallery of Scotland, Edinburgh, Scotland*

Antonio Canova was a leading artist working within the Classical movement that dominated European sculpture from the end of the eighteenth century through to the Victorian era. He settled in Rome in 1781, producing works of antique and mythological subjects and enjoyed the patronage of the Buonaparte family. In 1815 the sixth Duke of Bedford, one of his British patrons, commissioned Canova to create the group of **The Three Graces**, a celebrated sculpture, which recently achieved media attention by being saved from export out of Great Britain in autumn 1994. The intention was for the statue to be housed in a purpose-built temple at Woburn Abbey, main home of the dukes of Bedford. It is probably the most famous of Canova's Neoclassical works and many preliminary drawings, prints and terracotta models exist to reveal the breadth of preparation that went into its creation. The unblemished smoothness of the marble heightens the languid sensuality of the figures. Soft lines and gestures flow rhythmically through the upper portion of the group, focusing on the attitude of the heads and emphasizing a mannered artificiality that excludes sentimentality.

OTHER MASTERPIECES Cupid and Psyche; *1787–1793; Musée du Louvre, Paris, France*
Pauline Bonaparte Borghese as Venus; *1807; Borghese Gallery, Rome, Italy*

Caravaggio Michelangelo Merisi da

Born Bergamo, Italy c.1572; died Porto Ercole, Italy 1610

Supper at Emmaus *c.1601; oil on canvas; 139 x 195 cm; National Gallery, London, England*

After a lacklustre apprenticeship Caravaggio went to Rome. By 1592 he was causing scandal, not only because of his volatile character and temper but because of his controversial painting methods. He rejected the lengthy preparations traditional in central Italy, preferring instead to work in oils directly from the subject – half-length figures and still life – as practised by the Venetians. He aimed to make paintings that depicted the truth and he was critically condemned for being a naturalist. In spite of adverse reactions, Caravaggio was commissioned to produce a number of large-scale paintings. However, certain of these after 1600 were made only to be rejected by patrons on the grounds of indecorum or theological incorrectness. His innovatory work nevertheless gained strong support and was a welcome antidote to Mannerism, or the limp compromises wrought by lesser artists working on religious themes. **Supper at Emmaus** is an example of Caravaggio's virtuoso talent. Not only are the protagonists and the still life rendered equally with impeccable technique but the attitude of the apostles as they react to Christ is a remarkable interpretation. The circumstances and heightened emotion of the narrative are given further expression with dramatic chiaroscuro and powerful foreshortening.

OTHER MASTERPIECES Conversion of St Paul; *1600–1601; Cerisi Chapel, Sta Maria del Popolo, Rome, Italy* Bacchus; *c.1593; Galleria degli Uffizi, Florence, Italy*

Caro Sir Anthony

Born New Malden, England 1924

Night Movements *1987–1990; steel stained green, varnished and waxed; 276 x 211 x 229 cm; Tate Collection, London, England*

Anthony Caro is recognized as a leading pioneer in the development of British sculpture of the post-war era. He was educated at the University of Cambridge (1937–1944), where he studied engineering, attending Farnham School of Art during vacations. His competence as a sculptor was developed by studying at the Regent Street Polytechnic and at the Royal Academy Schools from 1947 to 1952. While still a student, he was employed as an assistant to Henry Moore. His mind was set on a figurative course, admiring Picasso's sculpture and the painting of Bacon, de Kooning and Dubuffet. However, less than a decade later, following a trip to New York, he oriented his ideas toward a radical alternative in abstracted, constructed steel sculpture. The work he produced during the 1960s was the stuff of revolution in artistic terms. He constructed his pieces in a similar way to a painter composing an abstract painting. Independent elements – planes, shapes, and lines – coloured and combined together form an autonomous whole, occupying a defined space on the ground, rather than elevated on a base or pedestal. **Night Movements** reveals the figurative tendencies that have returned to Caro's work from the 1950s.

OTHER MASTERPIECES Early One Morning; *1961; Tate Collection, London, England*
Yellow Swing; *1965; Tate Collection, London, England*

Carrà Carlo

Born Quargnento, Italy 1881; died Milan, Italy 1966

Lot's Daughters *1919;*
oil on canvas; 110 x 80
cm; Private Collection

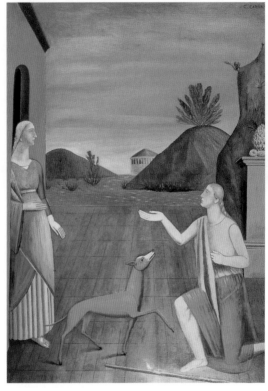

A signatory with Balla of the Futurist Manifesto in 1910, Carlo Carrá's earliest work showed the Futurist's preoccupation with movement. During his Futurist phase, Carrà studied the work of Giotto, noting in particular the earlier Italian artist's magical stillness of form. **Lot's Daughters** with its simple, sculpted, solid forms is a work that was produced in 1915 when Carrá was strongly influenced by Giotto. In 1917, while recovering from a nervous disorder in a military hospital, Carrá met Giorgio de Chirico and out of this encounter Pittura Metafisica evolved. This movement sought to define a new way of looking at reality, of looking beyond what is in front of our eyes to the "metaphysical aspect" of things. Placing disturbing and incongruous imagery such as faceless mannequins and outsize fish in claustrophobic rooms, Carrà's work of this period has a distinctly Surrealist feel. From 1921, he reverted to a more contemplative style while assimilating some of the heightened realism of his friend Giorgio Morandi. Carrà taught at the Milan Academy and was a leading influence on Italian painters between the two world wars.

OTHER MASTERPIECES The Bewitched Room; *1917; Collection Dr Emilio Jesi, Milan, Italy*
Woman with Dog; *1938; Galleria Nazionale d'Arte Moderna, Rome, Italy*

Carracci Annibale

Born Bologna, Italy 1560; died Rome, Italy 1609

The Assumption of the Virgin *c. 1587; oil on canvas; 130 x 97 cm; Museo del Prado, Madrid, Spain*

Annibale Carracci was the greatest painter of the Carracci family, which included his brother Agostino and cousin Ludovico. In 1585 all three artists founded an Academy in Bologna which went on to establish itself as the school for seventeenth-century Baroque painting, and which included Guido Reni and Domenichino amongst its pupils. In 1595 Annibale Carracci went to work for Cardinal Farnese in Rome on the decoration of the Farnese Palace. This series of frescoes, taking subjects from classical mythology, helped establish Carracci's reputation, ranking alongside Michelangelo's Sistine Chapel ceiling and Raphael's decorations in the Vatican Stanze in importance. **The Assumption of the Virgin** captures the dramatic moment of the occasion, revealing through its figures something of the artist's keen observational skills. In his smaller works he featured ideal classical landscapes. Everything in a Carracci composition is balanced; each element contributes to the overall harmonious design. To achieve this end, Carracci attempted to revive the Classical tradition while drawing upon the naturalistic advances he admired in the works of Titian. Annibale Carracci was an important influence on many artists, including Nicolas Poussin and Caravaggio.

OTHER MASTERPIECES The Virgin Mourning Christ; *c. 1605; National Museum, Naples, Italy* **Christ Appearing to St Peter on the Appian Way**, *1601–1602; National Gallery, London, England*

Carrington Leonora

Born Clayton Green, England 1917

Baby Giant c.1948, oil on canvas; Private Collection

Leonora Carrington now lives and paints in Mexico and the States. In the 1930s and 1940s she was closely associated with the Surrealists, producing paintings on childhood themes featuring magical elements. In 1942 Carrington settled in Mexico where she worked alongside Varo, a female Spanish painter who shared her interest in fairytales and alchemy. Carrington's central concern is with women's creativity, using her work to explore the female psyche. Investigating her interior life, she draws upon the intermediate state between sleeping and waking. Her narrative paintings of figures and animals in the landscape show the influence of the Early Renaissance and contain allegorical images from mythic and literary sources that do not lend themselves to easy interpretation. **Baby Giant** depicts an outsize infant towering over the landscape. In her hands she is cupping an egg, while birds flap in and around her protective shawl. It is a curious image that refuses absolute meaning, while suggesting creativity and nurturing as well as the more malign face of nature.

OTHER MASTERPIECES The Inn of the Dawn Horse (Self Portrait); 1936–1937; Collection Pierre Matisse, Paris, France **The Magic Works of the Mayas**; 1963; National Museum of Anthropology, Mexico City, Mexico

Cassatt Mary

Born Pittsburgh, USA 1844; died Paris, France 1926

Mother and Child
1893; pastel on paper;
81 x 65 cm; Pushkin
Museum, Moscow, Russia

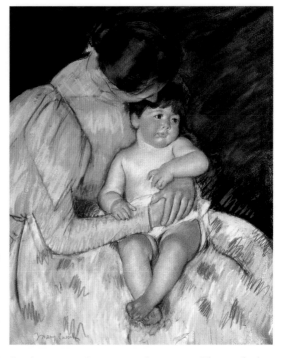

Mary Cassatt studied
art in Philadelphia
between 1861 and
1865 before travelling
to Europe and settling
in Paris in 1874. Here
she made contact with
Manet and the
Impressionists, with
whom she exhibited at
the Salon and
elsewhere between
1877 and 1881. Degas
was a lifelong friend
and her admiration for
his work was reflected
in her own pastel
studies. With Degas, she shared an interest in Japanese art and composition. This is explicitly
revealed in the character of her lithographs and etchings, print being a medium in which she
excelled. Perhaps because of her subjects, or her gender, or both, Cassatt has not been
recognized for the talented artist she was. A recurring motif was the relationship between
mother and child, softly delineated to express sensitivity but tautly contained to keep sweetness
in check. Degas wrote, in around 1890, that her preoccupation was the study of "reflections and
shadows on skin and costumes for which she has the greatest feeling and understanding". In
Mother and Child, the focus of attention is the emotional tie between baby and mother, who
is totally enraptured by her infant. Cassatt's vision is projected like a photograph, capturing an
instant that defies words or description.

OTHER MASTERPIECES La Loge; *c. 1882; National Gallery, Washington DC, USA*
Lady at the Tea Table; *1885; Metropolitan Museum of Art, New York City, USA*

Castagno Andrea del

Born Castagno, Italy c.1422; died Florence, Italy 1457

Portrait of Dante
*1447; fresco; Palazzo del
Proconsolo; Florence, Italy*

Andrea del Castagno
was a Florentine
painter in the mould
of Masaccio but
whose work reveals a
close affinity with the
sculpture of
Donatello. His earliest
work dates from 1442
when he worked on a
series of frescoes in
Venice. He returned
to Florence two years
later where he carried
out most of his
important work. After
undertaking
commissions for the
cathedral, Castagno
was asked by the
Carducci family to
decorate a room in their villa. For this commission, Castagno chose to paint a series of famous
men and women, of which **Dante** is one. These portraits are distinguished by their size, literally
larger than life and the shallow, fake marble surround which enhances the impression of these
as three-dimensional rather than as two-dimensional pieces. Realistic and monumental, these
portraits were an astounding leap forward and were of great significance to later Florentine
artists such as Leonardo da Vinci and Michelangelo. Castagno also painted an impressive **Last
Supper**, which again is notable for the intense realism of its figures.

OTHER MASTERPIECES David; *c.1450; National Gallery of Art, Washington DC, USA*
Boccaccio, *c.1450; Convent of St Apollonia, Florence, Italy*

Caulfield Patrick

Born London, England 1936

After Lunch *1975;*
acrylic on canvas; 224 x
213.4 cm; Tate
Collection, London,
England

Patrick Caulfield
studied at Chelsea
School of Art in
London from 1956 to
1960. The next three
years were spent at
the Royal College of
Art, in the year below
David Hockney,
Derek Boshier and
Allen Jones, leading
Pop artists of their
generation. The New
American Painting
exhibition at the Tate
Gallery in 1959 had a
major impact on
young British artists.
Caulfield was particularly impressed by the lyrical and evocative work of Philip Guston.
Caulfield's own, as yet unresolved personal style, was nevertheless recognized for its potential
and his work was included in the Young Contemporaries exhibition of 1961. Rather than
celebrate popular culture, Caulfield sought to provide a critique of it, to explore the mechanics
of the imagery used in a consumer society from a culture where everything is mass-produced.
His paintings began to mimic printed rather than painted imagery, wrought in household paint
on board rather than oil on canvas. His pictures, such as **After Lunch**, appear like clichés from
Ideal Home advertisement photos – chic but rather empty. The inclusion of still life or a scenic
view – here as an incongruous photographic image – is a reference to traditional, art historical
subject matter.

OTHER MASTERPIECES Still Life with Red and White Pot; *1966; Harry N. Abrams Family*
Collection, New York City, USA **Pottery;** *1969; Tate Collection, London, England*

Cézanne Paul

Born Aix-en-Provence, France 1839; died Aix-en-Provence, France 1906

Still life with Plaster Cast *c. 1895; oil on paper on board; 70 x 57.3 cm; Courtauld Institute Galleries, London, England*

The son of a banker, Paul Cézanne moved to Paris in 1861 where he met Camille Pissarro and worked to get his painting accepted by the Salon. Cézanne's early paintings, influenced by Daumier and Delacroix, were dark and dramatic, the paint roughly applied with a palette knife. In 1870 he retired to L'Estaque in the south of France where his landscapes showed a new subtlety. Of the older generation of painters only Pissarro was interested in Cézanne, both men taking part in the First Impressionist Exhibition of 1874. Cézanne shared the Impressionist's fascination with light, but his work is significant for exploring beyond the surface analysis of colour and tone to articulate the underlying forms. His radical reappraisal of the relationship between surface and depth can be seen in **Still Life with Plaster Cast**. The upper half of the twisting plaster figure is seen from a different dimension to the apples on the table, which in turn are viewed separately from the floor. Cézanne recreates the picture space to show how these objects exist independently while combining to make up the whole. The single most important influence on Cubism, Cézanne prepared the way for painting in the twentieth century.

OTHER MASTERPIECES Bathers; *1898–1905; Philadelphia Museum of Art, USA*
La Montagne Sainte-Victoire; *1886–1888; Courtauld Institute, London, England*

Chadwick Helen

Born Croydon, England 1953; died London, England 1996

Meat Abstract No 4 *1989;*
colour Polaroid; 51 x 61 cm;
courtesy of the Zelda Cheatle
Gallery, London, England

Helen Chadwick trained at
Brighton Polytechnic
before completing an MA
at Chelsea College of Art.
In 1978, she had her first
solo show in London.
Much of her work focuses
on the body and she made
use of a wide variety of
media – backlit projections,
casts, prints – to explore her concerns. She was an artist whose work literally tended to
transform its environment. In the mid-1980s, her giant glass case containing rotting and
fermenting vegetable matter commanded space at the Institute of Contemporary Arts. It split
and leaked through the floorboards. Her molten chocolate fountain, **Cacao**, cast a sickly sweet
pall over the Serpentine Gallery – while her work, **Piss Flowers**, cast first in white plaster, then
in bronze, derived from urinating in the snow and pushed at boundaries beyond the literal. In
1992, she made an acclaimed television film about the artist Frida Kahlo. **Meat Abstract No 4**
is a recent, richly coloured and unnerving photo-work, in which she has juxtaposed the natural
with the artificial; the animal insides and outsides with the electric bulb and synthetic, luxuriant
material. She manages to combine wit with seriousness, pleasure with revulsion and curiosity
with satisfaction. Her early death was a tragic loss to the art world.

OTHER MASTERPIECES Ego Geometria Sum IX: High School – Age 13; *1983; Arts*
Council of Great Britain, London, England **Cacao**; *1994; British Council, London, England*

Chagall Marc

Born Vitebsk, Russia 1887; died Saint Paul-de-Vence, France 1985

The Poet Reclining
1915; oil on canvas; 77.2 x 77.5 cm; Tate Collection, London, England

From a devout Jewish background, Marc Chagall entered art school in St Petersburg in 1907. Throughout his career he worked as a signpainter, and the influence of these techniques are evident in his paintings. His early style combined the primitive representation of folk art with the more sophisticated influence of Gaugin and the Fauves, whose work he saw in St Petersburg. In 1910 Chagall went to Paris. Back in his home town of Vitebsk by 1914, Chagall joined the Knave of Diamond group. Declaring their admiration for French painting, the group mounted an exhibition designed as a protest again the Moscow Art School. After the revolution in 1917, Chagall briefly became director of Vitebsk art school before designing murals for the Jewish State Theatre in Moscow. In works such as **The Poet Reclining**, Chagall painted rural scenes remembered with a childlike nostalgia. His richly coloured lyrical paintings depict objects and people in unusual juxtapositions, often floating in space. His later work produced designs for the ballet, stained glass windows and paintings for the ceilings of the Paris Opera.

OTHER MASTERPIECES *I and the Village; 1911; Museum of Modern Art, New York City, USA*
Paris Through the Window; *1913; Solomon R Guggenheim Museum, New York City, USA*

Chardin Jean-Baptiste-Siméon

Born Paris, France 1699; died Paris, France 1779

The Scullery Maid
*1738; oil on canvas;
45.4 x 37 cm; Glasgow
Art Galleries and
Museums, Glasgow,
Scotland*

Jean-Baptiste
Chardin trained in
the Rococo tradition,
and worked as a
restorer, although
from an early age his
own work bore little
relation to this
prevailing French
style. Chardin was a
master of simple still
life and genre painting. Using ordinary subjects, Chardin avoided sentimentality by concerning
himself with morality, namely the importance of truth, education and the dignity of labour.
Many of Chardin's genre paintings, such as **The Scullery Maid**, feature a woman engaged in a
single task. The room is empty and seemingly windowless. In his depiction of a hard and frugal
existence, the artist emphasizes the maid's industry. The unfussy intensity of Chardin's still life
gives his work a remarkably modern feel. Even the humblest of objects such as a metal pan, a
loaf of bread, or a pear, have a significance beyond the representational. Chardin was elected a
member of the French Academy in 1728. He became its treasurer and hung exhibitions there
over the next twenty years. Finding favour once the ornate court art's popularity was on the
wane, Chardin's timeless compositions had an enormous influence on Courbet and Manet.

OTHER MASTERPIECES The House of Cards; *c.1736–1737; National Gallery, London,
England* **Self-Portrait**; *1771; Musée du Louvre, Paris, France*

Chia Sandro

Born Florence, Italy 1946

Water Bearer *1981, oil and pastel on canvas, 207 x 170 cm, Tate Collection, London, England*

Sandro Chia was one of a generation of Italian artists who rejected the minimal and conceptual concerns of artists during the 1970s. In the early 1980s, Chia and his contemporaries, the Italian Transvantgarde, proved influential to other European and American artists in their concern to return to figuration and to revive interest in traditional materials. Resurrecting subject-matter based in the physical, as opposed to intellectual, world had an impact on the art market; painting became a more saleable art form and established artists, whose work had been neglected, were again fashionable. Chia trained at the Instituto d'Arte (1962–1967) and the Accademia di Belle Arti, Florence (1967–1969). He references his wide, art-historical knowledge to formulate his painting and transforms artistic traditions to "make them new". A Neo-Expressionist spirit is at the heart of his approach, which is energetic and decorative. The heroic figures of his images, such as those in **Water Bearer**, often refer to the artist himself. Here, the fish is a visual metonym for water, a symbolic metaphor for virility, perhaps, or the life-affirming load one carries. The work reveals Chia's imaginative technical abilities and his skill in the evocation of emotionally charged colour.

OTHER MASTERPIECES The Idleness of Sisyphus; *1981; Museum of Modern Art, New York City, USA* Bluish Fish Splash; *1996; Private Collection*

Chicago Judy

Born Chicago, USA 1939

The Dinner Party *1979;
mixed media; 14.4 x 14.4 x 14.4
metres, San Francisco Museum of
Modern Art, San Francisco, USA*

Judy Chicago was educated at the University of California, Los Angeles between 1962 and
1964. A pioneering American feminist, Chicago came to prominence in the 1970s through
work that challenged orthodox notions of what constitutes art, while promoting women as
artists. She chose to explore women's sexuality, often through explicit images based on female
bodily functions. In 1972, with Miriam Shapiro, she was the driving force behind
Womanhouse, a collective project to convert an abandoned Los Angeles house into a space for
performances and installations dealing specifically with the female experience. Her **Fantasy
Rejection Drawings** (1974) were based on female genitalia and intended as a coded reference
to woman's strength and vulnerability. Her most celebrated work, **The Dinner Party**,
represented the collective effort of around four hundred women, whose contributions ranged
from embroidery to ceramic decoration. The result was an elaborate, triangular table to which
thirty nine famous women – drawn from art and history – are gathered together for an
imaginary dinner party to celebrate female achievement. Chicago referred to the multimedia
piece as, "a sort of reinterpretation of the Last Supper from the point of view of those who'd
done the cooking."

OTHER MASTERPIECES Sheet Closet *(from* **Womanhouse***, recorded on film); 1971; California
Institute of the Arts, Valencia, USA* **Fantasy Rejection Drawing** *(from the* **Rejection Quintet***); 1974;
San Francisco Museum of Modern Art, San Francisco, USA*

Chillida Eduardo

Born San Sebastian, Spain 1924; died Spain 2002

Modulation of Space *1963;*
metal; 546 x 698 mm; Tate
Collection, London, England

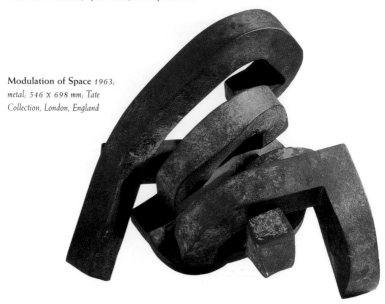

Eduardo Chillida was a leading abstract sculptor of the twentieth century. He studied architecture at Colegio Mayor Jienez in Madrid (1943–1946), training that formed a solid basis from which to formulate his art. In 1947, he studied drawing at a private academy and moved to Paris in 1948. He returned to Spain in 1951. Chillida's small- and large-scale sculptures and public plazas have the same monumental grandeur to them. Forged from unyielding materials – steel, iron, stone – each appears to interlock with the space around it. Like pieces of giant jigsaws, his public and private sculptures seem to be waiting for the final bit to complete each form. Such gaps are positive, unifying elements. **Modulation of Space** is a descriptive title, suggesting that its function is to affect the space around it, while acknowledging that it exists because of it. Chillida worked with people in mind, in spite of his work being non-figurative. His pieces, "steles", were often conceived as memorials to specific ideas or individuals – Giacometti, Neruda and Goethe, for example. He also strove to express concepts such as liberty and tolerance and to reference his passion for Greek sculpture and the spirit of the Basque people.

OTHER MASTERPIECES Monument of Basque Rights; *1980; Vitoria, Gasteiz, Spain*
Our Father's House; *1986–1988; Guernica, Spain*

Chirico Giorgio de

Born Volo, Greece 1888; died Rome, Italy 1978

Piazza d'Italie:
Malincornia *c.1948;*
oil on canvas; 49.5 x
40 cm; Private Collection

Giorgio de Chirico
studied painting in
Athens and Munich. In
Germany he discovered
Nietzsche and the
imaginative work of
Bocklin and Klinger,
which destroyed his
interest in naturalistic
painting. From 1911 to
1915 de Chirico was in
Paris and first began to
develop his metaphysical
style. **Piazza d'Italie:**
Malincornia exemplifies

his innovative approach to landscape. The square is deserted but for a classical sculpture and an
ominous human shadow. Time is suspended, focusing attention on the empty stage. In asking
the viewer to consider what lies beyond physical appearance, de Chirico remarked that "dead
voices speak to us from nearby, but they sound like voices from another planet". De Chirico
met Carlo Carrá and formed Pittura Metafisica while both artists were recovering in hospital
from injuries sustained during the First World War. The paintings that de Chirico produced in
this period are characterized by their claustrophobic interiors and the juxtaposition of
incongruous objects. His often bizarre and mysterious works were greatly admired by the
Surrealists. De Chirico continued to make work that expressed his metaphysical concerns until
the late 1920s when, in a complete volte-face, he embraced a new mannered naturalism.

OTHER MASTERPIECES The Philosopher and the Poet; *1915; Conte Alfonso Orombelli,
Milan, Italy* **The Archaeologists;** *1927; Private Collection, Venice, Italy*

Christo

Born Gabrovo, Bulgaria 1935

Wrapped Reichstag
*1978; Project for Der
Deutsche Reichstag, Platz
der Republik, Reichstag
Platz, Schiedemann
Strasse, Friedens Allee,
Berlin, Germany*

Christo Javacheff was
born into a Bulgarian
industrialist family. On
the same date, June 13,
his wife and
collaborator, Jeanne-
Claude, was born in
Casablanca. Christo
studied at the Fine Arts
Academy in Sofia
(1953–1956) and then
arrived in Prague,
undertaking a brief
period of study at the
Vienna Fine Arts
Academy. In 1920,
Man Ray wrapped a
sewing machine in material and tied in with string: Christo went to Paris in 1958 where, in a
similarly Surrealist spirit, he developed his idea to make art of objects, enigmatically packaged
and wrapped. At the beginning of the 1960s, Christo expanded his artistic ambitions to include
the wrapping of public buildings. He settled in New York in 1964. His out-sized, dramatic
projects were recognized as a significant contribution to a period when "Happenings" had taken
art beyond the modernist arena. Christo first conceived the **Wrapped Reichstag** project in
1971, before the Berlin Wall came down – a major artistic and political achievement. Like all
Christo's projects, the funds raised were made by selling many elaborate preliminary drawings
and maquettes. His major project for the early twenty-first century was **The Gates, Central
Park, New York City**, due for completion in 2005.

OTHER MASTERPIECES Valley Curtain; *1970–1972; Colorado, USA* The Pont Neuf
Wrapped; *1975–1985; Paris, France*

Christus Petrus

Born Baerle, Netherlands c.1410; died Bruges, Belgium c.1472

Lamentation over the Dead Christ c.1460; oil on wood; 98 x 188 cm; Museé Royeaux des Beaux-Arts de Belgique, Brussels, Belgium

Petrus Christus grew up in the northern Netherlands where there were no reputable painting workshops. In order to train as a panel painter, he had to travel south to Bruges, where he became a citizen in 1444. It is almost certain that Christus used a version of the same subject by Roger van der Weyden as the basis for this **Lamentation over the Dead Christ**. However, Christus broke new ground by integrating figures into their setting. They are not depicted as a block of people artificially placed in the foreground of a landscape, but rather in small clusters set apart from one another as if they actually inhabit the scene. His figures have a self-contained quality that gives the scene an appropriate sense of melancholy. Because masters of workshops and their apprentices collaborated so closely, and the cult of the individual painter did not exist at the time, it makes it difficult to ascertain precisely who painted what. What is certain is that Christus was one of the greatest fifteenth-century painters of northern Europe. He was probably Jan van Eyck's pupil and certainly his chief follower, and after van Eyck's death in 1441 became the foremost master in Bruges.

OTHER MASTERPIECES Portrait of a Lady; c.1470; Staatliche Museen zu Berlin, Germany
Portrait of a Young Man; c.1450–1460; National Gallery, London, England

Cimabue Giovanni

Born Florence, Italy 1240; died Florence, Italy 1320

**Madonna and Child
Enthroned** c.1280;
*tempera on panel; 385 x
223 cm; Galleria degli
Uffizi, Florence, Italy*

Cimabue is revered as the
greatest Florentine artist before
Giotto, whom it is believed that
he taught. He worked within
the Byzantine tradition –
religious figures portrayed flatly
and stiffly within a hierarchical
setting. Under the influence of
Romanesque sculptors and the
nascent classical revival in
Rome, he made the first
tentative steps toward a more
realistic style based upon
personal observation. Cimabue's early contribution to the movement toward greater naturalism
is qualified by doubts over many of the works assigned to him. The only work that is reliably
attributed to him is **Saint John** in the Pisa Cathedral, although it is highly probable, because of
its style, that **Madonna and Child Enthroned** is also one of his works. In this image he uses
fine gold lines to model the drapery, emphasizing the rhythmic qualities within the
composition. He has attempted to paint the architectonic throne receding in space, he even
paints a foot overhanging the platform – not because he was aware of the rules of perspective
but through careful observation.

OTHER MASTERPIECES Saint John, c.1302; *Pisa Cathedral, Pisa, Italy*
Madonna and Child, c.1280; *Musée du Louvre, Paris, France*

Claude Lorraine

Born Nancy, France 1600; died Rome, Italy 1682

The Adoration of the Golden Calf *1660; oil on canvas; 122 x 157 cm; Manchester City Art Galleries, Manchester, England*

Claude Lorraine is thought to have first trained as a pastry cook but other details of his early life remain uncertain. He lived in Rome from the age of 27 and it was there that he began to produce some of the great classical landscapes on which his reputation rests. Less concerned than his contemporary Nicholas Poussin with the construction of his compositions, Claude concentrates on the evocation of mood and atmosphere. His many large compositions of biblical, mythological and pastoral subjects evince calmness and a wistful nostalgia. This is largely because of the artist's ability to recreate soft and subtle lighting effects. Claude worked outside and made numerous studies of dawn and dusk, which are acclaimed for their free handling. He mainly conceived of his paintings in pairs. **The Adoration of the Golden Calf**, however, is not part of a pair. It retells the biblical story of Aaron's construction of a heathen image, although for Claude, the spacious Roman countryside becomes the real subject of the work. Claude Lorraine was a great inspiration to other later landscape artists, in particular Turner whose **Dido Building Carthage** was a homage to the Frenchman.

OTHER MASTERPIECES Landscape with Aeneas at Delos; *1672; National Gallery, London, England* Seaport, with the Embarkation of the Queen of Sheba; *1648; National Gallery, London, England*

Clemente Francesco

Born Naples, Italy 1952

Midnight Sun II *1982; oil on canvas; 200 x 250.8 cm; Tate Collection, London, England*

Francesco Clemente began painting in the late 1970s, achieving recognition in the early 1980s as one of the Italian Transavant-garde painters. He, like his contemporaries Cucchi, Chia and Paladino, was keen to redress the balance in favour of painting that employed the figure as an expressive site of meaning. Figuration had been neglected in the 1960s and 1970s under the weight of attention given to Conceptualism and Arte Povera. In addition to Clemente's revival of traditional art media – oil paint on canvas, watercolour, pastel and fresco – his significance lies in the metaphysical and cross-cultural aspects of his work. He has travelled widely and spent periods of time absorbed in different cultures; he maintains studios in Madras, Rome and New York. In the nostalgic spirit of Post-Modernism, he draws freely on art from the past and the ghosts of his Italianate history. In addition he freely plagiarizes imagery of non-European philosophies and religions, leading to criticism of him as a pasticheur. **Midnight II** appears to be a bizarre erotic or spiritual hallucination, with the artist represented in the narrative. It is one of Clemente's, "endless stream of images that seem to generate each other".

OTHER MASTERPIECES Paradigm; *1988; Sperone Westwater Gallery, New York City, USA*
Scissors and Butterflies; *1999; Guggenheim Museum, New York City, USA*

Constable John

Born East Bergholt, England 1776; died London, England 1837

Seascape Study with Rain Clouds *1824–1828; oil on paper laid on canvas; 222 x 310 cm; Royal Academy of Art, London, England*

The son of a prosperous Suffolk mill owner, John Constable was, with Joseph Turner, the major English landscape painter of the nineteenth century. Constable admired Claude and Ruisdael for their ability to draw directly from nature. After a spell at the Royal Academy, Constable returned to Suffolk and, declaring that there was "room enough for a natural painture [sic]", began an intense study of his native countryside. Constable was not a natural draughtsman. Making sketches outside in the fields in the summer, he then tried to reproduce the exact time and weather conditions of a particular moment in his London studio during the winter months. He was a painter of the particular rather than the general and wanted to show that "no two days were alike, nor even two hours; neither were there ever two leaves of a tree alike". Regarded by Constable as preparatory work for his large paintings, his oil sketches, including the inspired **Seascape Study with Rain Clouds** are now greatly valued in their own right. Constable never travelled abroad, but his large composition, **Haywain**, caused a great stir when it was exhibited at the Paris Salon in 1824.

OTHER MASTERPIECES Haywain; *1821; National Gallery, London, England*
The Leaping Horse; *1825; Victoria and Albert Museum, London, England*

Cooper Eileen

Born Glossop, England 1953

Baby Talk *1985; oil on canvas; 121.9 x 91.4 cm; Jason Rhodes Gallery, London, England*

Eileen Cooper studied at Goldsmiths' College and the Royal College of Art in the 1970s. Her paintings take women as their central theme and often depict the mother-child relationship. There is a strong narrative thread in Cooper's paintings which are at once autobiographical and universal, containing stories that defy any single or obvious interpretation. Cooper's paintings, with their use of vivid colours and primitive figures engaged in simple rituals, are celebratory in tone. Some commentators have been critical of her uncomplicated vision, suggesting that in her presentation of "a golden age where even the first get tickled pink with enjoyment", she ignores the harshness and brutality of life. Cooper herself has remarked that her paintings are not "restricted to a logical description of the world". **Baby Talk** comes from a series of startling orange, red and blue paintings made in 1987 in which Cooper explores her own status as a mother. The babies only form part of the picture: they begin to investigate the world giving the mother figure space to continue with her own activities.

OTHER MASTERPIECES If the Shoe Fits; *1987; Jason Rhodes Gallery, London, England*
Crawling Woman; *1990; Jason Rhodes Gallery, London, England*

Cornell Joseph

Born Nyack, New York, USA 1903; died Flushing, Michigan, USA 1972

Guiditta Pasta *1950; mixed media in a box; 305 x 457 x 10 cm; Tate Collection, London, England*

Joseph Cornell had no formal art training. In the 1930s he became known for his assemblages, most commonly glass-fronted boxes in which he juxtaposed an assortment of disparate objects and artefacts. Exquisitely arranged, these compilations featured a surprising and often random collection of items including matchboxes, postage stamps, compasses and newspaper cuttings. His work sometimes utilized heavy picture frames and also mirrors. In a reference to his own work, Cornell said, "these shadow boxes become poetic theatres or settings wherein are metamorphosed the elements of a childhood pastime". After the Second World War, Cornell associated with the Surrealists and his work was featured in the exhibitions at the Julian Levy Gallery in New York. He also made a number a number of Surrealist films. **Guiditta Pasta** is dedicated to the memory of Guiditta Pasta, a famous Italian opera singer. Wooden tracts support two loose balls above a row of wine glasses – three containing rock crystals and balls, symbolizing air, water and ice. While the box is a metaphor for a private world sealed in time and space, the two globe-like panels – representing the northern and southern hemispheres – allude to a world outside.

OTHER MASTERPIECES Chocolate Menier; *1952; New York University Collection, New York City, USA* Hotel Du Nord; *c.1953; Whitney Museum of Art, New York City, USA*

Corot Jean-Baptiste-Camille

Born Paris, France 1796; died Paris, France 1875

Recollections of Mortefontaigne *1864; oil on canvas; 65 x 89 cm; Musée du Louvre, Paris, France*

Known as Camille Corot, this painter of landscape and portraits trained in the classical tradition of Nicholas Poussin. Corot went to Italy in 1925 and returned there several times. The sketches he made on these visits have a remarkable freshness, although these were never seen by Corot as anything other than reference material for his large compositions. The direct, bold Italiante landscapes of the early part of his career were superseded in the 1850s by hazy wooded and waterside scenes which, with their soft grey-green tones and dreamy atmosphere, found immediate favour with the French public. **Recollections of Mortefontaigne** was painted after a visit to the great park just north of Paris. Watteau had also gone there for inspiration. In setting this scene against the lake in the early morning, Corot evokes an air of sleepy tranquillity. The painting's title refers to the image as a mere recollection; the painter attempts to capture this ephemeral scene as he remembers it. His late portraits and studies of women, such as **Woman with a Pearl**, were free of his diffuse style and are much admired.

OTHER MASTERPIECES Peasants under the Trees at Dawn; *c.1840–1845; National Gallery, London, England* The Lady in Blue; *1874; Musée du Louvre, Paris, France*

Correggio Antonio Allegri da

Born Correggio, Italy c.1489; died Correggio, Italy 1534

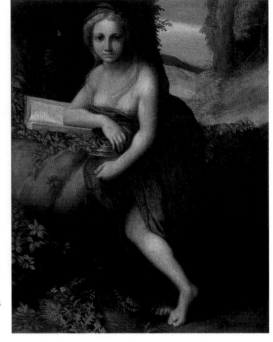

The Magdalene
*c.1517–1519; oil on
canvas; 38.1 x 30.5 cm;
National Gallery, London,
England*

Active chiefly in the
small northern Italian
town of Parma,
Correggio was regarded
by his successors as the
most "progressive" and
innovative painter of his
period. The sensuous
handling of the nude,
and the soft modelling
of flesh and draperies made him popular in the eighteenth century as a precursor of Rococo
style. The formal qualities of Correggio's early paintings suggest that he may have studied
Mantegna's work in Mantua. Similarly, Correggio employed illusionist techniques for various
commissions undertaken within architectural spaces. In the **Assumption of the Virgin** in the
dome of Parma Cathedral, c.1520, such daring trompe l'oeil effects are employed with dramatic
foreshortening, rendered in fresco enlivened by tempera. The influence of the Renaissance
masters, Raphael and Michelangelo is likely to have inspired Correggio indirectly via drawings
and prints familiar throughout Italy. The impression made upon him by Leonardo is evident in
the sweet lyricism with which **The Magdalene** is depicted. Correggio's sensitive interpretations
of religious themes are elegantly composed. The apparent ease with which they are constructed
lends a simple grace to complex figure groups as seen, for example, in the **St George Altar**.

OTHER MASTERPIECES Holy Night; *c.1530; Gemaldegaleries, Dresden, Germany*
Mercury Instructing Cupid; *c.1525; National Gallery, London, England*

Cotán Juan Sánchez

Born Toledo, Spain 1561; died Granada, Spain 1627

Still Life with Quince, Cabbage, Melon and Cucumber *c.1602; oil on canvas; 69 x 84 cm; San Diego Museum of Art, San Diego, California, USA*

Juan Sánchez Cotán was amongst the earliest of all European still life painters. He was a disciple of the artist Blas de Prado and an acquaintance of El Greco. Cotán became a friar at the age of 43, by which time he was already renowned for his dramatic still life. Based on strict mathematical principles, his arrangements of fruits and vegetables were made within a frame. In **Still Life with Quince, Cabbage, Melon and Cucumber** this framing device appears to be a shelf or a window. Strong perspective and dramatically lit forms help to further the illusion. In hanging the produce from strings, Cotán refers to the contemporaneous practice of keeping the fruit from rotting, while adding an extra note of realism to the arrangement. This is one of five still lifes bought by King Philip III from the estate of the Archbishop of Toledo. In 1813 it was taken by King Joseph Bonaparte with him into exile in America. Exhibited in America in 1818, this superb painting was only rediscovered in 1945. Cotán also painted religious works.

OTHER MASTERPIECES The Bearded Woman of Penaranda (**Brigida Del Rio**); *1590; Museo del Prado, Madrid, Spain* Still Life with Game Fowl, Fruit and Vegetable; *1602; Museo del Prado, Madrid, Spain*

Cotman John Sell

Born Norwich, England 1782; died London, England 1842

Chirk Aqueduct, Wales
c.1804; watercolour on paper;
31.7 x 23.2 cm; Victoria
and Albert Museum, London,
England

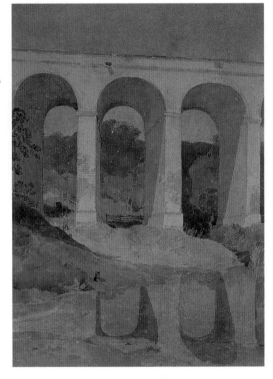

John Sell Cotman was a
watercolourist and oil
painter whose work was
unusually stark and
austere for the early
nineteenth century.
Cotman left Norwich for
London in 1798, where
he worked as a copyist.
He continued to produce
architectural and
archaeological drawings
throughout his career. In
1800 he exhibited at the Royal Academy. His painting tours of Wales and the West Country
were followed by visits to Yorkshire between 1803 and 1805. For watercolours such as **Chirk
Aqueduct, Wales**, Cotman laid clean flat washes of pure colour, mainly working indoors from
pencil notes made outside. This landscape could have been the product of Cotman's tour of
Wales in 1802, although there is no evidence that he actually visited the site. He probably
transplanted the image of the aqueduct from a print. It is clear from the work that he was
especially drawn to the rhythms of the arched shapes, and it is this sense of pattern and
abstraction of form that makes his work so distinctive. In later years his work lost some of its
freshness when he began to mix paste with his watercolours.

OTHER MASTERPIECES Duncombe Park; *1808–1810; Tate Collection, London, England*
Greta Bridge; *1807; British Museum, London, England*

Courbet Gustave

Born Ornans, France 1819; died Tour de Pietz, France 1877

Burial at Ornans *1850; oil on canvas; 315 x 668 cm; Musée du Louvre, Paris, France*

Courbet is credited with giving the name Realism to the style of painting with which he revolutionized art in Paris in 1850. He came to Paris in 1839 and, instead of official art training, copied seventeenth century naturalist paintings by Caravaggio, Velasquez, Ribera and Zurbaran. Following their example Courbet claimed to be a disciple only of truth. His principles condemned the pretentiousness of official, academic commissions and shunned the exotic elements of Romanticism. He alludes to these concerns in **Bonjour Monsieur Courbet**, a painting considered shocking because the artist depicts himself like a tramp being greeted by a patron. He concentrated on subjects from contemporary life for their pictorial rather than emotional value, earning praise from the political socialist Proudhon and from the novelist Emile Zola. **The Burial at Ornans**, exhibited at the Salon of 1850, is a monumental composition which caused outrage when it was first exhibited. The painting concentrates on the burial as a secular occasion and Courbet's depiction of the community was criticised for being "common, trivial and grotesque". His paintings of landscape, still-life and nudes are, however, no less remarkable for their chiaroscuro, impasto and rich colouring.

OTHER MASTERPIECES The Painter's Studio; *1855; Musée du Louvre, Paris, France*
Proudhon and His Children, *1865; Petit Palais, Paris, France*

Cozens John Robert

Born London, England 1752; died London, England 1797

Valley with Winding Stream *1778; watercolour on paper; 37.1 x 53 cm; Victoria and Albert Museum, London, England*

John Robert Cozens was a pupil of his father Alexander, who is best known for his method of composing landscapes out of accidental ink blots. Both father and son were associated with William Beckford, a leading protagonist of the trend towards sensibility of feeling in landscape in the late eighteenth century. John Cozens was more concerned to convey the poetry and drama that he found in landscape than he was with exact representation. He almost exclusively painted in watercolour – there is only one surviving oil painting – adopting a muted palette of predominantly blue-green and blue-grey. His work influenced Turner and Girtin and, in particular, Constable who referred to him as "the greatest genius that ever touched landscape". Cozens visited Switzerland and Italy, where he was especially drawn to the grandeur of the Italian lakes and the Swiss Alps. **Valley with Winding Stream** shows how his watercolours manage to emphasize the monumentality of the landscape at the expense of detail. There is a melancholic aspect to Cozens, which eventually was to overwhelm him. Psychiatric problems brought about his death when he was only forty-five years old.

OTHER MASTERPIECES View of Lake Albano; *c.1778; Ashmolean Museum, Oxford, England*
Valley of the Eisah Near Brixen in the Tyrol; *c.1776; Whitworth Art Gallery, Manchester, England*

Cragg Tony

Born Liverpool, England 1949

On the Savannah *1988; bronze; 225 x 400 x 500 cm; Tate Collection, London, England*

Tony Cragg came to prominence in the early 1980s with his wall-pieces fashioned from multicoloured fragments of plastic items. He studied at Gloucestershire School of Art, Wimbledon School of Art and the Royal College of Art, London. The wall-works were a sculptural response to the energy that surged back into figurative painting as a reaction against the minimalism and conceptualism that had knocked the tactile passion out of art since the end of the 1960s. Cragg's interest is in industry and the resulting products that shape our environment. Plastic, in particular, has become emblematic of a culture based on consumerism and obsessive materialism. Cragg exploits the unlikely, but nevertheless valid, aesthetic potential of the materials he uses. To emphasize our "metaphysical" relationship to the manufacturing processes on which we rely, Cregg has often created assemblages of scrap and rubbish, the detritus of mass production. **On the Savannah** is a graceful family of forms. The large-scale pieces derive from "the idea of mutation", here a metamorphosis of vessels commonly used within a science laboratory.

OTHER MASTERPIECES Britain Seen From The North; *1981; Tate Collection, London, England* **Complete Omnivore**; *1993; Marian Goodman Gallery, New York City, USA*

Cranach Lucas

Born Kronach, Germany 1472; died Weimar, Germany 1553

Adam and Eve
*c. 1518; oil on limewood
panel; 49.5 x 35 cm;
Kunsthistorisches
Museum, Vienna, Austria*

Lucas Cranach the Elder was of the same generation as fellow countryman, Dürer, but not much is known of his initial years or about his training. He was painting in Vienna in around 1500 where he produced portraits and religious panels of considerable inventiveness. His importance lies, however, in his ability to integrate figures within a natural environment. This is probably most significantly shown in his **Rest on the Flight to Egypt**, 1504, which combines charming fantasy with the familiar religious narrative. The so-called Danube School is thought to have originated from the inspiration engendered by such painting. After 1505 the poetic lyricism and inventiveness of Cranach's art diminished when he became court painter to the Elector of Saxony in Wittenberg. The formal requirements of commissioned portraits and religious works extracted fluidity and original spirit from Cranach's work. However, his paintings were fashionable and his friendship with Martin Luther gained him notoriety. His nudes, as in **Adam and Eve**, are more curious than classical. Their contrived gestures, awkward deportment and occasional, partial clothing often place them in the realm of the erotic.

OTHER MASTERPIECES Cupid Complaining to Venus; *early 1530s; National Gallery, London, England* **The Nymph of the Fountain**; *1534; Walker Art Gallery, Liverpool, England*

Crivelli Carlo

Born Venice, Italy c.1430; died c.1495

The Annunciation, with St Emidius *1486; oil on canvas; 207 x 146 cm; National Gallery, London, England*

Despite training in Venice, Crivelli remained at a distance from the developing Venetian tradition, living in Ascoli, Ancona and other towns of the Marches. Crivelli always signed himself as a Venetian painter, though he never actually returned to Venice. His work suggests little knowledge of the developing Renaissance art in Tuscany, or the startling work being produced in Umbria by Piero della Francesca. Crivelli's style shows a number of diverse influences. In his decorative handling of gold as well as in the stiff, linear quality to his figures, he owes much to the International Gothic style. He was also influenced by the sculptural qualities he discovered in the paintings of Mantegna. Combining such different elements, Crivelli's religious paintings have a concentration and a dramatic intensity that can be quite clearly seen in **The Annunciation, with St Emidius**. In rendering the grand decorative facade of the architectural construction in such deep perspective, the artist reveals his knowledge of the contemporary science of foreshortening. Patterned carpets, a peacock's tail and strategically placed fruit indicate Crivelli's mastery of ornamentation and trompe l'oeil.

OTHER MASTERPIECES Madonna and Child; *c.1472; Metropolitan Museum of Art, New York City, USA* La Madonna Della Rondine; *c.1490–1492; National Gallery, London, England*

Cuyp Aelbert

Born Dordrecht, Netherlands 1620; died Dordrect, Netherlands 1691

Dordrecht, Evening *c.1650; oil on canvas; 98 x 138 cm; Kenwood House, London, England*

There were six or seven painters in the Cuyp family, although Aelbert Cuyp was the most original and accomplished. He was influenced by earlier Dutch landscape painters, in particular van Goyen. Cuyp never visited Italy himself, but it is likely he learned from Dutch painters such as Jan Both who had been there. From these painters Cuyp assimilated an Italianate handling of light. In his use of golden light, Cuyp revealed the influence of Claude and became known as the Dutch Claude. By the 1640s, Cuyp was producing much larger canvases in which he showed an interest in different effects of light at various times of the day. He painted a wide range of subjects, including portraits, still life, landscapes and town scenes, but is best known for portraying cows shown grouped on the lowlands or simply chewing the cud. **Dordrecht, Evening** is one of many paintings that Cuyp made of the watery landscape in and around in his native town. Cuyp's work was much admired in the nineteenth century by the English artists Constable and Turner.

OTHER MASTERPIECES Cattle with Horseman and Peasants; *c.1650; National Gallery, London, England* **The Maas at Dordrecht**; *c.1660; National Gallery of Art, Washington DC, USA*

Dali Salvador Felipe Jacinto

Born Figueiras, Spain 1904; died Barcelona, Spain 1989

Lobster Telephone *1936; mixed media; 178 x 330 mm; Tate Collection, London, England*

In 1922 Salvador Dali entered the Special School of Painting, Sculpture and Engraving in Madrid. By 1926 he had been expelled for extravagant behaviour. Such artistic anarchy set the tone for his life. He was quick to explore a variety of avant-garde trends, working his way through phases of Cubism, Futurism, Purism and the metaphysical style of de Chirico. Self-portraits abound. From the late 1920s the influence of Picasso, whom he met in Paris, became increasingly important and he dallied between using a classical, figurative style and working in a Cubist manner. Individual and perverse features make their way into the paintings, heralding a dramatic change in 1927. A crisis in his ideas about representation coincided with his entanglement with Surrealism. Works of 1929 are the culmination of his exploration into desires, dreams and the unconscious mind. Freudian symbolism and other elements combined to produce extraordinary imagery that seemed to be the visual equivalent of hallucinatory experience. Translated into sculpture, this was realized in such incongruous juxtapositions as the **Lobster Telephone**. He was repudiated by Breton and other, more traditional Surrealists when from the late 1930s he adopted a more classical style.

OTHER MASTERPIECES Soft Construction with Boiled Beans; Premonition of Civil War; *1936; Philadelphia Museum of Art, USA* The Persistence of Memory; *1931; Museum of Modern Art, New York City, USA*

Daumier Honoré

Born Marseille, France 1808; died Valmondois, France 1879

Washerwoman
1863–1864; oil on panel;
49 x 33.5 cm; Musée d'Orsay,
Paris, France

Honoré Daumier was a caricaturist who employed his graphic skills satrizing bourgeois French life and politics in the nineteenth century. He studied painting and lithography in Paris before making his living as a cartoonist for various satirical journals. His attacks on the government resulted in a short spell of imprisonment, after which he attempted to establish himself as an oil painter. Retaining his radical political sympathies and a keen sense of injustice, Daumier painted ordinary people going about their daily life. **Washerwoman** exemplifies his unsentimental approach. Other subjects included the occupants of a third-class railway carriage and the audience at a theatre. Boldly painted with harsh brush strokes, his compositions have a dramatic intensity due to the strong chiaroscuro. His sketches and oil paintings of **Don Quixote** are reminiscent of Goya and Rembrandt in their free handling and intensity of light and shadow. Daumier made watercolours and wash drawings of the Courts of Justice. He also worked as a sculptor on a number of clay busts and statuettes. Toward the end of his life, he started to go blind.

OTHER MASTERPIECES The Republic; *1845; Musée du Louvre, Paris, France*
La Fine Bouteille; *1856–1860; National Museum, Stockholm, Sweden*

David Jacques-Louis

Born Paris, France 1748; died Brussels, Belgium 1825

Madam Récamier 1800; oil on canvas; 174 x 244 cm; Musée du Louvre, Paris, France

Jacques-Louis David was the most important and successful of the Neoclassical painters. He trained in the Rococo tradition of his distant relation, François Boucher. After winning the Prix de Rome in 1774, David spent six years there. This inspired an enthusiasm for ancient sculpture which, combined with his admiration for the work of Nicholas Poussin, formed the basis of his Neoclassical style. **The Oath of the Horatii**, shown in Rome and Paris in 1784, indicated the depth of David's rejection of the Rococo tradition. A monumental work expressing an austerity that commended it to the leaders of the Revolution, it helped to establish David himself as a revolutionary leader. It was followed by other cool classical compositions featuring the martyrs of the Revolution, such as **The Death of Marat** (1793). David also painted portraits including that of the famous beauty and conversationalist, **Madam Récamier**, which, with its cool colouring and elegant simplicity, is a Neoclassical masterpiece. In 1798 David met Napoleon and became an ardent Bonapartist, fleeing to Brussels after the Battle of Waterloo in 1815. Gérard, Gros and Ingres were among David's many pupils.

OTHER MASTERPIECES The Oath of the Horatii; 1784; Musée du Louvre, Paris, France
The Death of Marat; 1793; Musées Royaux des Beaux-Arts de Belgique, Brussels, Belgium

Deacon Richard

Born Bangor, Wales 1949

This, That and The Other *1985;*
2 parts, laminated hardboard and canvas,
galvanized steel; 228 x 396 x 182 cm;
Private Collection, London, England

Richard Deacon undertook his art training in London at St Martin's School of Art, from 1969 to 1972, and then at the Royal College of Art, from 1974 to 1977. He studied art history at Chelsea School of Art during 1979. Along with Tony Cragg, Deacon is recognized as one of the most significant British sculptors of his generation. Although his work is essentially abstract, there is a sense of figuration in the linear constructs and biomorphic forms that distinguish his work. Rather than focus on a particular range of subjects within the real world, Deacon works as a "fabricator", exploring the convoluted nature of sculpture itself by emphasizing the manufacturing process. He uses a variety of materials – metal, wood and, occasionally, cloth – and employs a diverse range of construction methods – welding, riveting and gluing – to create complex structures that somehow seem familiar. As in **This, That and The Other**, the interplay of solid shapes and fluid lines sets in motion interior relationships within the piece. Deacon enquires into the nature of forms in space and of the hidden spaces within those forms. The associations that we bring to our experience of this enquiry also become an integral part of it.

OTHER MASTERPIECES Fish Out of Water; *1987; Hirshhorn Museum and Sculpture Garden, Washington D.C., USA* **After**; *1998; Tate Collection, London, England*

Degas Hilaire Germain Edgar

Born Paris, France 1834; died Paris, France 1917

Woman Ironing *c. 1885;*
oil on canvas; 81 x 75 cm;
Walker Art Gallery,
Liverpool, England

Edgar Degas abandoned
a training in law to
study art. His tutor was
a pupil of Ingres and
passed the exemplary
draughtsmanship of the
eighteenth-century
master on to Degas. In
1856 the artist visited
various Italian cities
where he took the
opportunity to study and
copy the drawings and
frescoes by great
Renaissance artists. He
returned to produce
works with historical
themes wrought in a classical manner and exhibited these with the Impressionists. Contact with
Manet's circle from 1861 encouraged Degas to concentrate on scenes from contemporary life,
particularly those that offered the opportunity to depict movement. Contemporary experiments
with photography and the current vogue for Japanese prints made an impression on Degas'
composition. Unusual angles of vision, off-centre focal points, figures cut by the frame and a
assertion of linear qualities contributed to Degas' inimitable style. Degas is best known for his
exquisite pastel studies of the ballet, theatre and circus. Drawing allowed him to work rapidly,
capturing transient activity, a passing mood, a languid yawn. Degas has been accused of
misogyny in his dispassionate treatment of women. **Woman Ironing** demonstrates Degas
concern only to express what was real with a technical ability that remains unsurpassed.

OTHER MASTERPIECES Awaiting the Cue; *1879; Private Collection, New York City, USA*
At the Races; *1869–1872; Musée du Louvre, Paris, France*

Delacroix Ferdinand-Victor-Eugène

Born Charenton-St-Maurice, France 1798; died Paris, France 1863

Liberty Leading the People *1830; oil on canvas; 260 x 325 cm; Musée du Louvre, Paris, France*

By the early 1850s Eugène Delacroix had affirmed the position he had held as the leader of the Romantic movement – albeit a rebellious one. He visited Morocco in 1832 and considered himself a dandy. He was denied membership of the Academie des Beaux-Arts until 1857 despite being regarded as a key artist by all but the most conservative critics and had received numerous state commissions throughout his career. In addition to directing large decorative mural projects he produced many memorable, smaller works. In his later years he wrote the bulk of his celebrated *Journal* and continued to publish art criticism. He was probably the last great artist to consider himself primarily as a history painter, preferring to tackle exotic or heroic major themes. **Liberty Leading the People** is one such triumphant composition. It appears like an allegory but was conceived to act like a poster illustrating the contemporary life of the 1830 Revolution. The avant-garde of his time respected him as an older, independent artist and Baudelaire was included among his loyal admirers. He is often regarded as the greatest colourist of French painters.

OTHER MASTERPIECES Algerian Woman; *1833; Musée du Louvre, Paris, France*
Massacre at Chios; *1823; Musée du Louvre, Paris, France*

Delaunay Robert

Born Paris, France 1885; died Montpellier, France 1941

Windows Open Simultaneously *1912; oil on canvas; 457 x 375 cm; Tate Collection, London, England*

Robert Delaunay started to paint in 1904. His early work showed the influence of the Neo-Impressionists and the Fauves but in 1908, enlarging upon Cubist principles, he began his own influential investigation into colour. Delaunay's painting **Saint Sèverin** (1909) is regarded as the starting point of his new theories of colour. Believing he could create movement and depth purely through contrasts of colour, Delaunay declared that "colour is form and subject". His paintings of the city of Paris and the Eiffel Tower echoed these concerns. He generally worked in series and moved beyond the conventional notions of landscape to show the dynamism of city life, often from a high vantage point. **Windows Open Simultaneously** (first part of Triptych, 3rd motif) uses contrasting colours to break up space in an entirely new way. The poet Apollinaire was the first person to use the term Orphism to describe this movement, which was also closely related to music. His wife, Russian-born Sonia Terk Delaunay, was also a notable artist. Delaunay was a considerable influence on the Blaue Reiter group.

OTHER MASTERPIECES The Eiffel Tower; *1910; Guggenheim Museum, New York City, USA* **Paris, Ste Severin**; *1909; Private Collection, USA*

Denis Maurice

Born Grandville, France 1870; died Paris, France 1943

Homage to Cézanne *1900; oil on canvas; 180 x 240 cm; Musée d'Orsay, Paris, France*

Maurice Denis was a member of the Nabis and an exponent of the contemporary Symbolist ideologies. He met with future Nabis artist Vuillard and Roussel at the Lycée Condorcet, before attending the Atelier Balla and the Academie Julian. Here he met Bonnard and Serusier, with whom he formed the Nabis in 1888. **Homage to Cézanne**, an unusually naturalistic painting, illustrates, in detail, identifiable members of the Nabis paying respect to the earlier master's work. Denis participated in group exhibitions and exercised considerable versatility, producing not only easel and large-scale decorative paintings but also designs for stained glass, stage-sets and theatrical costumes. These were in addition to illustrations, prints and numerous articles, including a published history of religious art in 1939. His collected art dictums prefigured those of Modernist art theorist Clement Greenberg. Denis probably made his most valuable contribution to the history of painting when he stated that before it is anything else, "… a picture… is essentially a flat surface, covered with colours assembled in a certain order".

OTHER MASTERPIECES The Blessing of the Boats; *c.1895; Josefowitz Collection, Switzerland*
Bathers; *1899; Musée du Petit Palais, Paris, France*

Derain André

Born Chatou, France 1880; died Garches, France 1954

Barges on the Thames *1906; oil on canvas; 81.3 x 99 cm; City Art Gallery, Leeds, England*

André Derain first became acquainted with fellow painter Maurice de Vlaminck when he was a student. Derain met Henri Matisse in 1899 and introduced his friend Vlaminck to Matisse a couple of years later. Although all three artists recognized the important similarities between them it was not until 1905 that they entered the Salon d'Automne for the first time as part of a large group. The boldness of these painters' work led to their nickname of the Fauves (wild beasts). Derain's work of this period, with its expressive use of pure colour and mosaic surfaces, marked him out as one of the most original and important of the Fauves. **Barges on the Thames** is one of a number of Derain's works that took London landmarks as its theme. In his use of strong colour Derain transforms the scene, making the setting subordinate to its lively expression. Between 1908 and 1910, Derain's work showed the influence of Cubism. He met Picasso and worked with him at Cadaquès. After 1919, Derain retreated from the avant-garde and reverted to a more traditional style, adopting a much more restrained and sombre palette.

OTHER MASTERPIECES Fishing Boats, Collioure; *1905; Metropolitan Museum of Art, New York City, USA* **St Paul's from the Thames** *1906–1907; Minneapolis Institute of Arts, Minneapolis, USA*

Diebenkorn Richard

Born Portland, USA, 1922; died Portland, USA 1993

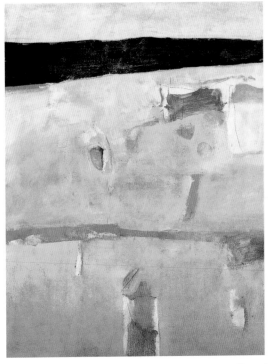

Albuquerque II 1951;
oil on canvas; 143.5 x
113 cm; Acquavella
Contemporary Art Inc,
New York City, USA

Richard Diebenkorn, like painter Robert Motherwell, swam calmly against the tide of Abstract Expressionism that saturated the American art scene of the 1950s and 1960s. The contemporary fascination with popular culture also left Diebenkorn's art unscathed. The subtle nuances of the European Modernist movement, however, infused his work. Sensitivity and compositional structure, informed by emotional and sensual concerns, infiltrated his painting. **Albuquerque II** was produced shortly before Diebenkorn radically changed direction toward figuration. This beautiful abstract is at once soft and hard, elegantly composed and grounded by the rich ultramarine wedge near the base. The visible element of drawing in the painting was realized more overtly in his subsequent representational style, which influenced successive generations of Californian artists. Diebenkorn's respect for the Modernists – Henri Matisse in particular – and the bold canvases of the colour-field painters, Clifford Still and Barnett Newman for example, resulted in later canvases that have much in common with the Symbolist tradition of equivalents; sensation and harmony are described in terms of colour, line and form.

OTHER MASTERPIECES City Scape 1; *1963; Museum of Modern Art, San Francisco, California, USA* **Ocean Park No.66;** *1973; Albright-Knox Art Gallery, Buffalo, New York State, USA*

Dine Jim

Born Cincinnatti, USA 1935

Jumps Out at You, No? *1993; etching and softground with hand-colouring; paper, 53.2 x 71.2 cm, image 31.5 x 53.6 cm; edition of seventy five; Jim Dine and the Alan Cristea Gallery, USA*

A prominent figure in the genesis of Pop Art in America, Jim Dine worked in the spirit of Dada as a multimedia artist. A negation of the traditional boundaries of art became the basis for his work. He trained at the University of Cincinnati, at the Boston Museum School and graduated from Ohio University in 1958. Dine propelled the Duchampian notion of the "ready-made" into his practice. Like Robert Rauschenberg, he created assemblages by attaching objects – a piece of clothing or a domestic appliance – to painted canvases. Items of the real world thereby became displaced from it; they were integrated with, and distinguished as, fine art objects. This was a concept he took further via his involvement with "Happenings", beginning at the end of the 1950s. These psychodrama collaborations heralded the all-embracing cultural aspects of Pop, while remaining cognisant of the physical action that is so much a part of Abstract Expressionist practice. A precursor of Performance Art, they were oriented toward combining the visual arts with free improvization. From the mid-1970s, Dine turned to a more traditional, representational mode of painting and printmaking, embodying himself in the image of the robe as in **Jumps Out At You, No?**

OTHER MASTERPIECES The Toaster; *1962; Whitney Museum of American Art, New York City, USA* **Child's Bright Blue Wall,** *1962; Albright-Knox Art Gallery, Buffalo, New York State, USA*

Dix Otto

Born Untermhausen, Germany 1891; died Singen, Germany 1969

Die Grosstadt *1928; (centre panel); mixed media on wood; 181 x 200 cm; Galerie der Stadt, Stuttgart, Germany*

Otto Dix studied in Dresden, where his early work declared an interest in pictorial realism and a refusal to idealize his subjects. In 1914 he was called up to fight in the First World War. At the front he experienced the horrors of trench warfare and gas attacks. He returned to study in Dresden and Düsseldorf, producing collages from materials chosen for their ugliness. His anti-war compositions, fifty etchings published as **The War** in 1924, and a large painting of trench life, now lost, are unsparing in showing the decay and carnage of the trenches. His triptych **Die Grosstadt** (Metropolis) depicts the corruption of modern urban society and in particular its night life. In his portraits, Dix investigates human nature with the critical detachment of a surgeon. It was this determination to root out truth as well as an unflinching attention to detail that led to Dix's inclusion in the New Objectivity movement with Beckmann and Grosz. After being appointed a professor at the Dresden Academy, Dix was dismissed by the Nazis in 1933. In the 1930s he slipped back into Romanticism, before entering a post-Second World War phase of Expressionism with religious overtones.

OTHER MASTERPIECES Homage to Beauty; *1922; Von Der Heydt-Museum, Wuppertal, Germany* **The Art Dealer Alfred Flechtheim**; *1926; National Galerie, Berlin, Germany*

Donatello

Born Florence, Italy c.1386; died Florence, Italy 1466.

*St George c.1417; white marble;
209 x 67 cm; Museo Nazional dell
Bargello, Milan, Italy*

Donatello was the greatest
Florentine sculptor before
Michelangelo, and the most
influential artist of the
fifteenth century. Along with
Masaccio and his friend
Brunelleschi he was the
leading figure of a new
humanist movement which
relocated man to the centre of
the Universe; with this came a
dramatic shift in how objects
and people could be
represented. These artists
made sense of a rapidly
changing world through their
own observations and styles,
galvanized by an increasing
knowledge of ancient Rome
and Greece. From 1416 he
worked on this sculpture of **St
George**, commissioned by the
Guild of Armourers whose
patron saint it represents. It
was destined for a space on
the outside of the church of
Or San Michele in Florence.

Donatello portrays St George as a heroic, lifelike figure, calm yet alert, watching warily for
approaching danger. More significant is the relief below of St George killing the dragon; this is
the earliest known example of the new science of perspective being used to create a believable
space for the figures to inhabit.

OTHER MASTERPIECES Herod's Feast; *1427; Siena Cathedral, Italy*
Magdalen; *c.1455; Baptistry, Florence, Italy*

116

Duchamp Marcel

Born Blainville, France 1887; died Neuilly, France 1968

The Bride Stripped Bare by Her Bachelors, Even – The Large Glass *1966; oil and lead wire and glass; 264.8 x 175.6 cm; Tate Collection, London, England*

Duchamp is usually associated with his ready-made sculptures, which feature one or two everyday objects, a urinal, for example, or a stool topped by a bicycle wheel. The artist's designation of these objects as art proved a highly influential ideology which remains pertinent for many artists working today. However, Duchamp first achieved notoriety for **Nude Descending a Staircase**, 1912, a painting in which he combined the principles of Cubism and Futurism. With Picabia, Duchamp was the leader of the New York Dada movement and his invention of the ready-made was a manifestation of Dada's anti-art dictum. In 1915 Duchamp began creating his major work, **The Bride . . .** He declared it "definitively unfinished" in 1923. This was another manifestation of his abandonment of conventional media and his interest in three-dimensional objects suggesting the technology of machines or instruments. These appeared to be scientific gadgets but neither functioned such nor served any purpose. **The Bride...** is elaborate and impressive, concocted of varnish, lead and dust mounted between glass panels. It is an obscure, symbolic work, a coded presentation of the sexual act as a mechanistic and endlessly frustrating procedure.

OTHER MASTERPIECES Fountain; *191˙*   *Jannis Gallery, New York City, USA*
In Advance of a Broken Arm; *1915; Yale*   *Art Gallery, New Haven, Connecticut, USA*

Dufy Raoul

Born Le Havre, France 1877; died Forcalquier, France 1953

The Pier and Promenade at Nice *c.1924; oil on canvas; 38 x 46.5 cm; Musée National d'Art Moderne, Paris, France*

Raoul Dufy studied in Le Havre, where his early work showed the influence of Impressionism. He moved to Paris in 1900 where he met Georges Braque and Henri Matisse. Matisse's painting **Luxe, Calme, et Volupté** had a great impact on Dufy who regarded it as "a miracle of the creative imagination at play in colour and line". Adopting the newly formed ideas of Fauvism, Dufy started to produce paintings with strong colour and heavy black outlines. He only exhibited with the Fauves twice – in 1906 and 1907. In 1908 he worked with Braque, before turning to themes that showed upper-class life. After 1920, Dufy's work is characterized by joyous scenes of racecourses, regattas and esplanades, typified by **The Pier and Promenade at Nice**. Painted in vibrant colours, these works are distinguished by their lively, frivolous, decorative style and their rapid, calligraphic brush strokes. Dufy also designed textiles and ceramics. He was essentially a light-hearted artist who never dwelt on the sad or unseemly side of life.

OTHER MASTERPIECES Placards at Trouville; *1906; Musée National d'Art Moderne, Paris, France* The Artist and his Model in the Studio at Le Havre; *1929; Stedelijk Museum, The Hague, Netherlands*

Dürer Albrecht

Born Nuremberg, Germany 1471; died Nuremberg, Germany 1528

Wing of a Hooded Crow *1512; watercolour on vellum with gold; 19.7 x 20.1 cm; Graphische Sammlung Albertina, Vienna, Austria*

Albrecht Dürer's father, a goldsmith, undoubtedly introduced him to detailed drawing with silverpoint, a medium of which he became a precocious master, shown by his remarkable self-portrait made in 1484. He was apprenticed in 1486 to the leading Nuremburg painter and book illustrator, Wolgemut. The master taught him the techniques of his trade which included woodcut. Dürer was also in contact with humanist thinkers who widened his vision of the world. He travelled across Italy, which brought him into contact with the paintings of Bellini, Leonardo's drawings and Mantegna's engravings, all of which had their effect on his work. He sought the company of scholars in preference to artisans and he inevitably became occupied with contemporary thought on perspective, proportion and beauty. **Wing of a Hooded Crow** is an exquisite example of Dürer's refined observation, graphic and colourist skills. He acknowledged the legacy of the Reformation but, more importantly, he introduced Italian Renaissance forms and ideas to the North, reinforcing his practical achievements by producing a number of theoretical treatises.

OTHER MASTERPIECES Melencolia I; *1514; Whitworth Art Gallery, Manchester, England*
Self-Portrait; *1498; Museo del Prado, Madrid, Spain*

Dyck Sir Anthony van

Born Antwerp, Belgium 1599; died London, England 1641

Charles I *c.1632–1633; oil on canvas; 100 x 81.8 cm; Philip Mould Historical Portraits Ltd, London, England*

Anthony van Dyck trained in Antwerp where he became chief assistant to Rubens. He visited Britain briefly from 1620 to 1621, before touring Italy where he undertook a number of church commissions. He returned to Antwerp in 1625 and started to develop his portraiture before settling in England in 1631. His years in England were enormously successful. Welcomed into the court of Charles I, van Dyck received a knighthood and unlimited access to the aristocracy as models for his portraits. Among the best known of his English portraits are his various paintings of **Charles I**. In these works, van Dyck strives hard to flatter the King, lending him dignity and intelligence. Sensitive to his royal sitter's individuality, van Dyck's portrait betrays something of the artist's own introspective disposition. Beneath the elegant and refined surface of this and many other of his portraits, there is a hint of nervous tension. His portraits established the style of British portraiture for the next 200 years, through Lely, Reynolds and Gainsborough to Lawrence. Van Dyck also painted a number of religious and mythological subjects.

OTHER MASTERPIECES Lord John and Lord Bernard Stuart; *c.1638; National Gallery, London, England* **Charles I in Hunting Dress**; *c.1635; Musée du Louvre, Paris, France*

Eakins Thomas

Born Philadelphia, USA 1844; died Philadelphia, USA 1916

The Champion Single Sculls *1871; oil on canvas; 81.9 x 117.5 cm; The Metropolitan Museum of Art, Purchase, The Alfred N Punnett Endowment Fund and George D Pratt, 1934*

Thomas Eakins was a prodigious draughtsman who studied art at the Pennsylvania Academy of Fine Arts, as well as anatomy at Jefferson Medical College. He travelled from Philadelphia to Paris in 1866 and entered the Ecole des Beaux-Arts, where he was influenced by the realism of Manet. Four years later in Spain, his exposure to the works of Velasquez and Ribera also had an impact on his painting style. On his return home, Eakins became one of the major American Realists. He was also a highly regarded art teacher, insisting that his students draw from the nude and attend anatomy lessons. Eakins pursued his own interest in scientific realism and his objective and faithful representations of surgeons operating caused an uproar when they were first shown. **The Champion Single Sculls (Max Schmitt in a Single Scull)** focuses on a single rower. Eakins loved sports, as demonstrated by other works that feature boxing and baseball. Above all, this work shows Eakins' ability to render a human figure based on sound anatomical knowledge. As a photographer, Eakins also continued Eadweard Muybridge's pioneering experiments concerning movement through sequential photography.

OTHER MASTERPIECES Starting out after Rail; *1874; Museum of Fine Arts, Boston, Massachusetts, USA* **Baseball Players Practising**; *1875; Museum of Art, Rhode Island, USA*

Eardley Joan

Born Warnham, England 1921; died Killearn, Scotland 1963

Catterline in Winter *c.1963; oil on hardboard; 120.7 x 130.8 cm; Scottish National Gallery of Modern Art, Edinburgh, Scotland*

Joan Eardley moved to Glasgow from the south of England when war broke out in 1939. Her involvement with the war effort prevented her from receiving her post-graduate diploma from Glasgow School of Art until 1948. With it she received a scholarship to travel to France and Italy. Returning to "the living part of Glasgow", she became involved in the local community, making studies of the tenements and of the children she befriended. Her work provides a socio-documentary record of the poor environment, which is poignant without being voyeuristic or sentimental. In 1950 Eardley visited the east Scottish fishing village of Catterline where she settled in 1956. Here she produced some of her most evocative images, focusing on the local land and seascapes and the changes wrought by the seasons. She often incorporated detritus into her paintings to increase an understanding of her experience. Her zest for the elements, for what was primitive and for humanity is comparable to that of van Gogh. The vigour and intensity of her vision is revealed in the fury and colour of **Catterline in Winter**, which verges on the abstract and confirms how she valued nature as her "greatest influence".

OTHER MASTERPIECES Street Kids; *1950; Scottish National Gallery of Modern Art, Edinburgh, Scotland* **Salmon Net Posts**; *c.1961–1962; Tate Collection, London, England*

Ensor James

Born Ostend, Belgium 1860; died Ostend, Belgium 1949

Death and the Masks *1897; oil on canvas; 78.5 x 100 cm; Musée des Beaux-Arts, Liége, Belgium*

In 1884 Ensor co-founded the international exhibiting group, Les Vingt. His relations with it were not entirely peaceful and he became increasingly isolated. He was an original but controversial talent and his feelings towards hostile critics and an uncomprehending public can be best explained by paintings such as **Death and the Masks**. Full of garishness and striking imagery it is constructed with slab-like handling of paint and crisply outlined forms. It represents a transitional phase which was partly the result of Ensor's changing position within artistic circles in Brussels. The painting incorporates the luminosity and graphic linear qualities that characterized his work from the early 1890s. It also looks forward to the increasingly facile, less inventive work made after 1900. The symbolism of masks, skeletons and pierrots in his work conveys the traditional meanings of dissimulation, death and despair. They are inventive devices of satirical, social criticism and reveal his cynicism. They link together theatrical tragedy and the grotesque, forcing the passage of Symbolism toward Expressionism and influenced the development of the Surrealist movement.

OTHER MASTERPIECES Christ's Entry into Brussels; *1888–1889; Koninklijk Museum voor Schone Kunsten, Antwerp, Belgium* **The Ray**; *1892; Musées Royaux des Beaux-Arts, Brussels, Belgium*

Epstein Sir Jacob

Born New York City, USA 1880; died London, England 1959

Genesis *1931; seravezza marble;*
162.5 x 83.8 x 78.7 cm;
Permanent loan of Granada Television
Group, Whitworth Art Gallery,
Manchester, England

Jacob Epstein was born of Russian-Polish Jewish parents. He studied at the Ecole des Beaux-Arts in Paris and at the Académie Julian. Visits to the Louvre engendered an interest in ancient and particularly primitive art, of which he was to become a notable collector. This and his knowledge of Rodin's work influenced the expressive power of his sculpture. He settled in London in 1905 and received a knighthood in 1954. His exploitation of nudity within his carving, emphasized by his rigorous handling of stone, marble and bronze, roused many objections, particularly when applied to religious subjects. However, the consternation did not reduce his reputation as a robust and imaginative talent, sculpting in the romantic tradition. He was a founder member of the London Group of artists in 1913 and his association with the Vorticists resulted in his creation of mechanistic figures such as The Rock Drill. Epstein began carving **Genesis** in 1929, "… with," he claimed, "no hesitations and no preliminary studies". The subject, pregnancy, was as controversial as the crude, anti-naturalistic carving. It is a raw, primitive vision and a bold testament to motherhood.

OTHER MASTERPIECES Jacob and the Angel; *1940; Tate Collection, London, England*
St Michael and the Devil; *1957; Coventry Cathedral, Coventry, England*

Ernst Max

Born Brühl, Germany 1891; died Paris, France 1976

Sea and Sun *1925; oil on canvas; 54 x 37 cm; Scottish National Gallery of Modern Art, Edinburgh, Scotland*

Max Ernst received no formal training as an artist, originally studying philosophy and psychiatry at the University of Bonn. During a visit to Paris in 1913 he met Macke, Delaunay, Apollinaire and Arp and began to develop a practice that involved working in a variety of media. Ernst founded the Cologne Dada group in 1919, introducing found objects into his fantasy-inspired ensembles. He was also responsible for a technique known as frottage, which involved drawing on a sheet of paper over a rough surface to allow the texture underneath to come through. **Sea and Sun** was painted in 1925, the year after the Surrealist movement was launched. Nature for Ernst was never a benign force; the single red eye casts a disturbing, all-seeing presence over the landscape. In paintings that frequently referred to nightmares and hallucinatory experience, Ernst continued to make irrational and bizarre juxtapositions of unrelated objects. Max Ernst was a leading Surrealist who, like many others, went to live in the United States during the Second World War. His last years were spent in France.

OTHER MASTERPIECES Two Children Are Threatened by a Nightingale; *1924; Museum of Modern Art, New York City, USA* **Petrified City**; *1933; City of Manchester Art Galleries, Manchester, England*

Eyck Jan van

Active from 1422; died Bruges, Belgium 1441

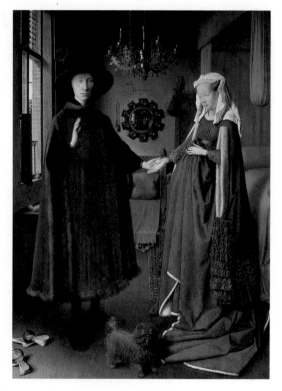

The Arnolfini Marriage
1434; oil on oak panel;
81.8 x 59.7 cm; National
Gallery, London, England

Jan van Eyck was the greatest artist of the early Netherlands school. He held high positions throughout his career, including court painter and diplomat in Bruges. So outstanding was his skill as an oil painter that the invention of the medium was at one time attributed to him, with his brother Hubert, also a painter. Van Eyck exploited the qualities of oil as never before, building up layers of transparent glazes, thus giving him a surface on which to capture objects in the minutest detail and allowing for the preservation of his colours. Nowhere is this better displayed than in this portrait of Giovanni di Arrigo Arnolfini, a merchant from Lucca and a frequent visitor to Bruges, and his wife Giovanna Cenami. The signature on the back wall – "Jan Van Eyck was here, 1434" – and his reflection in the mirror has led many to believe that he was a witness to their marriage. The carving of Saint Margaret, the patron saint of childbirth, on the bed, and the presence of the dog – a traditional symbol of faithfulness – accentuate the marital theme.

OTHER MASTERPIECES A Man in a Turban; *1433; National Gallery, London, England*
Madonna of Canon Van Der Paele; *1436; Groeningemuseum, Bruges, Belgium*

Fantin-Latour Henri

Born Grenoble, France 1836; died Buré, France 1904

Roses *1895; oil on canvas; 36.5 x 39 cm; National Gallery of Scotland, Edinburgh, Scotland*

Henri Fantin-Latour studied painting under both his father and Gustave Courbet. He exhibited regularly at the Paris Salon from 1861, but was also included, with Manet, Cézanne and Whistler, in the Salon des Refusés (1863). This was held as a protest against the number of works rejected by the Salon that year. A romantic streak, fuelled by a passion for the music of Wagner, meant that he began to move away from a hitherto academic approach. Fantin-Latour painted figure subjects, portrait groups and still life. His groups of figures include **Homage to Delacroix** (1864), a celebration of the great French Romantic painter and **Homage to Manet** (1870), which shows Manet and other leading artists of the period grouped round a portrait of Delacroix. His still life, such as **Roses**, were painted in the meticulous Dutch manner. Each petal of these cultivated blooms has been minutely observed. The delicacy of the pink flowers is further heightened by the dark background from which they emerge. Henri Fantin-Latour was friendly with most of the avant-garde French painters of his time and was an admirer of the Pre-Raphaelites.

OTHER MASTERPIECES Homage to Manet; *1870; Musée du Louvre, Paris, France*
White Roses in a Glass Vase; *c.1890; Guildhall Art Gallery, Corporation of London, England*

Feininger Lyonel

Born New York City, USA 1871; died New York City, USA 1956

Gelmeroda *1926; oil
on canvas; 100 x 80 cm;
Museum Folkwang,
Essen, Germany*

Born to German-
American parents,
Lyonel Feininger
moved to Germany
in 1887. He studied
music in Berlin before
working as a
cartoonist for various
magazines. On a visit
to Paris in 1911,
Feininger became
acquainted with
Robert Delaunay and
with Cubism.
Delaunay's study of the poetic possibilities of colour greatly influenced Feininger. The two men
also shared an interest in using urban architecture as the basis for their paintings. In 1913
Feininger was invited by Frans Marc to exhibit with Der Blaue Reiter. Feininger's romantic
streak found natural allies in Klee and Kandinsky. He taught at the Bauhaus but was forced to
return to the States when named as a degenerate artist by Hitler. His best works are his
visionary abstractions of architecture and seascapes. **Gelmeroda** is from a series of thirteen
paintings that take the village church at Gelmeroda as a starting point. Here, the tiny
foreground figures are dwarfed by a building seen simultaneously from several points of view.
Feininger gradually eliminates any natural elements from the series; the later work is simply
composed of a number of delicate, superimposed, translucent planes.

OTHER MASTERPIECES Gate-Tower II; *1921; Staatliche Kunsthalle, Karlsruhe, Germany*
The Steamship Odin II; *1927; Museum of Modern Art, New York City, USA*

Fischl Eric

Born New York City, USA 1948

Pizza Eater *1982;*
oil on canvas; 150 x
150 cm; Mary Boone
Gallery, New York
City, USA

Eric Fischl's reputation belongs to the 1980s, when a return to figuration usurped the monopoly that conceptual and Minimal art had on American painting through the 1960s and 1970s. He studied at the California Institute of the Arts, 1969 to 1972. Fischl followed in the spirit of the Social Realist painters of the 1930s, his work comprises scenes taken from a voyeuristic perspective. The viewer takes a complicit position as witness to the complicated narratives that unfold. A recurring mise en scène is of invaded privacy or emergent sexuality, as in **Pizza Eater**. A young girl, on the point of puberty, wanders naked through the sand, unaware of, or having contrived to orientate the males' gaze toward her. Typically, neither the beginning nor the end of this story is explained nor suggested and we are left with a sense of unease. Our response to this picture is dictated by our knowledge of contemporary society. Fischl seeks to denounce the attitudes that prevail in American culture, particularly toward women. His technique, which has been criticized on the grounds that it reveals a lack of skill, exacerbates the emotional awkwardness of his subjects and allows us some distance from the intimacy of the situation.

OTHER MASTERPIECES Bad Boy; *1981; Saatchi Collection, London, England* **What Stands Between the Artist and…**; *1994; Smithsonian American Art Museum, Washington D.C., USA*

Fontana Lucio

Born Santa Fé, Argentina 1899; died Varese, Italy 1968

Spatial Concept Waiting *1958; pastel on canvas; 163.8 x 123.6 cm; Tate Collection, London, England*

Lucio Fontana lived in Milan as a child and studied at the Brera Academy from 1927 to 1929. Fontana is noted for his controversial, slashed and otherwise vacant canvases of the 1960s, such as **Spatial Concept Waiting**. He first exhibited abstract sculptures from 1930 and turned his attentions to painting in the 1940s, often producing a series of monochrome pieces. He issued the White Manifesto in Milan in 1946 to coincide with his series of white paintings. A year later Fontana founded the Spazialismo group, reflecting his exploration of integrating spatial relationships with the development of two-dimensional media. He is connected with Dadaist ideology, producing as he did, works that would appear to negate traditional notions of art and aesthetics. His work is minimal to the point of presenting a negative presence. A slash in a bland, "colourless" canvas is less about violence than absence, a denial of creative application. The overt simplicity and reductive nature of Fontana's work belies great sophistication and has proved influential to successive generations of conceptual artists.

OTHER MASTERPIECES Spatial Concept; *1959–1960; Staditsches Museum, Munchengladbach, Germany* **New York 15**; *1962; Private Collection*

Fouquet Jean

Born Tours, France 1420; died Tours, France c.1481

Mary and Child c.1460s;
*wood panel; 91.8 x
83.3 cm; Koninklijk Museum
voor Schöne Kunsten,
Antwerp, Belgium*

Like Italy and the Netherlands in the fifteenth century, France too had its share of art schools
and eminent painters. Jean Fouquet, based in Tours, was perhaps their greatest painter during
the fifteenth century. He trained in Bourges and Paris between 1435 and 1445. It is almost
certain that he visited Italy, where he gained his knowledge of perspective and Piero della
Francesca's pictorial lighting effects. On his return to France, in 1475, he became an artist at the
French court. **Mary and Child** may in fact be a portrait of King Charles VII's mistress, Agnes
Sorel, who along with Etienne Chevalier, the Treasurer of France, painted on the left panel of
this diptych, were the most powerful French courtiers of the time. The naturalistic facial
features, the crown's jewels and throne adornment all show the influence of the French
miniaturist tradition. The delicately rendered folds of the Virgin's robe can be explained by
the fact that Fouquet also designed marble sculpture, despite his apparent disregard for
anatomical correctness. The icy stark whiteness of the Virgin's skin contrasts with the green
and fiery red of the cherubim and a seraphim close behind. It makes for a dramatic and
intensely serious devotional piece.

OTHER MASTERPIECES Saint Margaret and Olibrius; *c.1450; Musée du Louvre, Paris, France*
Portrait of Juvenal Des Ursins; *c.1460; Musée du Louvre, Paris, France*

Fragonard Jean Honoré

Born Grasse, France 1732; died Paris, France 1806

The Stolen Kiss c.1788; oil on canvas; 45 x 55 cm; Hermitage, St Petersburg, Russia

Fragonard is synonymous with eighteenth-century rococo style. He was, in fact, an artist of great versatility who worked in a variety of styles and used a range of techniques. These were a result of the breadth of the teaching he received and the works he studied on his travels. He was tutored by both Chardin and Boucher and when in Rome he studied under Tiepolo, whose influence in regard to the use of grandeur and spatiality can be detected in Fragonard's larger works. While in Italy he developed competent landscape paintings. Once back in Paris in 1761, he painted historical themes in the Grand Manner, becoming a member of the Academy in 1765. The elegance of the aristocracy and their gay abandonment to life's pleasures is portrayed with verve by Fragonard. Healthy foliage and outrageously fussy, decorative clothing all receive the same, painterly treatment; delicate observations of Watteau meet the robust fleshiness of Rubens. His images are rich, erotic and fanciful. In **The Stolen Kiss**, Fragonard rescues the subject from sentimentality, suggesting a more gallant approach. Subsequent attempts to conform to Neoclassical taste failed. He died in poverty.

OTHER MASTERPIECES The Progress of Love; c.1770; Frick Collection, New York City, USA
The Swing; c.1768; Wallace Collection, London, England

Frankenthaler Helen

Born New York City, USA 1928

Black Frame I *1992; acrylic on printed proof; 78.75 x 101.6 cm; Collection of the Artist*

Helen Frankenthaler attended the Bennington College in Vermont in 1949 and later studied under abstract painter Hans Hoffman. In 1951, she discovered the work of Jackson Pollock. This led, in the early 1950s, to the development of her own Abstract Expressionist style known as "stain-soak". These large paintings involved the application of washes and stains to unprimed canvas and were produced on the floor. The result of this innovatory technique was a delicate and fluid merging of forms, which have an ambiguous and improvisational quality due to the unpredictable absorbency of the canvas. Her key work from this period, **Mountains and Sea** (1952), influenced the stain paintings of Kenneth Noland and Morris Louis. **Black Frame I** is a later work that makes use of much stronger colour. Acrylic paint is used to create a sensuous and lyrical painting that seems to refer to seascape, while the overall effect is of a joyous, abstract composition, in which the artist's pleasure is revealed through the expressive brushstokes. Helen Frankenthaler was married to fellow Abstract Expressionist Robert Motherwell from 1958 until 1971.

OTHER MASTERPIECES Mountains and Sea*; 1952; on loan to the National Gallery of Art, Washington DC, USA* **Door***; 1976–1979; Tate Collection, London, England*

Freud Lucian

Born Berlin, Germany 1922

Standing By The Rags
1988–1989; oil on canvas;
168.25 x 138.5; Tate
Collection, London, England

The grandson of
psychoanalyst Sigmund,
Lucian Freud came to
England in 1932. He
studied at the Central
School of Arts and
Crafts, London,
(1938–1939) and at the East Anglian School of Painting and Drawing, Suffolk until 1942. He
then went on to study part-time at Goldsmith's College, London. Freud's early work was in a
harsh, realistic style, but painted with a flatness that lent emphasis to lineation. Quirky, surreal
elements infiltrated his portraits and still life. An unnerving distortion and washed-out palette
added to their potent charge. From the late 1950s, Freud's style began to alter, to satisfy his
need for paint "to work as flesh does". In his dedication to the human form, Freud has been
bracketed as a painter of the School of London. However, his personal approach to his subjects
– his mother, his daughters, friends and life models – is completely original. His paintings are
probing investigations of people, their skin, most commonly under electric light, their
expressions, their moods and their discomfort under scrutiny. **Standing By the Rags** reveals
how his paint-work has become increasingly impastoed, almost as if he is moulding or sculpting
from the very substance of what it is to be human.

OTHER MASTERPIECES Girl With Roses; *1947–1948; The British Council Collection, London,
England* **Naked Man With His Friend**; *1978–1980; Astrup Fearnely Museum, Copenhagen, Denmark*

Friedrich Caspar David

Born Greifswald, Germany 1774; died Dresden, Germany 1840

The Stages of Life *c. 1833; oil on canvas; 72.5 x 94 cm; Museum der Bildenden Kunst, Leipzig, Germany*

Caspar David Friedrich was a Romantic landscape painter who spent most of his life in Dresden. He trained at the Academy in Copenhagen, where he began to produce paintings that demonstrated his particular interest in light and the changing seasons. His landscapes were not, as he himself remarked, "the faithful representation of air, water, rocks and trees… but the reflection of the soul and emotion in these objects". In using landscape as a vehicle to convey deep, emotional feelings, there are parallels between Friedrich and his fellow countryman, Altdorfer, painting some three hundred years earlier. For Friedrich, nature was of religious and often symbolic significance. In **The Stages of Life** the sweeping perspective from the figure in the foreground right out to the ships on the horizon, not only suggests distance but the passage of time. The golden sunset imbues this melancholic scene with a sense of nostalgia. The empty, arctic wasteland depicted in another important symbolic work, **Wreck of the Hope**, conveys a profound sense of despair and desolation. In his attention to detail, Friedrich foreshadowed the work of the Pre-Raphaelite Brotherhood in the late 1840s.

OTHER MASTERPIECES Winter Landscape; *1811; National Gallery, London, England*
The Wreck of the Hope; *1824; Kunsthalle, Hamburg, Germany*

Frink Dame Elisabeth

Born Thurlow, England 1930; died Woolland, England 1993

Rolling Horse *1978; cast bronze; 17.8 x 35.6 cm; Private Collection*

Elisabeth Frink achieved national recognition as a celebrated sculptor of the post-war period. She trained at Guildford School of Art (1947–1949) and at Chelsea School of Art, London from 1949 to1953. While Paolozzi and William Turnbull were translating the aftermath of war into abstractions deviating from the real horror, Frink was producing more traditional images of death and human suffering, exuding pathos without sentimentality. Such genuine expression, although recognized, was not critically acclaimed, unlike the pioneering developments of Moore and Caro. Inspired by the art of Rodin and Giacometti, Frink's belief in the emotional charge of her work was her strength and guiding principle. The power and noble grandeur of her human figures was echoed in the many equine subjects she produced. **Rolling Horse** is an unusual example of Frink's interpretation of the animal, not poised or watchful, but caught in an unguarded moment, full of natural, untethered energy. Her figures and heads of the 1980s and early 1990s became more stylized and imbued with a stereotypical masculinity in marked contrast to the sensitivity of her earlier work.

OTHER MASTERPIECES Walking Madonna; *1981; Salisbury Cathedral, Salisbury, England* **Risen Christ**; *1992–1993; Liverpool Cathedral, Liverpool, England*

Gabo Naum

Born Briansk, Russia 1890; died Waterbury, USA 1977

Linear Construction No. 2
*1970–1971; acrylic; 114.9 x
83.5 cm; Tate Collection, London,
England*

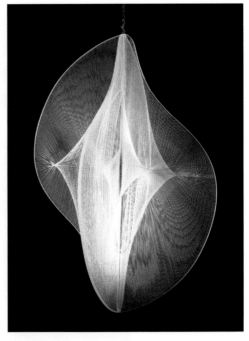

Under the name of Naum
Pevsner, the artist entered
Munich University in 1910,
originally to study medicine.
He then transferred to natural
sciences and attended art
history lectures. In 1912 he
moved to an engineering
school. He met Kandinsky
before going to Paris in 1913.
At the outbreak of war, and
until 1917, the artist lived in Norway under the name Gabo, making relief and sculptural
constructions. He returned to Moscow to join his brother, Antoine Pevsner, plus Tatlin,
Malevich and Kadinsky to form the Russian Constructivists. In 1920 Gabo's personal theory of
abstraction was published in the Realistic Manifesto, to coincide with an exhibition of his work.
Gabo later explained "…we were convinced that what we were doing represented a new
reality". He and the Constructivists saw that sculpture and architecture were closely linked.
Gabo's time in Berlin – 1922 to 1932 – and the contact he had with the De Stijl and Bauhaus
artists confirmed his thinking. The mechanics of forms existing in space and the tensions set
by sustaining this equilibrium are epitomized by **Linear Construction No. 2**. Constructed
from transparent plastic with nylon threads, the piece satisfies Naum Gabo's "search for an
art of pure space".

OTHER MASTERPIECES Head No. 2; *1917; Tate Collection, London, England*
Model for "Column", *1920–1921; Tate Collection, London, England*

Gainsborough Thomas

Born Sudbury, England 1727; died London, England 1788

The Morning Walk
*c.1785; oil on canvas; 236.2
x 179.1 cm; National Gallery,
London, England*

Although Gainsborough's
professional first love was
landscape, it is for his
elegant portraits of
eighteenth-century
aristocracy that he is most
popularly known. He was
brought up in rural
Sudbury and unlike his
contemporary and rival,
Reynolds, he did not travel
abroad to study works of
the great masters. He did
go to London in 1740,
where he worked with the French engraver, Gravelot, returning to Sudbury in 1746. He
established himself in Ipswich in 1752 as a portrait painter, including landscape elements into
the genre where possible, seen most clearly in his painting **Mr and Mrs Andrews**. When he
moved to Bath in 1760 he was able to develop this aspect of his work, focusing on full-length
portraits, producing paintings of inimitable style and sophistication. The influences of
engraving and of Dutch Landscape art are revealed in Gainsborough's command of a free and
spontaneous technique. The debt he owes to van Dyck is shown in his interpretation of the
married couple in **The Morning Walk**. Gainsborough's perceptive grasp of character and
natural feeling for harmonious composition make for a beautiful image. The painting
throughout is sensitively handled, charming and delicate without succumbing to sentiment.

OTHER MASTERPIECES Mr and Mrs Andrews; *c.1748—1749; National Gallery, London,
England* **Portrait of Miss Haverfield**; *c.1780; Wallace Collection, London, England*

Gaudier-Brzeska Henri

Born St Jean-de-Braye, France 1891; died Neuville-Saint-Vaast, France 1915

Bird Eating Fish *1914; plaster; 31.7 cm; Kettles Yard, University of Cambridge, Cambridge, England*

Born Henri Gaudier, the artist visited England in 1906 on a travelling scholarship and, on receipt of a second, undertook business studies in Bristol and Cardiff. During this time he kept sketchbooks, making drawings of architecture, plants, birds and animals. In 1909, he spent some time in Nuremberg and Munich. He returned to Paris in 1910 and met Sophie Brzeska; he adopted their joint names as his own. They were living in London from 1911 and gradually began to make significant contacts within artistic and literary circles. Key among these were artists Wyndham Lewis and Jacob Epstein. Following the example of the latter, Gaudier-Brzeska began stone carving. He was a significant figure within both the London Group and the Vorticists. A number of different interests and influences combined to make his stylized sculpture so compelling. He brought together the romanticism of Rodin, the crude forms of "primitive" arts and cultures, the sophistication of Brancusi and the formal concerns of Cubism. He amalgamated these influences to make extraordinary interpretations of the natural world such as **Bird Eating Fish**. His potential was cut short by his death in action with the French army.

OTHER MASTERPIECES Crouching Figure; *1913–1914; Walker Art Center, Minneapolis, USA*
Seated Woman; *1914; Musée National d'Art Moderne, Paris, France*

141

Gauguin Paul

Born Paris, France 1848; died Tahiti 1903

Two Women on a Beach *1891; oil on canvas; 69 x 91 cm; Musée d'Orsay, Paris, France*

As an ambitious stockbroker, Gauguin's initial interest in art was as a patron of the Impressionists. In 1876 he began exhibiting his own work and in 1883 gave up his business to be a professional painter. He settled in Brittany in 1886, becoming a central figure in a circle of artists whom he influenced with his strong personality and aesthetic ideals. Notable among these was van Gogh with whom a troubled friendship ended in Gauguin's famously fleeing from van Gogh's house in Arles to Paris. Gauguin had often fantasized about escaping the responsibilities and burdens of living in a civilized society. Encouraged by his brief sojourns in Martinique and Panama in 1887–1888, and resenting his inability to support a wife and family as an artist, he left for Tahiti in 1891. The lure of the exotic and the primitive fuelled his art, became his life and ultimately his death – over-indulgence in paradise gave him syphilis. His pursuits reflect the fin-de-siècle decadence and the interests of the Symbolists in Paris. **Two Women on a Beach** shows Gauguin's response to his "savage" surroundings. Flat areas of colour and clear outlines reveal his awareness of Japanese prints and stained glass techniques.

OTHER MASTERPIECES D'Ou Venons-Nous? Que Sommes Nous? Ou Allons Nous?; *1897; Museum of Fine Arts, Boston, Massachusetts, USA* **Vision after the Sermon**; *1888; National Gallery of Scotland, Edinburgh*

Gentile da Fabriano

Born Fabriano, Italy 1370; died Rome, Italy 1427

Adoration of the Magi
1423; wood panel; 173 x 220 cm; Galleria degli Uffizi, Florence, Italy

Gentile da Fabriano was the leading exponent of the International Gothic Style, which originated in the courts of Burgundy and France. By the early 1400s this had spread south across the Alps to Italy. It was a courtly art – richly coloured, highly decorative and textured and crammed with details of costumes, animals and paraphernalia associated with aristocratic society. His paintings were as charming as they were opulent and, although outwardly religious, were really chronicles of their time. They clearly reflected the lifestyle and aspirations of the patrons who commissioned them. Gentile worked in at least two courts, the Doge's Palace in Venice from 1408, and the Papal Court in Rome. From 1422 to 1425 he was in Florence, where he executed his best known work, the sumptuous **Adoration of the Magi**. From there he moved on to Siena and Orvieto, before his last trip to Rome. Gentile combines a religious narrative with the study of a hilly Tuscan landscape and its vegetation. The viewer's eye is drawn toward the same destination as the travellers – a castellated town.

OTHER MASTERPIECES Flight into Egypt (Part of the Adoration of the Magi); *1423; Galleria degli Uffizi, Florence, Italy* Madonna (Part of the Quaratesi Altarpiece); *1425; Royal Collection, Windsor, England*

Gentileschi Artemisia

Born Rome, Italy 1593; died Naples, Italy 1652

Judith and Holofernes
c.1620; oil on canvas;
199 x 162.5 cm; Galleria
degli Uffizi, Florence, Italy

Artemisia Gentileschi
worked mainly in
Florence and later in
Naples where she
finally settled. She was
taught by her father
Orazio, a follower of
Caravaggio, who in
turn engendered a
Caravaggesque realism and feel for dramatic subject matter in his spirited daughter. Gentileschi
joined her father in England and worked with him in the late 1630s on the decorations at the
Queen's House in Greenwich, London. She encountered a good deal of prejudice as a woman
artist in the seventeenth century – this was reinforced by the unusual and dramatic events of her
life, including a much sensationalized trial in which she accused her teacher of raping her many
times. The story of the Jewish heroine **Judith** decapitating Nebuchadnezzar's general,
Holofernes, after being offered to him as hostage was popular among Caravaggio's circle.
Gentileschi painted it herself several times. In this version, she portrays Judith as a courageous
and determined woman whose violent act is unromanticized. Criticized in her time for
depicting heroines who failed to conform to prevailing notions of elegant and delicate
femininity, Gentileschi's contribution to art has only recently been properly recognized.

OTHER MASTERPIECES Self-Portrait as La Pittura; *1630; Collection of HM The Queen,*
England Susanna and the Elders; *1610; Schonborn Collection, Pommersfelden, Germany*

144

Géricault Théodore

Born Rouen, France 1791; died Rouen, France 1824

Raft of the Medusa *1819; oil on canvas; 491 x 716 cm; Musée du Louvre, Paris, France*

Théodore Géricault was a painter and graphic artist who became a leading figure in the Romantic movement in France. He left the studio of Vernet in 1810 to study under Guérnin, whose pupils also included Eugène Delacroix. Delacroix became a great friend of Géricault and was strongly influenced by his art. Géricault visited Italy in 1816 and was in England from 1820 to 1822. His paintings of contemporary life reflected the poverty he saw in London, as well as his keen interest in racing and riding. Horses figure repeatedly in Géricault's paintings; whether in combat, racing or just rearing, they reveal a typical romantic preoccupation with drama and heightened emotion. His most celebrated work, the vast **Raft of the Medusa**, was shown at the Paris Salon in 1819. The painting is based on an actual shipwreck which cast a raft of survivors adrift, whose numbers then began to dwindle daily. Géricault is unsparing in his treatment of their plight: he visited hospitals and morgues to lend realism to his depiction of the dying and the dead. Between 1822 and 1823 Géricault painted a number of uncompromising and moving portraits of inmates at a Paris asylum.

OTHER MASTERPIECES The Mad Woman; *1822–1823; Musée des Beaux-Arts, Lyons, France*
Horse Frightened by Lightning; *c.1813; National Gallery, London, England*

Ghiberti Lorenzo

Born Florence, Italy c.1378; died Florence, Italy 1455

The Story of Jacob and Esau
1425–1452; bronze; 40 x 40 cm; Opera del Duomo, Florence, Italy

When Lorenzo Ghiberti was twenty-one years old, the Guild of Cloth Makers announced a competition for the making of the second set of bronze Baptistery doors in Florence. A year later, the little-known Ghiberti was declared the winner, having beaten Brunelleschi and other eminent artists. Ghiberti's workshop – the training ground for the next generations of artists, Donatello and Uccello among them – received enough commissions to guarantee security. The first set of doors was completed in 1424, after twenty-one years of work; the second set took from 1425 to 1452. **The Story of Jacob and Esau** is one scene from the cycle of the Old Testament used for Ghiberti's second set of doors. He includes numerous episodes from the same narrative as if they were occurring concurrently; the setting is a beautiful architectural structure. Ghiberti conveys a psychological relationship between the figures in order to give a feeling of authenticity to the scene. We can almost hear the conversation between the three women at the bottom left, and feel the unease of the woman on the far right as she watches her son's blessing. These bronzes, which synthesized expression and drama with movement and lucidity, inspired successive Renaissance artists. Michelangelo referred to them as "the Gates of Paradise".

OTHER MASTERPIECES Baptism of Christ; *1427; San Giovanni, Siena, Italy*
Saint Matthew; *c.1420; Orsanmichele, Florence, Italy*

Ghirlandaio Domenico

Born Florence, Italy 1449; died Florence, Italy 1494

An Old Man and his Grandson c.1490; oil on canvas; 57.4 x 46 cm; Musée du Louvre, Paris, France

Domenico Ghirlandaio trained as a goldsmith. In 1490, the Duke of Milan received a report that described a handful of good artists available for work in one region. Of Domenico Ghirlandaio it was suggested that he was a notable painter of panels and a master of fresco. It went on to commend his work and to describe him as an efficient and prolific artist. Ghirlandaio employed hordes of assistants – one of whom was Michelangelo – in his prosperous, family-run business. Ghirlandaio is best-known for his frescoes, in which he often set religious subjects in a secular setting and in which he included recognizable portraits. His largest commission, completed in 1490, depicting scenes from the lives of the Virgin and St John the Baptist, was in Santa Maria Novella, Florence. Ironically, in **An Old Man and his Grandson**, one of his best works, the identity of the protagonists remains a mystery. This naturalistic double portrait is an intimate and moving portrayal of a tender relationship between doting age and attendant youth. The loving young boy is oblivious to the old man's unfortunate physiognomy, a symptom of rhinophyma, from which he suffered.

OTHER MASTERPIECES Giovanna Albizzi Tornabuoni; 1488; Edel Ford Collection, Detroit, Michigan, USA **Adoration of the Magi**; 1487; Galleria degli Uffizi, Florence, Italy

Giacometti Alberto

Born Stampa, Grisons, Switzerland 1901; died Chur, Switzerland 1966

Jean Genet *1954; oil on canvas; 64.7 x 54 cm; Tate Collection, London, England*

Alberto Giacometti trained as an artist in Geneva and settled in Paris in 1922. Although he is primarily associated with the Existentialist philosophies of Jean-Paul Sartre, he was also significantly involved with contemporary avant-garde art developments in Paris.

His initial interest in Cubism and primitive sculpture gave way in the early 1930s to a more active participation with the Surrealists, headed by André Breton. Giacometti's jointed sculpture of this time, **Woman with her Throat Cut**, is in striking contrast to the later work for which he is best known. Its content, however, offers some indication of the artist's tendency to morbidity. His expulsion from the Surrealist movement in 1935 was a result of a dramatic change of direction. When Giacometti exhibited again, in 1948, his sculpture consisted largely of skeletal figures, excessively tall or extremely small. Each the width of the passage of a prolonged gaze, these spectres seem to be willing themselves not to exist. Giacometti's painting represents an equally powerful striving to sculpt a physical presence, in the knowledge that reproducing the essence of humanity with paint is impossible. It is appropriate that the subject of this passionately wrought portrait is writer **Jean Genet**, Sartre's protégé.

OTHER MASTERPIECES Femme De Venis IX; *1956; Tate Collection, London, England*
Portrait of Yanaihara; *1961; Galerie Beyeler, Basel, Switzerland*

Gilbert and George

Gilbert born Dolomites, Italy 1942; George born Devon, England 1943

Fear *1984; photomap on paper; 422 x 652 cm; Tate Collection, London, England*

Gilbert and George first met while they were both studying sculpture at St Martin's School of Art in London in the late 1960s. Since then they have worked as one. Their united activities first came to prominence with their notorious performance pieces as "living" and "singing sculptures". Dressed in a particular style of suit, without which they are not publicly recognized, they offered themselves as art. In 1969 this meant "performing", with hands and faces covered in metallic paint, to the song Underneath the Arches, originally by music-hall stars Flanagan and Allan. Photo and video pieces based on the pair gradually becoming drunk on Gordon's Gin followed. Their conservative appearance adds to the irony of their parodies of British taste and traditions. A narcissistic element is retained in more recent work, which makes overt reference to gay sexuality. Since the early 1970s their photo-pieces, by now large, highly coloured composite "pictures", such as **Fear**, appear to take provocative views to extremes. This has often been interpreted as a shocking celebration, rather than criticism, of right-wing, neo-fascist, racist and nationalist activity. Gilbert and George, however, claim to be, "trying to define the new morality".

OTHER MASTERPIECES England; *1980; Tate Collection, London, England*
The Nature of Our Looking; *1970; Tate Collection, London, England*

Giorgione Giorgio da Castelfranco

Born Castelfranco, Italy c.1477; died Venice, Italy 1510

The Sleeping Venus *c.1507; oil on canvas; 108 x 175 cm; Gemaldegalerie, Dresden, Germany*

Neither Giorgione's life nor his paintings are well-documented. There are few historical references to him and only a handful of paintings can be directly attributed to him. A pupil of Giovanni Bellini, his own work was assisted by Titian. He was a romantic figure – handsome, musical and poetic – who died of the plague in his early thirties. Leonardo da Vinci and Vasari believed him to be one of the founders of "modern art". In his work, subject matter is less important than inherent mood. Here, **The Sleeping Venus** is absorbed in private reverie. She lies resting in an idyllic country vista, a setting that the city-dwelling Venetians would have fully appreciated, given their penchant for retreating to the countryside. Giorgione was one of the earliest artists to complete work for private patrons rather than for churches or public commissions. The landscape may have been finished by Titian upon Giorgione's death. He is also thought to have painted in a cupid – who sat at the sleeping Venus' feet – that, because of ensuing damage, was painted out again years later.

OTHER MASTERPIECES Madonna and Child With St Liberale and St Francis; *c.1504; Church of San Liberale, Castelfranco, Italy* The Tempest; *c.1530; Galleria della Accademia, Venice, Italy*

Giotto Ambrogio Bondone

Born Florence, Italy c.1266; died Florence, Italy 1337

St Francis Preaching to the Birds
c.1296–1297; fresco; 270 x 200 cm; Upper Church, Assisi, Italy

Giotto was the son of a farmer. The painter Cimabue allegedly spotted him making rudimentary drawings of sheep and invited him to work with him. Under Cimabue's tutelage, Giotto quickly developed his own style, overshadowing that of his master. Dante wrote, "Cimabue was thought to hold the field in painting; but now Giotto is all the cry and Cimabue's style is badly dimmed". He became something of a legend in his own lifetime. Poets and commentators were united in their praise of his revolutionary naturalistic and narrative style. He broke free from the stylized linearity of the Byzantine tradition, and introduced solid forms and a sense of depth into his compositions. Giotto's understanding of colour and the way it changes in response to light has continued to ensure his reputation as a "modern" painter. **St Francis Preaching to the Birds** was part of a cycle of frescoes that he designed for the Upper Church in Assisi. It shows his humanistic approach and his ability to invest sacred figures with compassion and genuine emotion.

OTHER MASTERPIECES The Mourning of Christ, *c.1306; Scrovegni Chapel, Padua, Italy*
Madonna and Child, *c.1310; Galleria degli Uffizi, Florence, Italy*

Girtin Thomas

Born London, England 1775; died London, England 1802

White House, Chelsea *1800; pencil and watercolour on paper; 30 x 51.5 cm; Tate Collection, London, England*

Thomas Girtin did much to promote watercolour painting to a fine art in its own right. His watercolours were greatly admired during his short lifetime, not least by his friend Turner. The two men worked together for Dr Monro, copying topographical drawings, including those of Canaletto. The most important technical innovation for which Girtin had responsibility was the abandonment of the practice of monochrome underpainting. He favoured loose washes of pure colour, often applied to a semi-absorbent off-white paper. This gave his landscapes a freshness and daring that at times surpassed the work of Turner. Girtin travelled around Britain producing watercolours of landscape in his direct style. In 1801–1802 he visited Paris and made a number of etchings of the city. On his return to England he exhibited a vast panoramic painting of London. This work is now lost, but there are several sketches for it in the British Museum. Poetic and soft-edged, his painting of the **White House, Chelsea** is one of his finest works.

OTHER MASTERPIECES A Winding Estuary*, 1798; Tate Collection, London, England*
Porte St Denis*; 1802; Collection of Sir Edmund Bacon, England*

Gober Robert

Born Wallingford, USA 1954

Untitled *1989; mixed media; 30 x 16 x 51.5 cm; Tate Collection, London, England*

Robert Gober graduated in Fine Art from Middlebury College in Vermont in 1976. He moved to New York where he worked as a carpenter and a performer with a multimedia dance company. From 1978, in addition to painting, he also made plaster figures and small model houses. In 1984 Gober produced handmade replicas of household objects – sinks, doors, playpens, bags of cat-litter, wallpaper and body parts. He sited such objects and the body parts, cast from life, such as **Untitled**, the leg seen here, in room installations. Often these support other forms. Candles stand erect, drain holes burrow through, or a musical score is overlaid on the surface. Despite the hyperrealism of the leg, hairy, clothed and wearing an unremarkable shoe, its singularity and situation is initially humorous then incongruous and unnerving. Such work is laced with diverse contemporary meanings, bound with memories from childhood and gay erotic encounters. Perversion and subversion reside in Gober's skillful craftsmanship, **The Wedding Gown** being a prime example. Other installations incorporating newspapers, doorways and other seemingly banal items make tangible Gober's description of his work as "natural history dioramas about contemporary human beings".

OTHER MASTERPIECES The Wedding Gown*; 1989; Hamburger Kunsthalle, Hamburg, Germany* **Untitled***; 1998–99; Guggenheim Museum, New York City, USA*

Goes Hugo van der

Born Ghent, Belgium 1440; died Brussels, Belgium 1482

The Portinari Altarpiece c.1478; panel; 253 x 141 cm; Galleria degli Uffizi, Florence, Italy

Hugo van der Goes was one of the most gifted of the Early Netherlandish painters. His realism was recognized for its insight into psychological and religious intensity. He worked in the Guild of Ghent from 1467 and became Dean in 1473. He chose to take holy orders and join a monastery near Brussels from about 1477, but he lived a privileged life, continuing to travel and paint. He was prone to fits and suicidal depressions, contemporary chroniclers suggesting this was because he knew he would never match the brilliance of van Eyck's **Ghent Altarpiece**. He died in 1482. This is the left-hand wing of the unusually large **Portinari Altarpiece**, which was commissioned by Tommaso Portinari, the head of the Medici bank in Bruges, and is believed to be van der Goes's greatest work. Upon completion in 1478, it was delivered to Florence. In this panel the patron's wife, Maria Baroncelli, and daughter, Margherita, are kneeling, and behind them are grouped their patron saints. In the background the three Magi can be seen on their way to Bethlehem, which acts as a prelude to the Nativity scene depicted on the central panel of the altarpiece.

OTHER MASTERPIECES The Fall of Man; c.1470; Kunsthistorisches Museum, Vienna, Austria
Death of Our Lady; c.1470; Groeningemuseum, Bruges, Belgium

Gogh Vincent Willem van

Born Groot-Zundert, Netherlands 1853; died Auvers-sur-Oise, France 1890

Prisoners Exercising
1890; oil on canvas; 80 x 64 cm; Pushkin Museum, Moscow, Russia

Vincent van Gogh was an extraordinary Post-Impressionist whose contribution to painting was not recognized during his lifetime. The son of a Protestant pastor, his religious beliefs were a strong influence on his work. He became a lay preacher in 1878, working amongst the Belgian miners of the Borinage. He made his decision to become an artist after returning home to his parents in Etten in 1881. Until the end of his life a frenzied and prolific creative output ensued, charged with spiritual joy, anguish and religious fervour. The constant flow of correspondence with his brother Theo, who funded his living, provides a comprehensive diary and passionate expression of his activities and thoughts. He was impressed by the social subject matter and realist style of Millet. His meeting with Gauguin and other Post-Impressionist artists in Paris in 1886 was the catalyst for a dramatic change in his work. He settled in Arles in 1888, producing many purely coloured, stormy canvases and ink drawings, done in conditions of great poverty. Periods of recurrent mental disturbance led him to an asylum in St Rémy de Provence. **Prisoners Exercising** dates from this time, almost symbolic of the psychological trauma which imprisoned Vincent van Gogh until his suicide two years later.

OTHER MASTERPIECES Self-Portrait; *c.1886; Musée du Louvre, Paris, France*
The Artist's Room in Arles; *1889; Musée du Louvre, Paris, France*

Goldsworthy Andy

Born Cheshire, England 1956

Maple Leaf Lines
*1987; maple leaves
in a stream;
Ouchiyama-Mura,
Japan*

Andy Goldsworthy's stunning site-specific sculptural work has established his reputation as the
leading environmental artist working in Britain. He trained at Bradford College of Art from
1974 to 1975 and Preston Polytechnic from 1975 to 1978. Unlike more conceptually oriented
land artists such as Richard Long and Ian Hamilton Finlay, Goldsworthy works directly with
natural forms in their environment. He combines and juxtaposes contrasting shapes, textures
and colours to exploit their aesthetic qualities. The raw materials of his sculpture are the leaves,
seeds, ice, loose stones and branches he finds. The installations and objects he produces are
widely diverse in form and scale but are, without exception, of ephemeral beauty. They endure
only in photographs. His early work was made in Grizedale Forest, which is now a major
sculpture park for forest-generated art. Goldsworthy's international reputation is based on the
ingenuity and simplicity of pieces such as **Maple Leaf Lines**. Goldsworthy exploits the shapes
and saturated hues in nature to startling effect, making one wonder why artists ever needed to
turn to artificial materials.

OTHER MASTERPIECES Dome of Sticks Leaving a Hole Within a Hole in River Rock;
1991; Scaur Water, Dumfriesshire, Scotland Bamboo Leaves Edging a Rock for the Rising Sun;
1991; Ouchiyama-Mura, Japan

Golub Leon

Born Chicago, USA 1922

The Go-Ahead *1985–1986; acrylic on canvas; 304.8 x 487.9 cm; Saatchi Collection, London, England*

Leon Golub studied at the Art Institute of Chicago, between 1946 and 1950, and lived in Paris from 1959–1964. The imposing physical presence of his contemplative images, worked on the floor in acrylic on unstretched linen, is due to their large scale and high tonality. His political paintings present a paradox between form and content; although his themes focus on the horrors of war, such as mercenaries and interrogations, the paintings are elegant figurations with their foundations in classicism. Golub's ideas stem from media reports of the war in Vietnam and the immediacy with which violence and the perpetrators of torture are brought into the living room. The shocking dramas that Golub reconstructs are similarly direct and confrontational. Rather than focus on the specifics of El Salvador and Nicaragua, for example, they allude to universal themes of domination and power. Even **The Go-Ahead**, although not a scene of explicit action, is an evocative, disturbing image, with impending menace implicit in the attitudes and uniforms of the protagonists against a harsh, blood-coloured background.

OTHER MASTERPIECES Interrogation II; *1981; Art Institute of Chicago, USA*
Prisoners I; *1985; Private Collection*

157

Gorky Arshile

Born Khorkom, Armenia 1904; died Sherman, USA 1948

Agony *1947; oil on canvas; 101.6 x 128.3 cm; A. Conger Goodyear Fund, Museum of Modern Art, New York City, USA*

Arshile Gorky (born Vosdanik Adoian) has been credited with providing the link between European Surrealism and avant-garde art in America. He fled to the United States in 1920 after his mother's death as a result of the Turkish persecution of Armenians during the First World War. This enforced uprooting led to a preoccupation with his own identity. He adopted his familiar pseudonym and embraced the modernist art achievements of Miro, Picasso and Cézanne, seemingly insecure in his own potential for originality. His work was an eclectic mix of styles. Roberto Matta and André Breton particularly impressed Gorky and he adopted wholeheartedly the tenets of the Surrealists, most notably that of biomorphism, the creation of abstracted, organic – as opposed to geometric – forms. The automatic and intuitive nature of Gorky's approach had a specific impact on the development of Abstract Expressionism. Gorky interpreted form and translated it into organic, linear concoctions, suspended in fluid colours that melt and fuse. The dreamy lyricism of **Agony** belies its title, a reference, perhaps to the inner conflicts, exacerbated by the personal disasters – a fire, an operation and a car crash – that led to his suicide.

OTHER MASTERPIECES Waterfall; *1943; Tate Collection, London, England*
The Betrothal II; *1947; Whitney Museum of American Art, New York City, USA*

Anthony Gormley

Born London, England 1950

Untitled (for Francis)
*1985; mixed media, 18.8 x
11.9 cm; Tate Collection,
London, England*

Anthony Gormley has
achieved international
renown as a figurative
sculptor whose work
generates admiration
both in and out of the
gallery context. His
reputation was
established by the lone, lead figures that proliferated in his work for many years. These faceless,
featureless, humanoid forms were cast originally from his own body. Sheets of lead were laid
and then welded on to a hollow plaster body-cast. The subsequent symmetry of the join made a
grid-like map of the body. This echoed the poses and individual modifications the respective
figures assumed. This was true of **Untitled (for Francis)**, the attitude of which could be
interpreted as welcoming, submissive, or ecstatic. The physical context into which these figures
were sited – the city walls of Derry, the crypt of Winchester Cathedral, for example – gave
them a power, a rootedness that was uplifting and universally understood. With regard to the
use of the body in art, Gormley's aim was to place it, "in the sublime space created by
Modernism". From the 1990s, Gormley's work developed in new directions. His installation
Field, involving tens of thousands of small terracotta figures, attracted great public and media
interest, as did his monumental roadside sculpture **Angel of the North**.

OTHER MASTERPIECES Brickman (Model); *1987; Leeds City Art Gallery, England*
Angel of the North; *1995–1998; Gateshead, England*

Goya Francisco

Born Saragossa, Spain 1746; died Bordeaux, France 1828

Execution of the Defenders of Madrid, 3rd May 1808 *1814; oil on canvas; 266 x 345 cm; Museo del Prado, Madrid, Spain*

The most influential painter and graphic artist of the eighteenth century, Francisco Goya y Lucientes enjoyed a long and successful career. It is believed he visited Italy in 1771 to undertake commissions for churches, before settling in Madrid. Here he was influenced by Mengs' analytical approach to portraiture and by the decorative realism of Tiepolo. At first, Goya followed a conventional path, becoming a fashionable court painter to King Charles IV and producing charming if satiric works. The invasion of Spain by Napoleon's armies in 1808, however, offered him very different subject matter. **Execution of the Defenders of Madrid, 3rd May 1808** is one painting of a pair which depict two days in the people's resistance to French troops. Goya completed these works several years after the executions and yet manages to convey the scene with blood-red freshness. The expressions of panic and terror on the faces of the ordinary victims is reinforced by the harsh light reflected off the white shirt of the man kneeling. Goya exerted a major influence on the development of painting, inspiring artists as diverse as Delacroix, Manet, Daumier, Käthe Kollwitz and Picasso.

OTHER MASTERPIECES Dona Isabel de Porcel, *before 1805; National Gallery, London, England* **The Naked Maja**; *c.1797–1798; Museo del Prado, Madrid, Spain*

Goyen Jan van

Born Leyden, Netherlands 1596; died The Hague, Netherlands 1656

River Scene with an Inn *1630; oil on wood; 40 x 81 cm; Victoria and Albert Museum, London, England*

Jan van Goyen with Salomon van Rusydael, helped to establish the early school of Dutch landscape painting. He was the father-in-law and teacher of the Dutch genre painter, Jan Steen. Van Goyen visited France as a young man, before travelling extensively in Holland. On his trips he made sketches and drawings of various identifiable landmarks which he used as the basis for later paintings. After 1630 his work underwent a marked change. He simplified his compositions and began to adopt an almost monochrome palette. Later work is richer in colour and displays the poetic sensibility associated with the next generation of Dutch landscape painters, such as Jacob van Ruisdael. A prolific output did not, however, prevent van Goyen from dying insolvent. **River Scene with an Inn** provides a typical view of the Dutch lowlands. Van Goyen focuses on the low horizon and the reflections created in the expanse of water. The figure sitting on the fence lends the painting an air of wistful contemplation and nostalgia, reinforced by the warm glow of the setting sun.

OTHER MASTERPIECES A Windmill by a River; *1642; National Gallery, London, England*
A River Scene with a Hut on an Island; *1640–1645; National Gallery, London, England*

Greco El

Born Crete, Greece 1541; died Toledo, Spain, 1614

Christ Driving the Traders from the Temple *c.1600; oil on canvas; 106.3 × 129.7 cm; National Gallery, London, England*

In Crete, which was a Venetian colony at this time, El Greco (real name Domenikos Theotocopoulos), painted religious icons in the Byzantine tradition. In about 1560 he went to Venice, where he became a pupil of Titian. He also worked in Rome before settling in Toledo, c.1570. His early work, with its dramatic use of light and shade, reveals a strong Venetian influence. El Greco gradually evolved his mannered, highly individual style, featuring dynamic and distorted compositions with elongated figures, sweeping movement, as well as cold to acidic colours. The depth of the artist's fervent spiritual beliefs was reflected in his increasingly ecstatic and visionary treatment of the many religious subjects he painted. El Greco painted several versions of **Christ Driving the Traders from the Temple**. The story comes from the Gospel of St Matthew and depicts Christ purifying the house of prayer through the expulsion of the moneychangers and merchants. Despite its traditional and solemn subject matter, El Greco injects vigour into the scene, making it powerfully his own. Characteristically, the figure of Christ is elongated – his dramatic gesture and contrasting red robe occupy centre stage, while the other figures recoil from and rotate around him.

OTHER MASTERPIECES The Burial of Count Orgaz; *1586; San Tome, Toledo, Spain*
Resurrection; *c.1595; Museo del Prado, Madrid, Spain*

Gris Juan

Born Madrid, Spain 1887; died Paris, France 1927

The Bay *1921; oil on canvas; 686 x 975 mm; Tate Collection, London, England*

Juan Gris studied in Madrid before settling in Paris in 1906. Here he worked as an illustrator for French magazines. Meeting Picasso was a significant turning point and, from 1912, Gris became a leading Cubist. His work developed from the objective study of simplified, precise forms based on everyday items. His work was more calculated and intellectual than that of either Picasso or Braque. Like them, he collaged paper materials to represent their original function, not simply for their textural qualities. His logical approach was summarized in his own words, "Cézanne turns a bottle into a cylinder… I make a bottle – a particular bottle – out of a cylinder". During the last part of his career, he expressed an increasing preoccupation with colour. He also worked as a book illustrator, designed sets for Diaghilev and made several polychrome – multicoloured – sculptures. **The Bay** seems to conform to Gris's notion of himself as a classical painter. The harmonious composition is set on a stage; the curtain is drawn aside to reveal a selection of carefully delineated objects in a well-ordered combination of curves and straight lines.

OTHER MASTERPIECES The Chessboard; *1915; Art Institute of Chicago, Chicago, USA*
Still Life with Guitar and Clarinet; *1920; Kunstmuseum, Basel, Switzerland*

Grosz George

Born Berlin, Germany 1893; died Berlin, Germany 1959

Suicide *1916; oil on canvas; 100 x 77.5; Tate Collection, London, England*

George Grosz trained at the Dresden Academy between 1909 and 1912 before serving in the army in 1914. He was eventually declared "permanently unfit for service" and discharged. In 1917, Grosz was one of the founders of the Berlin club Dada, a movement identified with political radicalism that paralleled the Zürich Dada movement of 1916. Throughout his career, Grosz published collections of pen and ink drawings in which he directed his biting satire against the moral and social disintegration of society under the Weimar Republic. His oil paintings, such as **Suicide**, lay bare this aggressive social realism through brutal images of the modern city and those forced to exist on its margins. Here, Grosz presents a number of scenarios in one frightening image. A body hangs from a lamp post and the rotting corpse of a bowler-hatted businessman is overseen by the impassive stare of a prostitute. Grosz's fragmented approach to the picture space, rendered in garish complementary colours, is designed to show the artificial nature of urbanity. He also exploits theatrical elements that he found in the paintings of de Chirico and Carrà. Grosz lived in the USA between 1933 and 1959, dying just after his return to Berlin.

OTHER MASTERPIECES Portrait of Max Herrmann-Neisse; *1927; Museum of Modern Art, New York City, USA* Pillars of Society; *1926; Staatliche Museen, National Galerie, Berlin, Germany*

Grünewald Mathis

Born Würzburg, Bavaria, Germany c.1470; died Halle, Germany 1528

The Mocking of Christ
*1503; oil on panel; 109 x
73.5 cm; Alte Pinakothek,
Munich, Germany*

Little is known about
Mathis Grünewald's early
life, although he is
believed to have trained
in Alsace. He was court
painter to the
Archbishop-Elector of
Mainz from 1508, after
which he became court
painter to the Elector of
Mainz himself. His series
of religious paintings for the Isenheim altarpiece is generally regarded as his masterpiece.
Although familiar with Renaissance ideas such as perspective and solidity, Grünewald only
makes use of them to heighten the emotional impact of his work. He brings a unique and
subjective interpretation to late medieval German art, whether this is expressed through his
serene and tender Madonnas or the more tortured emotion of his various crucifixions. **The
Mocking of Christ** is a brutal and haunting image. This detail focuses on Christ's suffering. The
bloodstained bandages wrapped around his head and neck and the knotted rope directly reflect
his subjugation and abuse. Grünewald's interest is to lay bare the emotional truth of Christ's
torment. Grünewald was, with his contemporary Dürer, one of the greatest German painters of
the sixteenth century.

OTHER MASTERPIECES The Crucifixion; *c.1515; Unterlinden Museum, Colmar, Germany*
St Anthony and St Paul; *c.1515; Unterlinden Museum, Colmar, Germany*

Guardi Francesco

Born Venice, Italy 1712; died Venice, Italy 1793

Doge Embarking on the Bucintoro *1793; oil on canvas; 67 x 100 cm; Musée du Louvre, Paris, France*

Francesco Guardi was a contemporary of Canaletto and quite possibly his pupil. Like Canaletto, Guardi concentrated on painting views of his native Venice, initially with the idea of selling them to tourists. His landscape painting gradually evolved away from the architectural precision of Canaletto and closer to Turner. In his mature work, Guardi's vision of Venice is subjective and concentrated on the rendering of atmospheric effects, such as that of light on water. **Doge Embarking on the Bucintoro** records an actual ceremonial event, but is most notable for its evocation of atmosphere. Suffused with light, Venice appears out of the water like a mirage surrounded by a host of bobbing boats. This airy and poetic interpretation is given added potency through the use of loose and dynamic brushstrokes. Guardi collaborated with his brother Giovanni on some religious pictures – an altarpiece dating from after his brother's death in 1777 was only recently discovered. The great decorative Venetian painter, Tiepolo, was Guardi's brother-in-law. Guardi's son, Giacomo, continued his workshop after his father's death.

OTHER MASTERPIECES Ascent in a Balloon; *1783; Staatliche Museum, Berlin, Germany*
An Architectural Caprice; *c.1770; National Gallery, London, England*

Hals Frans

Born Antwerp, Belgium c.1580; died Haarlem, Netherlands 1666

Man with a Cane 633;
oil on canvas; detail; 2 x
61 cm; Kenwood Hou
London, England

Frans Hals was a painter who was ahead of his time. A contemporary of Rubens and Rembrandt, his seemingly spontaneous style could almost have come from a nineteenth-century Impressionist's hand. In 1591, Hals's parents settled in Haarlem and there he remained for the rest of his life. He is known for his extraordinary skills as a portraitist and although these were much in demand, particularly during the 1630s, he struggled financially throughout his career and died destitute. As little is known about him, it is intriguing to speculate on the influences to which he owes his inimitable painting technique. However, all that can be said with certainty is that he was aware of Caravaggio's innovatory work in Italy. In **Man with a Cane**, Hals captures the adventurous spirit of the merchant Pieter van den Broecke in a way that was unsurpassed by painters of the time. Without idealizing his subject, Hals cystallizes the vitality of a warm character with apparent ease. By the 1660s, Hals's lively approach had become tempered, his tonality darker. Most memorable are the **Regents and Regentesses of the Old Men's Alms House** (1664). These are sensitive and poignant group portraits, serving as prophetic images, indicative of Hals's own sad demise.

OTHER MASTERPIECES The **Laughing Cavalier**, *1624; Wallace Collection, London, England*
Head of a Young Boy, *c.1625; Royal Picture Gallery, Mauritshuis, The Hague, Netherlands*

Hambling Maggi

Born Sudbury, England 1945

Max Wall and his Image
*1981, oil on canvas, 167.6 x
121.9 cm, Tate Collection,
London, England*

Maggi Hambling is a versatile artist whose painting and sculpture cannot be defined in terms of a particular style or movement. Her fierce independence as an artist is complemented by her androgynous appearance and a vibrant personality that thrives on parties and living the good life. Her paintings are appropriately shot through with vitality. Her sunset pictures and abstracts based on laughter are brilliantly coloured and suffused with emotional intensity. From 1960, Lett Haines and Cedric Morris encouraged her development and her attendance at the Ipswich School of Art from 1962 to 1964. She went on to study at the Camberwell School of Art and The Slade School of Art. Her period as first Artist in Residence at the National Gallery in 1980 to 1981 established her as a significant contemporary artist. **Max Wall and his Image** is one of a number of portraits of the comedian that helped to secure popular recognition of her multifarious skills. Hambling also created a significant series of paintings devoted to her fascination with the Greek myth of the Minotaur. Despite its gruesome implications, Hambling injected sensitivity into the subject. "In the end", she has said, "there is only the physical reality of paint."

OTHER MASTERPIECES Max and Me (In Praise of Smoking), *1982, Birmingham City Museums and Art Gallery, Birmingham, England* **George Melly**, *1998, National Portrait Gallery, London, England*

Hamilton Richard

Born London, England 1922

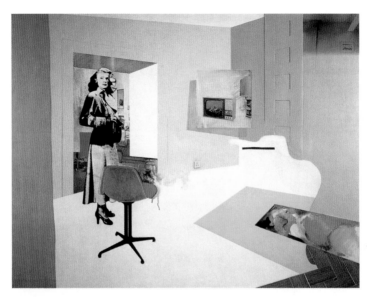

Interior II *1964; oil and acrylic, mixed media on wood; 121.9 x 162.6 mm; Tate Collection, London, England*

Richard Hamilton's art training did not follow the straightforward course enjoyed by his contemporaries. It was interrupted by war, expulsion from art school and his marriage. However, after he graduated from the Slade School of Art in London in 1951, he devised an exhibition at the Institute of Contemporary Arts (ICA) in London and co-founded the Independent Group at the ICA in 1952. The group's discussions and exhibition at The Whitechapel Art Gallery in 1956, This Is Tomorrow, signified the arrival of Pop Art in Britain. Hamilton's work was the eclectic juxtaposition of traditionally wrought and mechanically reproduced imagery. **Interior II** combines collage, paint and metal relief on panel, producing a composite image that accesses elements of nostalgia and the ultramodern. There is no doubt that this is pure artifice rather than illusion. In 1963, he first visited the USA and collaborated with Marcel Duchamp; he has since worked with artists Dieter Roth and Rita Donagh. Hamilton's engagement with issues surrounding Northern Ireland led to the production of numerous politically oriented paintings.

OTHER MASTERPIECES Just What is it That Makes Today's Homes So Different, So Appealing?, *1956; Collection E. Janss, Los Angeles, USA* **I'm Dreaming of a White Christmas**; *1967–1968; Kunstmuseum, Basel, Switerland*

Haring Keith

Born Kutztown, USA 1958; died New York City, USA 1990

Untitled *1989;*
acrylic and enamel
on canvas; 182.8
x 182.8 cm;
Estate of Keith
Haring

Keith Haring's earliest artistic creations as a child came from television cartoons. His high-school education was followed by attendance at the Ivy School of Art in Pittsburgh and, from 1978, a year's study at the New York School of Visual Arts. Among his teachers were experimental artist Keith Sonnier and conceptual artist Joseph Kosuth. In 1980, Haring eschewed more conventional outlets available to him to display his creativity and became a graffiti artist. He covered advertisements in the New York subway with stylized, marker pen and chalk drawings. His subjects were wide-ranging but had in common references to popular culture in a nuclear age. The strength of his graphic abilities, as shown by **Untitled** is contained in the linear element that dominated his complex images backed by saturated grounds. These have commercial rather than expressive roots, marking the transition of Haring's art from subway to T-shirts, badges, murals, official adverts and posters throughout the materialist 1980s. His universal popular imagery derived from a variety of ethnic and cultural sources, without being applicable to one in particular.

OTHER MASTERPIECES Ignorance = Fear; *1989; Estate of Keith Haring*
Silence = Death; *1989; Private Collection*

Hatoum Mona

Born Beirut, Lebanon 1952

Light Sentence *1992; 36 wire mesh lockers, electric motor, lightbulb; 198 x 185 x 490 cm; Jay Joplin, White Cube, London, England*

Mona Hatoum was forced by war to leave her native Beirut in 1975. Since then she has lived and worked in Britain extending her practice through various disciplines, installation, performance, video and sculpture. Her work has a political edge and discusses the physical, cultural and ethical boundaries which she has challenged or crossed. She often uses herself "as a site of metaphor or allegory for social constraints" engaging in ritualistic performances, that are physically demanding and often futile. Film footage of the interior of her own body forms the basis of a controversial manifestation of these preoccupations. Since 1989 Hatoum has concentrated on making installations and sculpture that implicate the viewer. In the absence of human presence, a sense of foreboding, torture and imprisonment pervades pieces such as **Light Sentence**. This minimalist construction comprises the wire skeleton of an institutional locker-room and a bare light bulb that mechanically patrols the length of the cage. The travelling light source throws sinister shadows of a perpetually changing grid that engulfs the spectator, reinforcing feelings of entrapment.

OTHER MASTERPIECES Corps Etranger; *1994; Musée National d'Art Moderne, Paris, France* **Incommunicado**; *1993; Tate Collection, London, England*

Hausmann Raoul

Born Vienna, Austria 1886; died Limoges, France 1971

The Art Critic *1919;*
photomontage, colour pencil
and newsprint; 31.8 x
25.4 cm; Tate Collection,
London, England

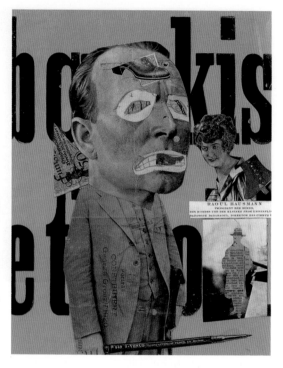

The son of a painter,
Raoul Hausmann
moved to Berlin in
1901. Here, in 1918, he
was one of the founders
of the Berlin Dada
movement, with
George Grosz and John
Heartfield. Hausmann
edited the first issues of
their magazine *Der Dada*
which, with its
disordered typography,
anticipated the
development of a new
artistic method, known
as photomontage. As a method of collage which involved pasting superimposed photographs,
photomontage showed an awareness of Cubist assemblage while retaining a distinctly political
and satirical edge. Hausmann explained that "this term translates our aversion at playing the
artist, and, thinking of ourselves as engineers…we meant to construct, to assemble our works."
The Art Critic, with its absurd and defaced figure, furthers this anti-art theme. He was a close
friend of Kurt Schwitters, who, like Hausmann, experimented with sound-poems and
typography. German artist Hannah Höch was Hausmann's companion during the Dada era.
Her witty collages are of equal merit to Hausmann's and sometimes featured portraits and
photographs of herself, Hausmann and other Dada luminaries. After the decline of Dada,
Hausmann abandoned painting for photography, writing and the study of optics.

OTHER MASTERPIECES Men are Angels and Live in Heaven; *c.1918; Berlinische Galerie,*
Berlin, Germany **Gurk**; *1919; Kunstarchiv Arntz, Haag, Germany*

Heckel Eric

Born Döbeln, Saxony, Germany 1883; died Radolfzell, Switzerland 1970

Bathers *1940; oil on canvas; 83 x 96.5 cm; Kunstmuseum, Bonn, Germany*

Erich Heckel was a German Expressionist whose graphic work, in the form of drawings, lithographs, woodcuts and engravings, is of equal importance to his painting. Between 1904 and 1906, Heckel studied architecture in Dresden, where he met Ernst Ludwig Kirchner and Karl Schmidt-Rottluff, with whom he founded a group known as Die Brücke (The Bridge) in 1905. Declaring Cézanne, van Gogh, Munch and primitive art to be their inspiration, the group began to produce paintings and graphics that combined a radical simplification of form with an increasingly strident colour sense. Like the Fauves, Die Brücke artists took their subjects directly from nature. Heckel's painting **Bathers** emphasizes harmony, the human figures are depicted as part of their natural surroundings. Although Die Brücke broke up in 1913, certain basic features of their expressive common style continued to influence Heckel's work. He served as a Red Cross orderly in the First World War, during which time he met Max Beckmann and the Belgian artist James Ensor. In later years, Heckel's style became more decorative and lyrical. Between 1949 and 1955, Heckel taught at the Karlsruhe Academy of Art.

OTHER MASTERPIECES Sleeping Negress; *1908; Yale University Art Gallery, New Haven, Connecticut, USA* **Landscape in Thunderstorm**; *1913; Tel Aviv Museum, Israel*

Heem Jan Davidsz de

Born Utrecht, Netherlands, 1606; died Antwerp, Belgium c.1683

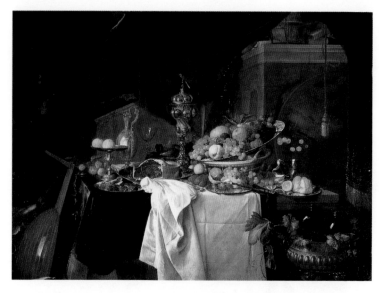

Still Life of Dessert *1640; oil on canvas; 149 x 203 cm; Musée du Louvre, Paris, France*

Jan Davidsz de Heem was part of a family of talented Dutch still life painters that included his father, David, and his son, Cornelius. He worked in Utrecht and Leyden before moving to Antwerp at a time of religious conflict. **Still life of Dessert** features the apparent remains of a sumptuous feast. In typical Baroque fashion, the composition emerges from dark shadow, in sharp contrast to the brilliant white cloth in the foreground. With plates and salvers poised precariously on the table, the picture has been contrived to give the impression of casual abandon. The luscious fruit and pies are deeply tempting and a testament to de Heem's skill of rendition. Henri Matisse made copies of this painting and was greatly influenced by it. Fruit, fancy goblets, shining metals dishes, luxurious cloth and a profusion of flowers were frequently featured in de Heem's still lifes. Less commonly, he included a human figure in his compositions, surrounded by memorabilia in the form of books and pictures. De Heem is widely regarded as the greatest Dutch still life painter.

OTHER MASTERPIECES Still Life with a Nautilus Cup; *1632; Barber Institute of Fine Arts, University of Birmingham, England* Still Life with a Lobster; *c.1645; Wallace Collection, London, England*

Hepworth Dame Barbara

Born Wakefield, England 1903; died St Ives, England 1975

Mother and Child *1934; stone; 23 x 18.9 cm; Tate Collection, London, England*

Barbara Hepworth trained at Leeds and the Royal College. She made both representative and abstract work but it is for the latter that she is best known. Trips to Italy and to Paris in the 1920s and 1930s introduced her to marble-carving techniques and to the work of eminent artists including Arp, Mondrian and Brancusi. In 1934 she abandoned figuration but continued to use nature and the **Mother and Child** theme as her inspiration. Her bronze and marble forms were conceived originally as abstract responses to her own vision of life. At this time, living in London, she came into contact with the artist, Naum Gabo, a refugee whose work affected her deeply. In 1939 she and her second husband the painter Ben Nicholson, settled in St Ives, Cornwall where they became the nucleus of an artistic community. Neolithic stones standing on the moors and the rugged coastline with its towering rocks and curving inlets made an impact on her ideas. She pierced holes in, hollowed out and painted forms, complementing their mass and volume by adding the tension of taught strings or wires. As somewhat of an outsider, that she gained recognition in a field dominated by men is a remarkable achievement.

OTHER MASTERPIECES Pelagos; *1946; Tate Collection, London, England*
Squares with Two Circles; *1963; Tate Collection, London, England*

Heron Patrick

Born Leeds, England 1920; died Zennor, Cornwall, England, 1999

Untitled 10–11 July *1992; oil on canvas; 198.1 x 274.3 cm; Tate Collection, London, England*

Patrick Heron described Matisse's **Red Studio** as, "the most influential single picture in my career". As he wrote, in 1958, that "Space in colour is the subject of my painting", his early admiration for Matisse's masterpiece was significant. Heron's art training was minimal – he attended the Slade School of Art part-time for two years. He worked as an assistant in the Bernard Leach Pottery in St Ives (1944–1945) and came into contact with Ben Nicholson and Barbara Hepworth. An art critic as well as a practitioner, his views were published in his book, *The Changing Forms of Arts* (1955). Until 1956, he produced figurative painting. This developed into a concern to make the paint, colour and spatial organization take precedence over content. Striped paintings of the late 1950s gave way to the "formal vocabulary" of square and lozenge shapes. An emphasis on drawing returned to his work during the 1960s. Works made through the 1980s and 1990s, **Untitled 10–11 July**, for example, provided a softer, looser focus on his primary concern, colour. However, there was a return to the graphic qualities of earlier work, emphasizing the unifying element of the ground on which the linear patterns rest.

OTHER MASTERPIECES Horizontal Stripe Painting; *1957–1958; Tate Collection, London, England* **Cadmium with Violet, Scarlet, Emerald, Lemon and Venetian**; *1969; Tate Collection, London, England*

Hilliard Nicholas

Born Exeter, England c.1547; died London, England c.1619

**Queen Elizabeth I
(Pelican Portrait)**
*c.1572; oil on panel;
76.8 x 59.6 cm;
Walker Art Gallery,
Liverpool, England*

Nicholas Hilliard
is the first English
artist whose life is
reliably documented.
The son of an Exeter
goldsmith, he
trained and worked
for a while as a
goldsmith himself.
By 1560 he was
practising as a
limner, that is, a
painter of portraits
in miniature; these
were often mounted
in lockets or worn
on the end of
jewelled chains. It

was a precise art which combined the need for fine brushwork with an unerring eye for detail.
He was appointed limner and goldsmith to Queen Elizabeth I in 1562. This portrait is one of
the few full-size portraits attributed to Hilliard. It has helped to define the popular image of
Queen Elizabeth, while providing a record of the courtly grace of the Elizabethan age. It is
known as the "**Pelican Portrait**" because the pendant around the Queen's neck features a
pelican. A traditional Christian symbol of Christ's sacrifice, the pelican has been known to feed
its young on its own blood and is therefore an appropriate symbol for a Queen who saw herself
as mother of her people. Until overtaken by his pupil Isaac Oliver, Hilliard was the most
successful limner in England.

OTHER MASTERPIECES Portrait of an Unknown Man; *c.1588; Victoria and Albert Museum,
London, England* Queen Elizabeth I (Ermine Portrait); *1585; Hatfield House, Hertfordshire, England*

Hilton Roger

Born Northwood England 1911; died St Just, England 1975

Oi, Yoi, Yoi *1963;*
oil on canvas; 152.4 x
127 cm; Tate Collection,
London, England

Roger Hilton's
declared goal was to
"reinvent figuration".
His attempts to do
so have established
his significant
contribution to the
development of
post-war painting in
Britain. Hilton
trained at the Slade
School of Art in
London. During the
1930s he attended
the Academie
Ranson in Paris,
where he began to
absorb the influence of progressive artistic ideas. Hilton served in the Commandos during the
war. He was captured and held prisoner until 1945. By 1950 he had returned to Paris and the
influence of the painters of the Paris School was reinforced by his study of Mondrian's work in
Amsterdam and The Hague. He had travelled there with Constant Nieuwenhuys, a painter of
the CoBra group whom Hilton referred to as a "humanized Mondrian". Hilton's own abstract,
"neo-plastic" paintings became more severe, forceful compositions of line produced from a
reductive palette. Impressed by his first visit to St Ives in 1956, he rented a studio at Newlyn,
and settled in Cornwall in 1965. He had announced that, "Abstraction in itself is nothing", and
his work began orienting toward colourful figuration, beginning with the landscape and
culminating in the vitality of recognizable subjects such as the dancing woman of **Oi, Yoi, Yoi**.

OTHER MASTERPIECES Large Orange, Newlyn, June 1959; *1959; The Syndics of the*
Fitzwilliam Museum, Cambridge, England **March 1961;** *1961; Whitworth Art Gallery, Manchester,*
England

Hirst Damien

Born Bristol, England 1965

The Physical Impossibility of Death in the Mind of Someone Living *1991; shark in a glass case; 210 cm x 640 x 213 cm; Saatchi Collection, London, England*

Damien Hirst has attracted controversy and respect in equal amounts. He is one of a generation of artists who have broken the boundaries between art and moral, ethical respectability. Initially noted for his work as a curator of alternative exhibitions while still a student at Goldsmith's College (1986–1989), it is for his art that he has achieved international recognition. **The Physical Impossibility of Death in the Mind of Someone Living** is an oft-quoted, notorious example of his work. A tiger shark, one of the most feared creatures in the sea, is preserved in formaldehyde in a glass tank and rendered a passive museum object, an icon for contemplation. Face to face with a killer, we ponder on the wonder that death preserved can look so alive. Hirst has specialized in using vitrines and animals living – butterflies and maggots – dead and dismembered (sheep and cows), conveying a mood at once confrontational, clinical and distanced. Hirst's conceptual work is less about conventional aesthetics and more about a willingness to take risks and explore the ambiguities inherent in human thoughts and desires. He has stated, "I sometimes feel I have nothing to say. I often want to communicate this".

OTHER MASTERPIECES Acetic Anhydride; *1991; Saatchi Collection, London, England*
A Thousand Years; *1990; Saatchi Collection, London, England*

Hitchens Ivon

Born London, England 1893; died Sussex, England 1979

Garden Cove *1952–1953; oil on canvas; 44 x 108 cm; Arts Council Collection, London, England*

Ivon Hitchens applied the principles of structural design to his painting. He coupled this with the exploration of colour as an integral element of pictorial composition. By his own admission he was ". . . a sucker for noble art" and his early admiration for Puvis de Chavannes and Piero della Francesca is reflected in his mural and stained glass designs. Hitchens studied at London's Royal Academy and held his first solo exhibition in 1925. The influence of Cézanne's painting and, by the early 1930s, of Braque's Cubism was complemented in Hitchen's work by exuberant colour experimentation inspired by Matisse. From 1940 onward West Sussex was his home and the inspiration for his painting. What interested him was not the subject but the way in which he could express it without resorting to descriptive realism. By orchestrating shapes and formal elements within two-dimensional space he painted a parallel for the natural world, evoking mood and creating beauty with lyrical, soft-edged abstractions. His so-called "tone poems" were barely tainted by changing artistic fashions. **Garden Cove** exemplifies this tendency and established his reputation within a painting tradition that was intimately English.

OTHER MASTERPIECES Winter Lawn and Fir Trees; *1978; Waddington Galleries, London, England* **Flower Piece**; *1943; Sheffield City Art Galleries, Sheffield, England*

Hobbema Meindert

Born Amsterdam, Netherlands, 1638; died Amsterdam, Netherlands 1709

The Avenue at Middelharnis *1689; oil on canvas; 103.5 x 141 cm; National Gallery, London, England*

Meindert Hobbema was both a friend and pupil of Jacob van Ruisdael. The two artists occasionally painted the same view, although Hobbema's landscapes lack the heightened drama of his master's. Hobbema achieved little recognition in his lifetime. He became an excise officer in 1668 and thereafter spent more time inspecting wine casks than painting. Originally thought to date from the late 1660s, this example of his work is dated 1689, and features Middelharnis, a village in south Holland whose flat and ordered lowlands have changed little over the centuries. The foreshortening of the avenue of young poplar trees draws us into the picture. The image of a path or road to suggest a journey and the passage of time is not new, but is used to especially powerful effect here. In Hobbema's tranquil scene, a man strolls with his dog, another tends his plants, two more stop for a chat. The brilliant contrast between the red roofs of the houses and the greyish-green foliage is one of the painting's many notable features. What makes this a truly exceptional painting is that the details combine to increase the harmony of the overall composition.

OTHER MASTERPIECES Stormy Landscape; *c. 1663; Wallace Collection, London, England*
The Watermill with a Red Roof; *c. 1670; Chicago Art Institute, Chicago, USA*

Hockney David

Born Bradford, England 1937

Man Taking a Shower in Beverly Hills
1964; acrylic on canvas; 167.3 x 167 cm; Tate Collection, London, England

David Hockney delights in contradictions. His name is synonymous with slick acrylic or coloured pencil portraits, renditions of still life, or variations on the theme of men in showers, as seen here in the stylized **Man Taking a Shower in Beverly Hills**, and swimming pools with spaghetti-like reflections. In the early 1960s, Hockney was an innovative student at The Royal College of Art. He delved into Pop Art, going against the tide of Abstraction from the US, which threatened to engulf art production in Britain. His larger painting projects were concerned more overtly with the major preoccupations of his early work. These were notably, his homosexuality and his absorption in the work and ideas of other artists, particularly Dubuffet, Bacon and Kitaj, who was an early associate at the Royal College of Art, and the writers Walt Whitman and Cavafy. Hockney had a fear of repetition and did not maintain allegiance to stylistic unity. In the 1980s his photographic works exemplified his enquiry into the nature of visual reality, incorporating Cubist ideology and questioning the Renaissance view of perspective. Subsequently he has worked with optical devices such as the camera obscura, exploring their use in the past and employing them in his own art.

OTHER MASTERPIECES We Two Boys Together Clinging; *1961; Arts Council Collection, London, England* **Mr & Mrs Clark & Percy**; *1970–71; Tate Collection, London, England*

Hodgkin Sir Howard

Born London, England 1932

Dinner at Smith Square *1975–1979; oil on wood; 94.6 x 125.1 cm; Tate Collection, London, England*

Sir Howard Hodgkin's contribution to British painting is difficult to define, as his work does not correspond to any particular art movement. He studied his craft at Camberwell School of Art, London, between 1949 and 1950 and at the Bath Academy of Art, Corsham, between 1950 and 1954. One of his tutors at Bath was William Scott, whose modernist aesthetic guided Hodgkin's notions of painting toward the consideration of it as a physical object. His early interest in Indian painting has undoubtedly informed the pure brilliance of his palette. His continued commitment and indebtedness to the culture behind the art form is shown by his collection of Mughal miniatures and frequent visits to India. His extensive travels elsewhere in the world have inspired his subject matter. Hodgkin's paintings, incorporating their frames, appear purely abstract. They are, in fact, based on experiences or encounters. **Dinner at Smith Square**, for example, implies that a complete narrative, suggested by the title, is held within the layers of colour and superimposition of brush marks, which are as varied as the words within a wide vocabulary, evoking a vivid story.

OTHER MASTERPIECES Interior at Oakwood Court*; 1978; Whitworth Art Gallery, Manchester, England* **Menswear***; 1980–1985; Saatchi Collection, London, England*

187

Hodler Ferdinand

Born Berne, Switzerland 1853; died Geneva, Switzerland 1918

Lake Thun and the Stockhorn Mountains *1910; oil on canvas; 83 x 105.4 cm; Scottish National Gallery of Art, Edinburgh, Scotland*

Ferdinand Hodler was, with Arnold Böcklin, the leading Swiss painter of the nineteenth century. He settled in Geneva in 1871, where he studied landscape and figure painting. His early work consists of landscapes, portraits and large allegorical and historical compositions. A visit to Paris in 1891 exposed him to the work of Corot and Courbet, but ultimately his flat, linear and sometimes decorative style owed more to Symbolism and Art Nouveau. In the 1880s Hodler's deep spirituality led him to develop a theory of Parallelism, which stressed the underlying unity rather than the diversity of all natural things. He was especially drawn to Alpine scenery and painted many views of the Swiss mountains around Lake Thun. These landscapes, from the last ten years of his life, are thought to be his finest work.

The elemental, timeless quality of nature is emphasized in this full-frontal view. The blue and purple tones in which the lake, mountains and sky are rendered help to imbue the scene with a sense of harmony and order.

OTHER MASTERPIECES The Chosen One; *1893–1894; Kunstmuseum, Bern, Switzerland*
Day; *c.1900; Kunsthaus, Zurich, Switzerland*

Hofmann Hans

Born Weissenburg, Germany 1880; died New York City, USA, 1966

Nulli Secundus *1964; oil on canvas; 213 x 131.8 cm; Tate Collection, London, England*

Hans Hofmann was an influential artist and teacher. He studied in Paris, where he met Delaunay, Matisse, Braque and Picasso. In 1915 he opened an art school in Munich. He emigrated to the USA in 1931, where he opened another art school in New York. Attended by many of the next generation of American painters, the school exercised a profound influence on the subsequent development of abstract painting. Hofmann was a major influence on Jackson Pollock. His own work was initially representational, showing Expressionist and Fauve influences. His vigorous abstract style emerged in the 1940s. **Nulli Secundus** is a painting from the last years of his life, when he began to paint with renewed zest. The title means "second to none". Hofmann always based his later work on nature, although the paintings themselves are often resolutely abstract. Built up from a series of underlying rectangles, the painting offers a curious and ambiguous sense of space. Hofmann himself believed form and colour to be inexorably linked, declaring "form only exists through colour, and colour only exists through form".

OTHER MASTERPIECES The Prey; *1956; Museum of Modern Art, New York City, USA*
Exuberance; *1955; Albright Art Gallery, Buffalo, New York State, USA*

Hogarth William

Born London, England 1697; died London, England 1764

The Countess's Morning Levée *c.1743; oil on canvas; 70.5 x 90.8 cm; National Gallery, London, England*

Hogarth's work exemplifies the British taste for acerbic social satire. His painting offers valuable insights into eighteenth-century English society. Hogarth was apprenticed in 1712 to an engraver working in the Rococo tradition and by 1720 was earning a living illustrating books. He studied painting in his spare time at the Academy in St Martin's Lane, eager to develop an entrepreneurial market for contemporary art by British painters. He predicted correctly that popular taste would favour topical narratives that were as critical of vanity as immorality. His series of conversation pieces and sequences of anecdotal paintings were commonly available by the early 1730s and were reproduced as engravings, making them widely affordable. **The Countess's Morning Levée** is the fifth of six scenes from *Marriage à la Mode*. This is a detail of the penultimate tableau of unsavoury characters, each of whom plays a significant part in the collapse of a marriage doomed from the start. Like a stage set, almost every detail has some direct or symbolic bearing on the plot, referring to social and moral indiscretions of the time. Hogarth's keen observations also contributed to his success as a spontaneous and uncompromising portrait painter.

OTHER MASTERPIECES The Graham Children; *1742; Tate Collection, London, England* A Rake's Progress; *c.1735; Sir John Soane's Museum, London, England*

Hokusai Katsushika

Born Asakusa, Japan 1760; died Honjo, Japan 1849

The Great Wave of Kanagawa *c. 1830; colour wood block print; 25 x 30 cm; Museum of Modern Art, New York City, USA*

Katsushika Hokusai was one of the most significant and creative wood-block printmakers of the first half of the nineteenth century. Recognized as a leading artist of the Ukiyo-e School, the most popular translation of Ukiyo-e being "pictures of the floating world", Hokusai's master was the eminent artist Shunsho. He worked during a period when art was made for and by the common people – artisans, traders and city dwellers. Since this work was widely available – due to its reproducibility – it was bound by the strictures of changing fashion. Popular prints featured courtesans and actors of the Kabuki theatre. Hokusai worked on such images until 1794. In 1798 he began a series of views of Edo, which formed a precursor to his serious interest in landscape. Through this subject, Hokusai exercised artistic sensitivity and imagination, rejecting the demand for the increasing garishness of theatrical subject matter. This demand ceased with the end of the eighteenth century and Hokusai's prints, such as **The Great Wave of Kanagawa**, became sought after. It is an ingenious and dramatic scene, the fishing boats and Mount Fuji itself are rendered tiny in the presence of the wall of water, threatening to break.

OTHER MASTERPIECES The Dream of the Fisherman's Wife; *c. 1820; British Museum, London, England* Snowy Morning at Koishikawa; *c. 1830; British Museum, London, England*

191

Holbein Hans

Born Augsburg, Germany c.1497–1498; died London, England 1543

Georg Gisze *1532; oak panel; 96.3 x 85.7 cm; Staatliche Gemalde-Galerie, Berlin, Germany*

Hans Holbein trained in his father's studio in Augsburg, a place famous for its goldsmiths. The Reformation had effected a crisis within the creative and decorative arts; knowledge of the Renaissance filtering into the North from Italy was welcomed by artists. By 1516 Holbein was painting portraits exquisitely rendered in a realist manner; in about 1520 he was the leading painter in Basel. However, the turmoil caused by the Reformation influenced a decline in patronage and Holbein's departure for England in 1526. A letter of recommendation from eminent scholar, Erasmus of Rotterdam, led to Sir Thomas More become Holbein's patron. The group family portrait that followed, of full-length figures in their own home, was a landmark in European painting. After a brief return to Basel in 1528, Holbein again worked in England from 1532. He found new patrons in the German Steelyard Merchants for whom he painted several portraits, including one of **Georg Gisze**. By 1536 he was official Court Painter to Henry VIII, providing detailed and vivid records of the period. Despite various decorative and fine art commissions that resulted from court patronage he died without having used the full range of his considerable talents.

OTHER MASTERPIECES The Ambassadors, *1533; National Gallery, London, England*
Artist's Wife and Children; *c.1528; Kunstmuseum, Basel, Switzerland*

Homer Winslow

Born Boston, USA 1836; died Prout's Neck, USA, 1910

The Gulf Stream *1899; oil on canvas; 71.4 x 124.8 cm; Catherine Lorillard Wolfe Fund, 1906, The Metropolitan Museum of Art, New York City, USA*

Winslow Homer's early life was spent on the New England coasts of Massachusetts and Maine. After training as a lithographer he moved to New York City in 1859, where he worked as an illustrator and war artist, spending several months with the Union army. He travelled to France and then to England, where he stayed in Tynemouth painting seascapes in watercolour. His style broadened and his brushstrokes loosened. In 1883 Homer settled in Prout's Neck, on the Maine coast. Although more tonal than the Impressionists, he observed the effects of light with equal interest. He travelled again, to the Bahamas, Florida and Bermuda, where his paintings of huntsmen, sea divers and fishermen record his fascination with man's struggle against the darker forces of nature. Watercolour studies of shark fishing and of an ominously derelict and dismasted schooner were used as the basis of **The Gulf Stream**. The painting has been described as a catalogue of marine catastrophe. A water spout compounds the danger already wrought by the hurricane which has snapped both mast and bowsprit. And, just below the surface, the sharks are waiting…

OTHER MASTERPIECES The Fox Hunt; *1893; Pennsylvania Academy of Fine Art, Philadelphia, USA* Fishing Boats, Key West; *1903; Metropolitan Museum of Art, New York City, USA*

Hooch Pieter de

Born Rotterdam, Netherlands 1629; died Amsterdam, Netherlands 1684

A Woman Peeling Apples *c.1663; oil on canvas; 67.1 x 54.7 cm; Wallace Collection, London, England*

Pieter de Hooch was a contemporary of Vermeer. Both painters worked mainly in Delft where they recorded domestic scenes from middle-class life. Like Vermeer, de Hooch was particularly interested in the fall of light upon surfaces. Typically, his paintings feature either a sunny courtyard juxtaposed with a view into the shadows of a house or a dim interior lit by bright natural light falling through a door or window. **A Woman Peeling Apples** is characteristic of the latter. Absorbed in her household duties the woman is watched silently by a small child. It is a comfortable and tranquil scene in which the gloom and heaviness of the dark room is relieved by the light steaming through the window, as well as the warmth of the woman's red skirt. De Hooch moved to Amsterdam in the early 1660s and, in place of his simple interiors, began to paint grandiose scenes of Dutch high life. His art declined from this point until his death in an asylum some 20 years later.

OTHER MASTERPIECES Courtyard of a House in Delft; *1658; National Gallery, London, England* The Pantry; *c.1658; Rijksmuseum, Amsterdam, Netherlands*

Hopper Edward

Born Nyack, USA 1882; died New York City, USA 1967

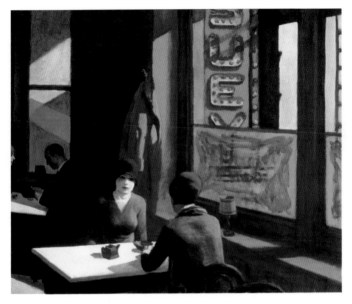

Chop Suey *1929, oil on canvas; 81.3 x 96.5 cm; Collection of B.A. Ebsworth, St Louis, USA*

Edward Hopper is recognized as a major realist painter of the twentieth century. In 1924, while working as an illustrator, he had his first solo exhibition. He studied at the New York School of Art from 1900–1906. Hopper then visited Paris and returned there during 1909 and 1910. The European lifestyle and the art he witnessed had a major impact on his painting; he claimed that it took him ten years to get over the experience. Looking at his work, it is clear that he never really did. The influence of the French Impressionists infiltrates his composition and his focus on light effects and social scenes. Hopper established his artistic identity by utilizing the "typically American subject matter" of hotel room interiors, gasoline stations, theatre foyers, apartments and cafe bars at night. Without resorting to narrative, a sense of contemplation, quietness or non-communication is suggested. **Chop Suey** is such a picture. It has a timelessness and the pervasive air of introspection is a reflection of Hopper's own character. The interior life of the city forms the content of most of Hopper's work and has, stylistically, inspired film makers and other artists searching for an essentially American mood.

OTHER MASTERPIECES Automat*; 1927; Des Moines Art Center, Iowa, USA*
Room in New York*; 1932; Sheldon Memorial Art Gallery, University of Nebraska, Lincoln, USA*

Horn Rebecca

Born Michelstadt, Germany 1944

Ballet of the Woodpeckers *1986, mixed media, size variable, Tate Collection, London, England*

Rebecca Horn is established as one of the most imaginative artists of her generation. Her truancy from school prophesied her independence and rejection of conventional art forms. From 1964–1969 she trained at the Fine Arts Academy in Hamburg. During this period she was employing toxic materials to make her work and their effect led to prolonged illness. While confined, she designed a series of surreal clothing. These included extensions for arms and for fingers that trailed on the floor, wings, a tall, cloth horn and a pulsating garment of veins. She transformed herself and friends into living sculptures wearing these and others on film. She continued her studies at St Martin's School of Art, London (1971–1972). Alongside her film, video and performance work she explores the possibilities of kinetic sculpture. These "symbols of people" are powerfully enigmatic automata, which Horn describes as "melancholic actors, performing in solitude". They incorporate all manner of objects – shoes, guns, pianos, motorized blue butterfly wings – and materials with alchemical significance. **Ballet of the Woodpeckers**, a sequence of mirrors spasmodically tapped by small hammers, is like birds flying toward, or destroying, their own image. It is a potent metaphor for desire, compulsion and isolation.

OTHER MASTERPIECES The Golden Bath, *1980, Stedelijk van Abbemuseum, Eindhoven, Netherlands* **Orlando**, *1988, Tate Collection, London, England*

Howson Peter

Born London, England 1958

A Night That Never Ends *1995; oil on canvas; 152 x 122 cm; Angela Flowers Gallery, London, England*

Peter Howson lives and works in Scotland. He trained at the Glasgow School of Art from 1975–1977 and 1979–1981. Here, the strong academic traditions of figurative art gave him and other painters of his generation a solid basis on which to formulate a recognized way of working. Howson was one of the driving forces behind the so-called New Image painting that revolutionized British art in the late 1980s. A return to narrative and to powerful figuration came from an acknowledgement of Glasgow's socio-economic difficulties at the time. A socialist element infiltrated Howson's painting, which tended to focus on the struggles of the working classes. **A Night That Never Ends** was a typical example of Howson's oeuvre of this period, a multi-figure scene comprising individuals representing. "the common man". They inhabit a tough, violent world where nihilism rules. There is little hope, little sun and no joy. Howson's assured, bold technique lends a note of reassurance; the viewer is in no doubt that this is not the real world. It is, however, an extraordinary visualization of humanity as both feared and fearful. In 1993 Howson was official British war artist in Bosnia, making some bleak images. His nude paintings of superstar Madonna, exhibited in 2002, excited a different form of controversy.

OTHER MASTERPIECES Patriots; *1991; Art Gallery and Museum, Kelvingrove, Glasgow, Scotland* **Cleansed**; *1994; Imperial War Museum, London, England*

Hunt William Holman

Born London, England 1827; died London, England 1910

The Scapegoat *1854; oil on canvas; 87 x 139.8 cm; Lady Lever's Art Collection, Port Sunlight, England*

William Holman Hunt first began to study art at the British Museum and National Gallery at the age of 16. In 1844 he entered the Royal Academy where he met Dante Gabriel Rossetti and John Everett Millais. The three founded the Pre-Raphaelite Brotherhood in 1848. Hunt alone remained true to its basic principle of expressing serious moral ideas through art, combined with a truthful and realistic approach to nature. He made several trips to Egypt and Palestine from 1854 to paint religious scenes within their original location. **The Scapegoat** dates from Hunt's first trip to Palestine and shows the animal alone on the shores of the Dead Sea. Hunt believed that a realistic treatment of this biblical allegory would enhance the spiritual message. Consequently he went to great lengths to ensure that every detail in his work was historically authentic, making use of strong colours and exact realism to enhance his depiction. In later years, Hunt's obsession with accuracy as well as his dogmatic convictions grew more pronounced, and the imaginative power of his paintings declined.

OTHER MASTERPIECES The Hireling Shepherd; *1851; Manchester City Art Gallery, England*
The Light of the World; *1854; Keble College, Oxford, England*

Immendorff Jorg

Born Bleckede, Germany 1945

Café Deutschland I *1987; oil on canvas; 282 x 330 cm; Galerie Michael Werner, Cologne, Germany*

Jorg Immendorff is a leading German Neo-Expressionist whose artistic career began in 1961 – the same year as the Berlin Wall was constructed – with a solo exhibition in Bonn at the New Orleans Club. Beginning in 1964, he attended courses at the Kunstakademie, Dusseldorf, studying under Joseph Beuys, whose polemic and direction profoundly affected his artistic development. Immendorff's social and political concerns marked the paintings he produced at the end of the 1960s, serialized by the nonsensical LIDL slogan, referring to the world of infancy. A more overtly political element underpinned the **Café Deutschland** paintings, which referred directly to the division of Germany and the increasing polarization of society. The motifs and harsh, satirical gestures in the German Expressionist art, seventy years before, provided Immendorff with inspiration. In addition, his experience of the realism of Renato Guttuso's **Caffé Greco** painting (1978) confirmed his approach to his subject. The high tonality, dark shadows and frenetic activity and imagery crammed into the pictorial space evoke anarchy and menace. Immendorff opened the Café La Paloma in Hamburg in 1984, which became a reputable exhibiting venue.

OTHER MASTERPIECES Eigenlob Stinkt Nicht; *1983; Michael Werner Gallery, New York City, USA* Cafe Deutschland Horerwunsch; *1983; Private Collection*

Ingres Jean-Auguste Dominique

Born Montauban, France 1780; died Paris, France 1867

La Grande Odalisque *1814; oil on canvas; 91 x 162 cm, Musée du Louvre, Paris, France*

Ingres began his artistic career as a pupil in Jacques-Louis David's studio in Paris. He won the Grand Prix de Rome, a four-year scholarship, in 1801 with a Neoclassical history painting. He painted **La Grande Odalisque** in 1814. In this, he reasserts the ideal of elegance, sensuousness and purification of line to which anatomical correctness was subservient without looking unnatural. Figure compositions and portraits were the mainstay of his oeuvre. The latter, in particular, allowed him to revel in the depiction of porcelain skin and luxurious materials and brocades and he epitomized the sumptuous lifestyle of the higher classes of nineteenth-century French society. He rarely painted landscapes. Draughtsmanship impregnated by the gothic and the archaic described his style and he was likened by one of his contemporaries to a "Chinese or Japanese artist who has strayed into Greece". After the fall of Napoleon in 1814 Ingres produced a series of small-scale paintings after medieval and Renaissance subjects and spent much of his time in Rome. He was the most admired painter of his day and was, as a teacher, one of the most influential.

OTHER MASTERPIECES Portrait of Madame Moitessier; *c.1850; National Gallery, London, England* **Nude From the Back;** *c.1815; Musée du Louvre, Paris, France*

Jawlensky Alexei von

Born Kuslovo, Russia 1864; died Wiesbaden, Germany 1941

**Spanish Woman with
Grey Background** *1913;
oil on cardboard; 64.5 x
53.2 cm; Private Collection*

A Russian aristrocat,
Alexei von Jawlensky
was initially an officer in
the Imperial Guard. He
studied at the St
Petersburg Academy
before moving to
Munich in 1896, where
he met Kandinsky. In
1905 he travelled to
Brittany and Provence. During a short stay in Paris, he worked with Matisse. Jawlensky's
paintings show a mixture of influences from the naive, bold style of the Fauves to the traditional
icon painting and peasant art of his native Russia. **Spanish Woman with a Grey Background** is
one of a number of head-and-shoulder portraits that Jawlensky first embarked upon in 1910.
Through its bold colours and expressive contours, Jawlensky reveals an interest in the universal
and mystical qualities of his sitter. Like Kandinsky, he was fascinated by the relationship
between colour and music, describing how "colours rang like music in his eyes". Unlike
Kandinsky, however, Jawlensky never became a wholly abstract painter, preferring to pursue his
meditative style of representation in portraits and landscapes. After the First World War, he
settled in Wiesbaden in Germany, where he formed the Blaue Vier (Blue Four) with Kandinsky,
Klee and Feininger.

OTHER MASTERPIECES The White Feather; *1907; Staatsgalerie, Stuttgart, Germany*
Portrait of Alexander Sacharoff; *1913; Stadtisches Museum, Wiesbaden, Germany*

John Gwen

Born Haverfordwest, Wales 1876; died Dieppe, France 1939

A Corner of the Artist's Room *1907–1909; oil on canvas; 32 x 26.5 cm; Sheffield City Art Gallery, Sheffield, England*

Gwen John studied at the Slade School of Art with her brother Augustus. She went to live in Paris in 1903 where she was taught by Whistler. A solitary and single-minded woman, she had an unhappy love affair with Auguste Rodin, whom she met in 1904. **A Corner of the Artist's Room** depicts her room at 87 rue du Cherche Midi in Montparnasse, Paris. She chose her accommodation carefully, taking into consideration the comfort of her cats as well as the view it offered. Augustus, whose own flamboyant lifestyle differed wildly from his sister's, was unhappy with her spartan choice. However, the image of her room portrayed by this canvas (she painted several versions) is of serenity and self-containment rather than neurotic, self-imposed isolation. The bright sunlight is diffused by the lace drape and attention is focused on the few possessions – a simple bunch of flowers, a wicker chair and a parasol. In 1913 John became a Catholic, declaring "My religion and my art, these are my life". She continued to live in relative isolation and painted many delicate, muted, introspective portraits, mainly of women and girls, of outstanding sensitivity. Her work is now held in higher regard than her brother's.

OTHER MASTERPIECES Self-Portrait; *c.1900; Tate Collection, London, England*
A Young Nun; *c.1920; Scottish National Gallery of Modern Art, Edinburgh, Scotland*

Johns Jasper

Born Augusta, USA 1930

Device 1962; oil on canvas with wood; 101.6 x 76.2 cm; purchased with funds provided by The Dexter M. Ferry, Jr. Trustee Corporation Fund and by Edith Ferry Hooper, Baltimore Museum of Art, Baltimore, USA

Jasper Johns is widely recognized as one of the most influential American artists of the post-war period. Following in the wake of the gestural but largely empty passions of the Abstract Expressionists, the simplicity of John's comparatively reductive art made a startling contrast. Johns settled in New York City in 1952 and met fellow artist Rauschenberg shortly after. Rather than focus on the vitality of popular culture, Johns exploited the banality of it, declaring "Take an object. Do something to it. Do something else to it". His favourite motifs were the universally familiar symbols of flags, targets, letters and numbers. Turning these into art, he provoked the viewer into considering the things the mind already knows in a different way, while highlighting the methods by which he turns such subjects into artifice. The enigmatic **Device** exemplifies Johns's techniques, which are rendered as signs and language in themselves. He is an exceptionally proficient painter and graphic artist, a master of a variety of media. His more recent work has increased in thematic and conceptual complexity, with an emphasis on more personal references.

OTHER MASTERPIECES Zero Through Nine; *1961; Tate Collection, London, England* **Zone**; *1962; Kunsthaus, Zurich, Switzerland*

203

Judd Donald

Born Excelsior Springs, USA 1928; died New York City, USA 1994

Untitled *1972; copper, enamel and aluminium; 916 x 155.5 x 178.2 cm; Tate Collction, London, England*

Donald Judd's art training began in earnest when, in 1949, he attended the Arts Students League in New York City. During the evenings he studied philosophy at Columbia University. He graduated with an MA in art history from Columbia in 1962. He commenced his artistic career as a painter during the 1950s and his familiarity with the contemporary art world was confirmed by his employment as art critic of *Arts Magazine* from 1959. His observations of the work of emerging avant-garde artists and the development of his own work led to the realization that the two-dimensionality of painting was severely limiting and lacked specific focus. In the early 1960s, therefore, he rejected the medium to construct wall reliefs and free-standing sculpture. He developed the simplicity of the work until his sculpture was reduced to "stacks" and "progressions" – boxes and bars arranged in a mathematical sequence. These "Specific Objects", mechanically reproduced to avoid the look of hand-made craftsmanship, quickly established him as a leader of the new Minimalist movement. **Untitled** is a typically sterile, single unit, made at a time when Judd was producing pieces in response to the content of specific environments.

OTHER MASTERPIECES Untitled; *1969; Solomon R. Guggenheim Museum, New York City, USA*
Untitled; *1973; Tate Collection, London, England*

Kahlo Frida

Born, Mexico City, Mexico 1907; died Mexico City, Mexico 1954

Self-Portrait with Cropped Hair *1940; oil on canvas; 40 x 27.9 cm; Gift of Edgar J. Kaufmann, Museum of Modern Art, New York City, USA*

Frida Kahlo's life was transformed at the age of fifteen when a trolley car plunged into the bus in which she was a passenger. She suffered terrible injuries that served to shape her painting for the rest of her life. On small canvases and rendered with miniaturist detail, her autobiographical paintings make literal and symbolic reference to the emotional and physical pain she had to endure. Kahlo married Mexican muralist Diego Rivera in 1929. Their stormy and tempestuous relationship led to a divorce in 1939 and reunion later in life. **Self-Portrait with Cropped Hair** was painted in response to one of Rivera's many infidelities. Kahlo represents herself in an angry and defiant mood. Dressed in a baggy man's suit she is surrounded by stands of her hair, that wriggle like snakes. The writing across the top of the painting mocks the lyrics of a popular song which declared that love was dependent upon their lover's beautiful hair. Fiercely proud, sensual and magnetic – these are all qualities associated with the legendary Frida Kahlo. Above all, however, her self-portraits provide an extraordinary insight into an intense and complex imagination.

OTHER MASTERPIECES Self-Portrait with Monkey; *1940; Collection of Mr and Mrs Jacques Gleman, Mexico City, Mexico* A Few Small Nips; *1935; Collection of Dolores Olmedo, Mexico City, Mexico*

Kandinsky Vassily

Born Moscow, Russia 1866; died Paris, France 1944

Improvisation 26 *1912; oil on canvas; 97 x 107.5 cm; Stadtische Galerie im Lenbachshaus, Munich, Germany*

Vassily Kandinsky is generally considered to be the pioneer of abstract painting. Much affected by an exhibition in Moscow of French Impressionists, he abandoned his legal career and went to Munich to study art. His early work showed a number of influences, including features of Art Nouveau, Russian folk art and the Fauves. Kandinsky was the driving force behind the formation of the Blaue Reiter group in 1912. With fellow-artists Marc and Macke, this influential group's primary commitment was to the intuitive and primitive qualities of painting, as well as to the symbolic importance of colour and line. Kandinsky began to make his first pure abstract works in 1910. **Improvisation 26** is from a series of paintings that took landscape as their starting point. Through a fluid blend of calligraphic lines and amorphous shapes, the artist expresses a sense of growing detachment from nature. The emphasis is on mood and harmony and reveals Kandinsky's fascination with the relationship between colour and music. Kandinsky taught at the Bauhaus from 1921–1933, when he left Germany for France. He was one of the most influential artists of his generation and an important art theorist.

OTHER MASTERPIECES Landscape with Church; *1913; Museum Folkwang, Essen, Germany*
Composition VIII No 260 *1923; Solomon R Guggenheim Museum, New York City, USA*

Kapoor Anish

Born Bombay, India 1954

Dragon *1992; limestone and pigments; various dimensions; Installation Art Tower Mito, Mito-shi, Japan*

Anish Kapoor's beautiful and contemplative abstract sculpture bridges the artistic gap between East and West. His work combines European modernist influences with the ritualistic traditions and objects associated with Hindu Tantrism. Kapoor trained at Hornsey College of Art, London from 1973–1977 and at Chelsea College of Art, 1977–1978. As an artist with both an Indian and European identity, Kapoor's work celebrates the differences and the similarities between the two. He does not approach the socio-cultural implications of his mixed identity with a political agenda. Work made during the 1980s appeared like strange fruit. Brightly coloured powdered pigment covered and settled around each piece like dust, fusing it with the floor. Later, rough-hewn stone pieces have the rich pigment clinging more closely, with gravity rather than colour being their grounding, elemental force. His organic forms, although essentially abstract, often take on a male or female identity, containing deep voids or protuberances or both. They exist as independent presences or become, like **Dragon**, comprising eleven pieces, part of a group dynamic, suggesting spiritual metaphors.

OTHER MASTERPIECES Mother as a Solo; *1988; Collection Musée St Pierre, Lyon, France*
Marsyas; *2002; Tate Collection, London, England*

Kauffman Angelica

Born Chur, Switzerland 1741; died Rome, Italy 1807

Self-Portrait Hesitating between the Arts of Painting and Music *1794; oil on canvas; 147 x 216 cm; reproduced by kind permission of the Winn family and the National Trust*

Angelica Kauffman's father was a painter who encouraged both her artistic and musical abilities. Travelling formed part of an unorthodox upbringing that included a visit to Rome in 1763, where she established her own Rococo-inspired decorative style of portraiture. Kauffman visited Venice in 1765 and London between 1766–1781. She became a friend of Joshua Reynolds and was influenced by his classical portraits. In England, she also worked with Robert Adam on interiors and became a founder member of the Royal Academy in 1768. **Self-Portrait Hesitating between the Arts of Painting and Music** refers to the difficult decision with which she was faced when choosing between a musical and an artistic career. However, the allegorical, idealized representation of the women tends to undermine the significance of this decision for Kauffman herself. The figure representing painting points to a distant classical temple; this is a reference to the wisdom of the ancient theorists as well as to the neo-classical movement to which she belonged. Kauffman married Zucchi, an Italian decorative painter, in 1781 and settled in Rome.

OTHER MASTERPIECES Fame Decorating Shakespeare's Tomb; *c.1772 Burghley House Collection, England* **Portrait of Johann Winckelmann**; *1764; Kunsthaus, Zurich, Switzerland*

Kelly Mary

Born Fort Dodge, USA 1941

Post-Partum Document VIa
*1978—1979; slate and resin; 35.6
x 27.9 cm per unit; 18 units;
Arts Council, London, England*

Part of the strength of the women's movement of the 1960s and 1970s, Mary Kelly progressed key developments in feminist art practice. She studied at the College of St Teresa, Winoa, Minnesota, the Instituto Pius XII, Florence, 1963–1965 and St Martin's School of Art, London 1968–1970. Her **Post-Partum Document** project spanned six years, focusing on the mother/child relationship, specifically that between her and her infant son. She was, "concerned to deal with an area of women's experience that I felt really hadn't been spoken". Rather than construct notions of femininity via painting or sculpture, Kelly operated within a conceptual art idiom. She distanced both herself and the viewer from the emotional intimacy of her relationship by offering a series of charts, graphs and diagrams, working like an analytical diarist, noting the feeding, growth, speech and mark-making developments of her son. Subsequent works, **Interim** (1985), for example, represent an exploration of women's experiences in their middle years. Comprising text and imagery, this witty and humorous work accesses both the stereotypical and the specific. Kelly uses photographic images and hand-written texts to explore her own concerns and those typically assigned to women – sex, ageing, fashion and relationships.

OTHER MASTERPIECES Corpus (Detail); *1984–1985; Collection of the Artist*
Gloria Patri; *1992; Collection of the Artist*

Kiefer Anselm

Born Donaueschingen, Germany 1945

Parsifal III *1973; oil on paper; 229.1 x 425.8 cm; Tate Collection, London, England*

Anselm Kiefer intended to study Law and French in 1965 but became more interested in painting. Study and travel led to the production of his first important series of paintings in 1970, **Historic Emblems**. A notable period of tuition followed under his mentor Joseph Beuys from 1970 to 1972. Kiefer did not travel down the path of Minimalism and Conceptual art taken by many of the European avant-garde in the early 1970s. Instead he responded to an increasing political polarization within West Germany by reviving the large, traditional format. He dealt subtly and symbolically with his country's past, its literature and music, and the heritage of Nazism. **Parsifal III** refers to Wagner's opera and to the legends that were the composer's sources. It exemplifies Kiefer's powerful exploration of the great myths of German tradition, hinting at his interest in depicting the physical space of landscape and in architecture. This is particularly prevalent in the works referring to the influence of Caspar David Friedrich and those describing the heroic grandeur of neo-classical interiors. Kiefer's use of different materials, particularly straw and lead, remind the spectator of the physical reality of the canvas and lend metaphorical and alchemical significance.

OTHER MASTERPIECES Bohemia Lies by the Sea; *1996; Metropolitan Museum of Art, New York City, USA* Let a Thousand Flowers Bloom; *2000; Museum of Fine Arts, Houston, USA*

Kiff Ken

Born Dagenham, England 1935; died London, England, 2001

Shadows (triptych) *1983–1986; acrylic on board; left and right panels, 116.8 x 88.9 cm; centre panel, 119.4 x 99 cm; Tate Collection, London, England*

Ken Kiff's work was largely ignored throughout the 1960s and 1970s, when minimal and conceptual tendencies in art were critically acclaimed. Highly imaginative and brightly coloured, Kiff's art came to prominence with the revival of figurative painting in Britain toward the end of the 1970s and during the 1980s. He was eloquent in various media including oil and acrylic paint, pastel, charcoal, woodcut and lithography, revealing himself to be a true visionary artist. The narratives in his paintings were derivative of a dream-world set apart from the physical reality of twentieth-century living. Kiff's imagery existed beyond an identifiable social context. However, his representation of the universal inner man was portrayed with reference to psychological and autobiographical material. This was accessed via Expressionist scenes from the subconscious. In spirit, he was, perhaps, closest to the Symbolist painter, Odilon Redon and, accordingly, offered motifs and colours in his pictures that were symbolic and emotionally charged. His **Shadows** triptych is an unusually sombre piece, with the shadows of the title providing a menacing presence in each scene. Together the three pictures suggest a day's journey through desires and fears, with elements of the natural world exerting vital and watchful forces.

OTHER MASTERPIECES Man Greeting Woman; *1965–1966; Arts Council Collection, London, England* **Orange Sun, Sequence No. 187**; *1973; Marlborough Fine Art, London, England*

Kirchner Ernst Ludwig

Born Aschaffenburg, Germany 1880; died Davos, Switzerland 1938

The Red Tower in Halle
1915; tempera on canvas; 120
x 90.5 cm; Museum Folkwang,
Essen, Germany

German Expressionist Ernst Ludwig Kirchner met Erich Heckel and Karl Schmidt-Rottluff while studying architecture at Dresden from 1901–1905. The three founded Die Brücke in 1905 – Kirchner was the dominant force behind the group, which lasted until 1913. Inspired by Gauguin, Munch, van Gogh and primitive art, the Brücke artists were concerned with the direct expression of human emotions. Kirchner developed an angular style that used simplified drawing and bold juxtapositions of complementary colour – a clashing mix of orange, blue, red, yellow and green. Aside from his paintings, he also produced woodcuts and coloured wooden sculpture. He moved to Berlin in 1911, where he painted a series of distorted street scenes, depicting the frenzy and chaos of urban life. The red tower of the title is the focal point of an intense, exciting image. The sloping roofs and slanting streets brought up against the picture plane in sharp, distorted perspective add a dizzying sense of urgency to the picture. Kirchner suffered a nervous breakdown while serving in the First World War. He convalesced in Switzerland, producing work that drew upon the elemental force of the Alpine landscape, and which became more abstract after 1928. Kirchner committed suicide in 1938.

OTHER MASTERPIECES Striding into the Sea; *1912; Staatsgalerie, Stuttgart, Germany*
Berlin Street Scene; *1913; Brücke Museum, Berlin, Germany*

Kitaj Ronald Brooks

Born Cleveland, USA 1932

The Wedding
*1989–1993; oil
on canvas; 182.9 x
182.9 cm; Tate
Collection, London,
England*

R.B. Kitaj studied art extensively in New York, Vienna, Oxford and at the Royal College of Art, London, from 1959 to 1961. He arrived in England after travelling widely as a merchant seaman. His experience of the world made him a charismatic character among fellow students at the RCA, who were in the thralls of Pop Art. Kitaj established an enduring friendship with the artist David Hockney at this time. The comparative superficialities of Pop did not significantly affect Kitaj's figurative work. His focus was more intellectual, looking for his subjects in his personal interests, Jewish history, the work of political activists, writers and other artists. The myriad of influences that inspired his art is complemented by the diverse imagery that appears in his oil paintings and, since 1975, pastels. His interest in the medium was instigated by a renewed admiration for Degas and the enthusiasm of his second wife, painter Sandra Fisher. **The Wedding** illustrates his marriage to her and reveals the construction of his composition. It is like a collage where the spatial relationships are disjointed and dream-like. Kitaj's later style has became more decorative, with an emphasis on flattened colour and expressive line.

OTHER MASTERPIECES If Not, Not; *1975–1976; Scottish National Gallery of Modern Art, Edinburgh, Scotland* Cecil Court, London, WC2 (The Refugees); *1983–1984; Tate Collection, London, England*

Klee Paul

Born Münchenbuchsee, Switzerland 1879; died Muralto, Switzerland 1940

The Castle in the Garden
1919—1920; 21 x 17 cm;
gouache on paper;
Kunstmuseum, Basel,
Switzerland

Swiss-born painter Paul
Klee lived in Germany for
most of his life after
studying in Munich. His
early work consisted of
etchings that showed an Expressionist influence as well as an element of fantasy, which he
discovered in Blake and Beardsley. He began teaching at the Bauhaus in 1906 and was an
inspirational and influential teacher. He also produced many theoretical volumes, including
Pedagogical Sketchbook (1923). From 1911 Klee was associated with the Blue Four, namely
Kandinsky, Feininger and Jawlensky. In 1914 he went to Tunisia with Macke and this visit,
combined with his contact with Cubism and Robert Delaunay, was instrumental in changing his
work. From then on, his work relied on a subtle and meditative arrangement of colour.
Stylistically he moved freely between figuration and abstraction, the constant theme of his
prodigious output being his feel for improvization and re-invention. His sensitive, fluid and
often witty paintings drew upon his love of primitive art, folk painting and children's drawings.
The Castle in the Garden is comprised of an abstract architecture of coloured shapes. The
delicate, tonal variations make up a prism through which the visible world is made remote.

OTHER MASTERPIECES Adventure of a Young Lady; *1922; Tate Collection, London, England*
At the Sign of the Hunter's Tree; *1939; Kunsthaus Zurich, Switzerland*

Klein Yves

Born Nice, France 1928; died Paris, France 1962

IKB 79 *1959; acrylic and photograph on wood; 139.7 x 119.7 cm; Tate Collection, London, England*

Yves Klein had no formal training in art. He was a jazz musician who, between 1952 and 1953 had lived in Japan, where he became a black belt in judo. In the 1950s Klein began to exhibit monochrome canvases covered in a distinctive shade of blue, which he referred to as **International Klein Blue**. This painting is one of these paintings, hence the title, **IKB 79**. The all-pervading colour is intended to act as a contemplative screen rather than to encourage the viewer to make subjective associations. Klein's minimalist exhibition of 1958 flouted every convention, presenting to the public an empty, white-washed Parisian gallery. Known as **The Void**, it was the scene of a near riot when it opened. Klein continued to shock, with his "happenings" known as **Anthropométries** 1958–1960. In these, nude models daubed in blue paint imprinted themselves on canvas to musical accompaniment – a single note sustained for ten minutes, alternated with ten minutes of silence. His works were produced using a variety of unorthodox methods, including a flame-thrower, and rainfall on to a prepared canvas. Klein died aged 34 from a heart attack. His innovatory work had a lasting impact on the development of twentieth-century art.

OTHER MASTERPIECES Fire F 45; *1961; Private Collection, Paris, France*
Trilogie Blue – Or Pink; *1960; Louisana Museum of Modern Art, Humlebaek, USA*

Klimt Gustav

Born Baumgarten, Austria 1862; died Vienna, Austria 1918

*Judith II 1909; oil on canvas;
178 x 46 cm; Museo d'Arte Moderne,
Venice, Italy*

Gustav Klimt enjoyed early
success as a decorative painter,
working on the staircase in the
Kunsthistorisches Museum in
Vienna in 1891. He resigned from
the conservative Viennese Artists'
Association in 1897 and, with
other artists, set up the Viennese
Secession. Klimt was their first
President. A leading Symbolist and
Art Nouveau painter, he exerted
particular influence on Oskar
Kokoschka and Egon Schiele.
Most of his portraits are of woman
– often archetypal, idealized
women – depicted in an array of
alluring poses. His work is highly
distinctive through its mosaic and
decorative patterning and
extensive use of gold. **Judith II** is
Klimt's second version of the story
of Judith and Holofernes in which
Judith, a pious and courageous
widow, is forced to decapitate the
army commander after being given
to him as a hostage. The work caused an outcry amongst Viennese critics because of the
unlikely portrayal of Judith as a femme fatale and the unmistakable eroticism of her semi-naked
torso, half-closed eyes and parted lips. This is a woman whose rapturous expression suggests
she has achieved orgasm at the point of Holofernes' death.

OTHER MASTERPIECES Beech Forest I; c.1902; Moderne Galerie, Dresden, Germany
The Kiss; 1907–1908; Osterreichisches Galerie, Vienna, Austria

Kline Franz

Born Wilkes Barre, USA 1910; died New York City, USA 1962

Meryon 1960–1961;
oil on canvas; 235.9 x
195.6 cm; Tate
Collection, London,
England

Franz Kline had much in common with the Abstract Expressionist group of artists with whom he is associated. However, in many ways, his painting was quite distinct from their work. He trained at Boston University (1931–1935) and travelled to London, where he studied painting and drawing at Heatherley's Art School. Back in New York, in 1940, he received various bar room mural commissions. It was not until 1946 that his awareness of developments in painting, specifically in the gestural works of de Kooning and the "Action Painting" of Jackson Pollock, for example, inspired him to veer toward abstraction. By 1950, he had begun producing the monumental, black and white canvases such as **Meryon**, for which he is best known. Like a small, calligraphic sketch magnified to monstrous proportions, the power of this image, typically produced with a house-painter's brush, is awesome. The white areas, the "negative" spaces, were equally as important as the black, positive blocks. However, Kline's palette was not limited to monochrome. The colourful, saturated hues he applied to some of his canvases were not merely decorative but satisfied his desire, "to feel free to work both ways".

OTHER MASTERPIECES Blueberry Eyes; 1959–1960; National Museum of American Art, Smithsonian Institution, Washington, DC, USA **Black Iris**; 1961; The Museum of Contemporary Art, Los Angeles, USA

Knight Dame Laura

Born Long Eaton, England 1877; died London, England 1970

Ruby Loftus Screwing a Breech-Ring *1943; oil on canvas; 86.3 x 101.6 cm; Imperial War Museum, London, England*

In 1890, Laura Johnson began as a full time student at Nottingham School of Art and had won silver and bronze medals for her portraiture by the age of sixteen. She lived in two artists' colonies – Staides, Yorkshire and Newlyn, Cornwall – before settling with husband, painter Harold Knight, in London in 1918. In 1927, she became the second woman to be made an Associate of the Royal Academy and became a full Royal Academician in 1936. She is known for her popular paintings of the circus and the ballet and was duly recognized for her technique, which satisfied conservative standards of the Academy. However, her most memorable achievements are encapsulated in the monumental painting of **Ruby Loftus Screwing a Breech-Ring**. Focusing on women's work in an armaments factory in 1943, Knight draws attention, with scrupulous detail, to the position of women in the war effort. Ruby is made a symbol of virtue and hard work, literally illuminated like a saint by her task, which was of national importance. Knight was made an official war artist in 1942 and was commissioned to paint the Nuremburg war trials in 1945. The sensitive interpretation of her lesser known works, featuring women and children, have largely been overlooked.

OTHER MASTERPIECES The Beach; *1908; Laing Art Gallery, Newcastle-Upon-Tyne, England*
Self-Portrait; *1913; National Portrait Gallery, London, England*

Kokoschka Oskar

Born Pöchlarn, Austria 1886; died Montreux, Switzerland 1980

Ambassador Ivan Maisky
*1942—1943; oil on canvas;
120 x 76 cm; Tate Collection
London, England*

Oskar Kokoschka trained
at the Vienna School of
Arts and Crafts from
1905 to 1909. Significant
to his development was
the artistic climate in
Austria, including the
recent introduction to Art
Nouveau, the work of
Gustave Klimt and the
existence of the craft
workshops "Wiener
Werkstatte". In response,
Kokoschka produced
lithographs and posters
that revealed his strong
graphic sense. He began
exhibiting in 1908. From
the beginning he imbued his Expressionist style with a highly original imagination. The
drawings he contributed to Berlin's avant-garde Der Sturm journal bear testimony to this. From
1919 to 1924 he taught at Dresden Academy, after recovering from wounds inflicted during the
war. Kokoschka travelled in Europe and North America and Prague. He moved to England in
1938. **Ambassador Ivan Maisky** was the Soviet Ambassador in London from 1932 to 1943.
Typical of Kokoschka's so-called "psychological portraits", the essence of the sitter's personality
is extracted with a frenetic play of colourful brush marks, seemingly assembled on the canvas at
random. This fresh, apparently spontaneous approach injects vitality into his subjects.
Kokoschka's land and cityscapes, often seen from a high viewpoint, are equally memorable.

OTHER MASTERPIECES Children Playing; *1909; Kunstmuseum, Duisberg, Germany*
View of the Thames; *1959; Tate Collection, London, England*

Kollwitz Käthe

Born Konigsberg, Germany 1867; died Moritzbur, Germany 1945

Tower of Mothers *1937–1938; bronze
statue; 27 x 27.5 x 28 cm; Baltimore
Museum of Art, Maryland, USA*

Käthe Kollwitz was a
graphic artist and
sculptor whose
powerful work
reflected her keen
left-wing political
sympathies. She
married a doctor in 1891 and
lived in a Berlin slum until it was
bombed in 1943. She started to make
etchings, woodcuts and lithographs that expressed her concern for the plight of those forced to
live and work in inadequate social conditions. Kollwitz had her own share of human suffering –
her son was killed in the First World War and her grandson in the Second – tragic events that
fuelled her own pacifism. In 1933 she was expelled from the Academy in Berlin by the Nazis. In
her later years she made some bronzes, including a war memorial at Essen in Flanders. Drawing
upon the great strength and humanity that she found in her mother and child relationship,
Tower of Mothers depicts an important recurring theme in her work. This small bronze
provides, through its amorphous and anonymous mass of mothers protecting their children, a
solid and authentic expression of empathy in a largely uncaring and alienated society.

OTHER MASTERPIECES Pieta; *1937–1938; Käthe Kollwitz, Berlin, Germany*
War Memorial; *1932; Dixmuiden, Flanders, Netherlands*

220

Kooning Willem de

Born Rotterdam, Netherlands 1904; died Long Island, USA, 1997

The Visit *1966—1967*
oil on canvas; 152.4 x
121.9 cm; Tate Collection,
London, England

Willem de Kooning
was apprenticed to a
firm of commercial
artists at the age of
twelve. In 1925, he
received his diploma
from the Rotterdam
Academy of Fine Arts
and emigrated to
America. He set
himself up in New
York, where the skills
he had acquired
enabled him to work as
a house painter and
commercial artist. He
met and established a
firm friendship with the Armenian artist, Arshile Gorky. They shared a studio and by 1936 de
Kooning was painting full time. Gorky's involvement with the Surrealist movement exerted a
notable influence on de Kooning's work. Black and white paintings of the late 1940s gave way
to a series of paintings of women. Although he was respected by fellow artists, it was not until
the early 1950s that de Kooning's paintings began to sell. The energetic, gestural qualities of
paintings such as **The Visit** established de Kooning as a notable figure among the Abstract
Expressionists. Veering on abstraction, they transform the figure while retaining classical
elements. De Kooning remained faithful to the interpretation of identifiable subject matter –
the figure or landscape. Even his late reductive paintings derive from his experience of man's
relationship with nature.

OTHER MASTERPIECES Rosy-Fingered Dawn at Louise Point, *1963; Stedelijk Museum,*
Amsterdam, Netherlands **Woman I**; *1950—1952; The Museum of Modern Art, New York City, USA*

Koons Jeff

Born York, USA 1955

Rabbit *1986; stainless steel sculpture; 104 x 48 x 30.5 cm; Saatchi Collection, London, England*

Jeff Koons's art could be said to epitomize late 1980s consumerist kitsch. A disciple of Duchamp's ideology concerning the ready-made, he came to fame with his frank presentations of consumer items, vacuum cleaners and basketballs. Also ornaments were reproduced, not by Koons himself, but by traditional craftsmen. These are often alarmingly outsized or rendered in materials that either blatantly mimic or deliberately subvert the original. **Rabbit**, for example, is fashioned on a toy balloon, which succumbs to touch and is essentially fragile. As an artwork it is hard, precious and iconic, shiny and expensive. Sculptures of cultural celebrities followed. From 1989–91 Koons worked with his then wife Ilona Staller "La Cicciolina" to produce the **Made in Heaven** project. Sculptures, paintings, posters and magazine photo-pieces depict the couple's sexual love. It is an uninhibited series that is shocking in its flagrant depiction of carnal activity. It at once mocks and becomes the pornography, labelled as eroticism, which is a traditional motif, intrinsic to art history. In spite of the often shocking content of Koons's work, it is a potent reminder that the human condition is frail, subject to materialistic desires, narcissism and sentimentality.

OTHER MASTERPIECES Michael Jackson and Bubbles; *1988; San Francisco Museum of Modern Art, California, USA* Lips; *2000; Deutsche Guggenheim Berlin, Germany*

Kossoff Leon

Born London, England 1926

Children's Swimming Pool After Afternoon *1971; oil on board; 1687 x 214 cm; Tate Collection, London, England*

Leon Kossoff was one of seven children born to Russian-Jewish immigrant parents. Based on his immediate environment, his lustrous paintings tacitly acknowledge his origins. Speaking about his work in 1974, he suggested that images of the city that fill his pictures similarly infuse his mind, "like a faintly glimmering memory of a long forgotten, perhaps never experienced childhood". He attended David Bomberg's evening classes at the Borough Polytechnic from 1950 to 1952 and studied at St Martin's School of Art, the Royal College of Art and Chelsea School of Art, finishing his formal art training by the mid-1950s. He had his first solo exhibition in 1957 and joined the London Group of artists in 1962. Stylistically similar to the work of Frank Auerbach, Kossoff's range of subject matter is also confined to his locality, friends and trusted models. Kossoff's thick, syrupy paint surface is the result of many layers of chalky coloured impasto. It is difficult to distinguish where drawing ends and painting begins. **Children's Swimming Pool After Afternoon** is typical of Kossoff's monumental appraisal of a complex subject, challenging in its perspective depth and changing light effects.

OTHER MASTERPIECES Booking Hall, Kilburn Underground, *1987; Tate Gallery, London, England* **Between Kilburn and Willesden Green, Winter Evening,** *1992; Scottish Gallery of Modern Art, Edinburgh, Scotland*

Kounellis Janis

Born Piraeus, Greece 1936

Untitled *1983; pen and ink on paper; 35.6 x 43 cm; Tate Collection, London, England*

Aged twenty, Janis Kounellis moved from Greece to Rome where he studied at the Accademia delle Belle Arti and became familiar with the work of modern Italian painters such as Alberto Burri and Lucio Fontana. In 1958, he embarked on a series of large paintings on paper that used graphic signs, numbers and letters. Two years later, these formed the basis for his first solo exhibition in Rome, where Kounellis literally accompanied his work by chanting notations derived from his paintings. In 1966, he started to make three-dimensional work in the form of installation and performances. In 1969, he tethered twelve horses to the Galleria L'Attico in an enquiry into the nature of certainty and chance. His temporary installations used commonplace but unusual sculptural materials such as cotton, coal and fire. In the late 1960s, he became the leading figure in Arte Povera, a post-minimalist art movement associated with the production of works from freely-available materials. In the late 1970s, Kounellis introduced classical motifs into his work. His recent large-scale, site-specific installations have made use of roughly-hewn wood, charcoal and bells, referencing a nostalgia for a historical and cultural past. He lives and works in Rome.

OTHER MASTERPIECES Untitled; *1987; Guggenheim Museum, New York City, USA*
Untitled; *1979; Tate Collection, London, England*

Kruger Barbara

Born Newark, New Jersey, USA 1945

We Don't Need Another Hero *1985; photographic silk screen/vinyl; 43 x 82.6 cm; Mary Boone Gallery, New York City, USA*

Barbara Kruger's feminist art is based upon the striking juxtaposition of text and photographic imagery, powerfully rendered in a propagandist poster format. In 1965, she began studying fine art at Parsons School of Design and the School of the Visual Arts, New York. She became disillusioned with her short-lived employment as a graphic designer for Condé Nast but the commercial spirit lived on in her own work. Her characteristic bombardment of the viewer with overt instructions and authoritative statements is exemplified by **We Don't Need Another Hero**. Such strident imagery has graced billboards, shopping bags – "I Shop Therefore I Am" – matchboxes, T-shirts and gallery installations. Similar to Jenny Holzer's digitized message of "universal truths", Kruger's line of communication has a dictatorial, pedantic spirit, visualized in the manifesto style of Russian Constructivism, in black and white, and often, red. The effect that the media have on our lives and their infiltration into our urban environment, with hidden codes and cryptic suggestions, is the substance of her work. It is "seeing how culture exists".

OTHER MASTERPIECES Untitled (**It's A Small World But Not If You Have To Clean It**), *1990; Museum of Contemporary Art, Los Angeles, USA* Untitled (**We Will No Longer Be Seen And Not Heard**), *1985; Tate Collection, London, England*

Landseer Sir Edwin

Born London, England 1802; died London, England 1873

Monarch of the Glen *1850; oil on canvas; 166 x 171.4 cm; Dewar House, London, England*

Sir Edwin Landseer was an infant prodigy who first exhibited at the Royal Academy at the age of 12. He enjoyed a successful career based upon paintings that lent their animal subjects a range of human expressions and virtues. His brother Thomas was an engraver whose many prints of Landseer's work helped to increase their popularity. Queen Victoria's favourite painter, he was knighted in 1850. **Monarch of the Glen** is Landseer's best known painting. It is a large work, which not only shows great skill in its rendition of a stag, but which embodied certain human virtues considered important in the Victorian age. The stag is the personification of nobility and heroism. The Scottish highland setting, already popularized by the novels of Sir Walter Scott, was given added status through Queen Victoria's residence there. Landseer's work lost some of its appeal in the twentieth century. Apart from accusations of sentimentality, the paintings have been attacked on the grounds that they frequently depict and often glorify the bloodsport of deer-hunting. Landseer also worked on several sculptures, including the lions at the foot of Nelson's Column in London's Trafalgar Square.

OTHER MASTERPIECES The Old Shepherd's Chief Mourner; *1837; Victoria and Albert Museum, London, England* Dignity and Impudence; *1839; Tate Collection, London, England*

Lanyon Peter

Born St Ives, Cornwall, England 1918; died St Ives, England 1964

Lost Mine *1959; oil on canvas; 183.2 x 152.7 cm; Tate Collection, London, England*

Peter Lanyon's home had, since the 1880s, been attracting the attention of artists who relished the light, land and seascape views of the Cornish town of St Ives. Lanyon, credited as a major painter of the St Ives school, attended the Penzance School of Art and, briefly, the Euston Road School in London. In 1939, the migration of artists to his locality brought him into contact with Ben Nicholson, Barbara Hepworth and Naum Gabo. This impacted on Lanyon's work and he rejected landscape studies in favour of making abstract, three-dimensional constructions. These and his free-standing sculptures subsequently influenced the direction of his painting. His response combined together the romantic lyricism of the Cornish landscape and abstraction. With a loose, expressive technique, he aimed to represent a spatial structure describing the complete experience of being in the landscape, rather than an observation from a single viewpoint. He exhibited his work in New York in 1959 and made friends with American Expressionists Kline and Rothko. **Lost Mine** dates from this time and has similar qualities to the work of his counterparts in the States. In the same year he took up gliding, literally giving a new angle on his landscape visions; it proved a fatal activity.

OTHER MASTERPIECES Porthleven; *1951; Tate Collection, London, England*
Bojewyan Farms; *1951–1952; British Council Collection, London, England*

227

La Tour Georges de

Born Vic-sur-Seille, France 1593; died Lunéville, France 1652

The Magdalene with Nightlight c. 1650; oil on canvas; 128 x 94 cm; Musée du Louvre, Paris, France

It is believed that Georges de la Tour lived and worked for most of his life in the Duchy of Lorraine. Little is known of his life, although he did enjoy the patronage of the Duke of Lorraine from 1623. Curiously, he was completely forgotten until his belated rediscovery in 1915. La Tour is now greatly admired for his religious and genre paintings, particularly the nocturnal scenes, which often make use of a candle or lamp as a single light source. **The Magdalene with Nightlight** is a prime example of a candlelit scene whose dramatic shadows recall the work of the great Italian master, Caravaggio. The sombre and monumental mood of the painting is enhanced through the use of smooth and simplified forms. The Magdalene is dressed in everyday, humble clothing and appears lost in thought. There is a quiet mysticism to the work, despite the presence of the ghoulish skull. Although there is uncertainty over the dating and attribution of some of his work, his classically inspired simplicity has prompted comparisons with Piero della Francesca and Poussin.

OTHER MASTERPIECES Penitent St Peter; *1645; Cleveland Museum of Art, Ohio, USA*
St Jerome; *1635; Musée de Grenoble, France*

Leonardo da Vinci

Born Vinci, Italy 1452; died Amboise, France 1519

Cartoon for Virgin and Child with St Anne
1499—1500; charcoal on tinted paper; 141.5 x 104.6 cm; National Gallery, London, England

Painter, sculptor, draughtsman, writer, architect, inventor, scientist, musician – Leonardo da Vinci was the most accomplished Renaissance artist. The illegitimate son of a Florentine notary, Leonardo's extraordinary artistic ability allegedly so impressed his master, Verrochio, that he gave up painting. Leonardo spent 17 years in Milan from 1482, working mainly for the Duke of Milan. He then returned to Florence, where he painted the renowned **Mona Lisa** between 1503–1506. His last years were spent in triumph at the French court of Francis I. One of the most important works in the National Gallery's collection, **Cartoon for Virgin and Child with St Anne** is kept in a darkened room to prevent it from fading. Cartoons were preparatory large-scale drawings to be transferred to a wall or canvas as a guide to the final painting. This cartoon was never actually transferred. Covering eight sheets of paper, it is drawn in charcoal with white chalk highlights. The extraordinary features of this work is the intense interplay of emotion within the tightly knit group of figures. Leonardo's particular skill was to endow his mainly religious subjects with a spirituality and enigmatic beauty unsurpassed in the history of fine art.

OTHER MASTERPIECES Mona Lisa; *1503–1506; Musée du Louvre, Paris, France*
Virgin of the Rocks; *before 1483; Musée du Louvre, Paris, France*

Lewis Percy Wyndham

Born Nova Scotia, Canada 1882; died London, England 1957

A Reading of Ovid (Tyros)
*1920–1921; oil on canvas; 165.2 x
90.2 cm; Scottish National Gallery of
Modern Art, Edinburgh, Scotland*

Wyndham Lewis was the formidable
energy behind the British Vorticist
movement. After the breakdown of
his parents' marriage, in 1893, he
lived in London with his mother.
He studied for three years, from
1898, at the Slade School of Art
and then spent six years travelling
around Europe. In 1911 he joined
the Camden Town Group, and, in
1913, the Omega Workshops. In
1914, the avant-garde magazine,
Blast, of which Lewis was editor,
published his Vorticist manifesto.
This was the literary counterpart of
the modern, emphatically
mechanistic paintings he was
producing at the time. The war, in
which Lewis served as both active
participant and later, official war
artist, quelled the power of the
Vorticist movement. Lewis's success
as a writer also gained momentum,
earning praise from the poet, T.S.
Eliot. **A Reading of Ovid (Tyros)** is
one of a series of mythological paintings containing robotic figures, leading up to his move in
1939 to the United States and Canada. It represents a partial and diluted version of Lewis's
earlier explorations of an advanced, modernist visual language, reflecting the machine
technologies of the age. Lewis became blind in 1951 and devoted his creative energies to art
criticism and teaching.

OTHER MASTERPIECES The Dancers; *1912; Manchester City Art Galleries, Manchester, England*
A Battery Shelled; *1918; Imperial War Museum, London, England*

Le Witt Sol

Born Hartford, Connecticut, USA 1928

Two Open Modular Cubes *1972; enamel on metal; 160 x 305.4 cm; Tate Collection, London, England*

Sol Le Witt's position as a sculptor was central to the Minimal and Conceptual Art movements in New York during the 1960s. After completing his studies at Syracuse University, graduating in 1949, he eschewed the artistic trend toward Abstract Expressionism to concentrate on developing an intellectual approach to sculptural construction. Paradoxical elements in the two-dimensional work of Jasper Johns proved influential. John's art, concerning issues of perception, repetition and language, fed into Le Witt's. His earliest works focused on the relationship between the idea and its physical realization through process. Cerebral, non-referential sculpture remains at the root of his production. Early hybrid wall structures began to extend further into space to develop into the free standing format, of which **Two Open Modular Cubes** is a prime example. His use of the cube as a primary unit, and of the grid, was inspired by the emerging New Mathematics, which introduced diagrammatic methods, the matrix and sets, among others, into mathematical study. By the 1970s, Lewitt's inert, monumental structures had become part of a range of media that included drawings, prints, wall drawings and artist's books. "Seriousness and it's claim to modernity", was his work's strength.

OTHER MASTERPIECES 3x3x3; *1969–1983; Crex Collection, Schaffhausen, Switzerland*
Complex Form 6; *1988; National Museum of Japan, Tokyo, Japan*

Lichtenstein Roy

Born New York City, USA 1923; died USA 1997

Whaam! *1963; acrylic on canvas; 172.7 x 406.4 cm; Tate Collection, London, England*

Roy Lichtenstein created the imagery that has the widest appeal of the work produced by the American Pop artists during the 1960s. His name has become synonymous with the "comic strip" canvases with which he launched his career in 1962. His tuition began at the Art Students League in 1939. Studies at the Ohio State University were interrupted by a period spent serving with the US Army from 1943–1946. He began exhibiting in 1949, with paintings inspired by American history and Cubism. Later, he moved into Abstract Expressionist mode. It was not until he came into contact with experimental artist Allan Kaprow, while teaching at Rutgers University in the early 1960s, that he developed an interest in consumer culture and "Happenings". The cheap printing methods of comic production and the stylized drawing of the melodramatic narratives that proliferated these publications became Lichtenstein's main source of inspiration. **Whaam!** epitomizes the genre in which the crises of war, the pain of love and the horror of explosions become removed from reality. The meticulous reproduction of the printed dots highlights the artificiality of the episode described and the limitations of both the comic medium and the two-dimensionality of paint on canvas.

OTHER MASTERPIECES M-Maybe (**A Girl's Picture**); *1965; Museum Ludwig, Cologne, Germany* **Big Painting No.6**; *1965; Kunstsammlung Nordrhein-Westfalen, Dusseldorf, Germany*

Liebermann Max

Born Berlin, Germany 1847; died Berlin, Germany 1935

Terrace at the Restaurant Jacob in Niestedten on the Elbe *1902; oil on canvas; 70 x 100 cm; Kunsthalle, Hamburg, Germany*

Painter and graphic artist Max Liebermann studied in Amsterdam and Paris. One of the first German artists from his generation to respond to foreign painters, he was influenced by Courbet, Millet and the landscape painters of the Barbizon school. On his return to Germany in 1878 he became the leading German Impressionist. Liebermann painted scenes of peasants and elderly people. The influence of Impressionism on his predominantly realistic landscape style can be seen in **Terrace at the Restaurant Jacob in Niestedten on the Elbe**. In this painting, the sunlight filtering through the dark canopy lighting the sketchy background figures is reminiscent of Renoir. The colours, however, are more tonal and the overall effect is less spontaneous than works by his French Impressionist counterparts. Liebermann founded the Berlin Secession in 1899 and became its President. Although he was an important intermediary between the new painting in France and the older narrative tradition in Germany, his work was quickly made to look outmoded. He was a supporter of the conservative tradition against which Nolde and the members of Die Brücke revolted.

OTHER MASTERPIECES The Parrot Keeper; *1902; Museum Folkwang, Essen, Germany*
Schweinmarkt in Haarlem; *1891; Staditsche Kunsthalle, Mannheim, Germany*

Limbourg Paul, Jean and Herman de

Born Limbricht, Netherlands c.1385, died Netherlands c.1416

January (from the Très Riches Heures du Duc de Berri) *1413—1416; manuscript; 29 x 21 cm; Musée Condé, Chantilly, France*

Paul, Jean and Herman de Limbourg were introduced to the rich world of the Burgundian dukes by the their uncle, Malouel, who was court painter in the late 1300s. In Paris they were apprenticed as goldsmiths but by 1411 were working as book illuminators for the bibliophile, the Duke of Berry. It was in the duke's employ that they produced what is now considered to be the greatest achievement of the International Gothic Style, the **Très Riches Heures**. This page from the illuminated devotional *Book of Hours* describes the duke's secular, festive activity in the month of January. It reveals how the aims of painting were moving away from traditional depiction of religious subjects. No longer was the interest solely in telling a sacred story, but rather in attempting to represent man in his environment. Here the Limbourgs capture the gaiety of a medieval banquet scene. The duke sits in profile against a white firescreen whilst the High Steward orders on the next course. The Limbourgs and their patron died of the plague in about 1416; the book was never finished.

OTHER MASTERPIECES Belles Heures; *c.1408—1409; Metropolitan Museum of Art, New York City, USA* **February; Tres Riches Heures**; *c.1413; Musée Condé, Chantilly, France*

Lippi Filippino

Born Florence, Italy c.1457; died Florence, Italy 1504

**Virgin and Child
with Saint Jerome
and Saint Dominic**
*c.1485; oil and tempera
on poplar; 203.2 x
186.1 cm; National
Gallery, London, England*

Filippino was the son
of Fra Filippo Lippi,
who trained him.
At the age of
twelve he set off for
Florence, and within
a couple of years
was working
alongside Botticelli, whom his father may have taught. His major commissions include the
completion of Brancacci Chapel frescoes, the **Vision of Saint Bernard**, and the fresco cycles at
the Strozzi and Caraffa Chapels. He enjoyed great fame during his lifetime but ultimately his
style of painting, marked by a linear clarity, fell out of fashion, to be replaced by the dramatic
eccentricities of the Mannerist painters. The **Virgin and Child with Saint Jerome and Saint
Dominic** altarpiece comes from a Florence chapel dedicated to St Jerome. It was unusual for the
Virgin and Child to be located in such an expansive landscape as this, but the artist's father, Fra
Filippo Lippi, had a penchant for similarly bleak settings which may have informed his choice.
Most notable is Filippino's masterful rendition of facial expressions and his skill in finely painted
textures, both of which are traditionally associated with northern schools.

OTHER MASTERPIECES Vision of Saint Bernard; *c.1484; Badia, Florence, Italy*
Adoration of the Magi; *c.1496; Galleria degli Uffizi, Florence, Italy*

Lippi Fra Filippo

Born Florence, Italy c.1406; died Spoleto, Italy 1469

The Celebration of the Relics of Saint Stephen
1452–1466; fresco, Prato Cathedral, Prato, Italy

Fra Filippo Lippi was an orphan who was put into a monastery in his teens, but was temperamentally unsuited for monastic life – he was tried for fraud, and also abducted a nun who bore him a son, Filippino. In the 1420s he worked with Masaccio painting the Brancacci Chapel. In Lippi's early works, such as **The Relaxation of the Carmelite Rule**, the heaviness of the figures, derived from Masaccio, is clearly evident, but this was soon to be overlaid by a more descriptive and decorative tendency. Both Fra Angelico and Lippi knew of Netherlands painting and made oblique references to specific northern features in their own work. **The Celebration of the Relics of Saint Stephen** shows attendance at a celebration of St Stephen, Christianity's first martyr. This saint was stoned to death for blasphemy after claiming to see the figure of Jesus in the sky. The beatific choristers are portrayed in an unidealized way. His playful studies of the Virgin and Child were particularly highly thought of, and set the style for the next half century.

OTHER MASTERPIECES Tarquinia Madonna; *1437; National Museum, Rome, Italy*
The Annunciation; *c.1430; San Lorenzo, Florence, Italy*

Lissitzky El

Born Smolensk, Russia 1890; died Moscow, USSR 1941

Victory Over the Sun
1923; colour litho on paper;
51.1 x 42.9 cm; Tate
Collection, London, England

In 1909 the Italian
Futurists published their
manifesto in the Parisian
newspaper, *Le Figaro*.
Their ideas filtered to
Russia and the artist
Malevich and his
followers, one of whom was Lissitzky, responded with ideas of their own. Lissitzky studied
engineering and architecture from 1909–1914. After being a painter, illustrator and designer of
Soviet flags, he taught with Malevich at Vitebsk and at art workshops in Moscow. He arrived in
Berlin in 1921 and set up exhibitions of art by the post-revolutionary avant-garde, working also
as a writer and designer for international magazines. His achievements acted like a campaign to
forge links between artists in Russia and in the West, between Weimar's De Stijl and
Constructivism. His own **Proun** paintings, Proun being an anacronym signifying "for the new
art", express his vision of a world of physics inspired by modern spiritualist thought. They were
produced at the same time as **Victory Over the Sun**, which suggests similar concerns. His
work was intended to be a catalyst to encourage "the broad aim of forming a classless society".
His publications include *Die Kunstismen*, with Hans Arp, an issue of *Merz* magazine, with
Schwitters, other books and independent contributions.

OTHER MASTERPIECES Beat the Whites with the Red Wedge; *1919–1920; Lenin Library,
Moscow, Russia* Proun R.V.N. 2; *1923; Kunstmuseum mit Sammlung Sprengel, Hanover, Germany*

241

Long Richard

Born Bristol, England 1945

Norfolk Flint Circle
1990; flint, 8 metres in diameter; installation view; Tate Collection, London, England

Richard Long is known globally for his environmental art, which is relayed into a gallery context via photographs, texts, statements, stone installations and wall paintings. He was educated at the West of England College of Art, Corsham (1962–1965) and St Martin's School of Art, London, (1966–1968). Like American Land Artist Robert Smithson, Long has stretched the boundaries of conventional art practice to integrate natural elements into his work. His use of the Earth goes far beyond the wildest, romantic imagination of traditional landscape artists, referencing both conceptualist and Minimalist ideas. Distance, time and place also play a major part in his work. He has made several "walking sculptures" by travelling between specified places, here and abroad, on foot. The visible "results" of these landscape forays have been charted for exhibition. More tangible evidence of his interventions are the materials he collects from various locations for formal exhibition. **Norfolk Flint Circle** is such a piece. The contrived arrangement is suggestive of the order man seeks to impose on nature. However, the circular shape, which Long also uses in wall-paintings made with his hands and mud, for example, is a universal organic symbol of regeneration, harmony and fecundity.

OTHER MASTERPIECES Spring Circle, *1992; British Council Collection, London, England*
A Hundred Mile Walk; *1971–1972; Tate Collection, London, England*

242

Lorenzetti Ambrogio

Born Siena, Italy c.1313; died Siena, Italy 1348

Good Government (detail) *1338–1340; fresco; detail; 300 x 700 cm; Palazzo Pubblico, Siena, Italy*

Ambrogio Lorenzetti's and his brother Pietro's lives are not well-documented although they are both known to have perished in the Black Death plague of 1348. Both were believed to have been pupils of the great Sienese decorative master Duccio, although the solidity of their figures and the narrative qualities of their work show a greater debt to Giotto. Through their connections to Giotto and Duccio, the brothers also provide a link between the hitherto separate Schools of Siena and Florence. Ambrogio was the more accomplished artist of the two. His innovative fresco series **Good and Bad Government** was painted for the Town Hall in Siena between 1338–1340. The panel reproduced here is a detail of this large allegorical work and records the streets of Siena with a mastery of perspective unusual for its time. The clusters of small figures engaged in conversation were also a significant advance in naturalism for the early fourteenth century. The depth, balance and detail of the overall composition indicate the extraordinary range of Ambrogio Lorenzetti's fertile imagination.

OTHER MASTERPIECES The Presentation of the Temple; *1342; Galleria degli Uffizi, Florence, Italy* **The Annunciation**; *1344; Pinacoteca, Siena, Italy*

Lowry Lawrence Stephen

Born Manchester, England 1887; died Glossop, England 1976

Going to the Match *1946; oil on panel; 25.3 x 47 cm; Private Collection*

In 1909, Lowry and his parents moved to Pendlebury, Salford, which was then a busy and unkempt region of the great Lancashire cotton-manufacturing complex. For some years after 1910, Lowry was employed as a rent collector in Manchester. He claimed that contact with working-class life was to inform his art. At the Manchester Municipal College of Art, Lowry drew from life in a traditional manner, producing refined, naturalistic works that offer no inkling of the dramatic change that was to come. In 1915, intense dislike of the Salford area developed into an obsession with the scenery, mills and collieries that made the urban environment and the people who lived and worked within it; a painting style was consolidated that remained virtually unchanged for nearly fifty years. **Going to the Match** is typical of the thickly painted, lugubrious imagery that established Lowry's reputation. The painting epitomizes the mood of the Depression in the 1920s and 1930s in the stark depiction of trudging masses of match-stick figures. Lowry provides a satirical, evocative view of the proletariat on a day out of their factories, which is as acute for its time as Hogarth's or Bruegel's own visions were for theirs.

OTHER MASTERPIECES Coming from the Mill; *1930; Salford Art Gallery, England*
Outpatients, Ancoats Hospital; *1952; Whitworth Art Gallery, Manchester, England*

Magritte René

Born Lessines, Belgium 1898; died Brussels, Belgium 1967

The Reckless Sleeper
1928; oil on canvas; 115.6 x 81.3 cm; Tate Collection, London, England

René Magritte initially worked in wallpaper design and fashion advertising. His early paintings were inspired by Futurism and Cubism but, under the influence of de Chirico, he turned to Surrealism in 1925. Between 1927 and 1930 Magritte worked in Paris with the other Surrealists. He then settled in Brussels for the rest of his life. He painted convincing illusionistic images in a flat, deadpan style of disturbing clarity. His paintings presented a range of bizarre juxtapositions of ordinary objects in strange and incongruous surrounds. **The Reckless Sleeper**

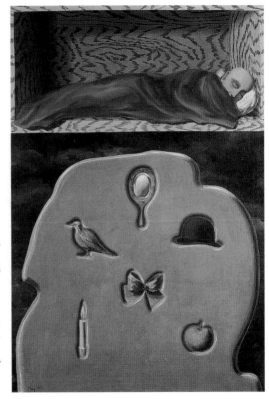

exploits the ambiguity of dreams, typically making use of unexpected distortions of size and scale as well as humour. Magritte frequently featured paintings within paintings in his work, as well as names and labels to question the relationship between painted and real objects. In his absurd and unnerving world, there are many recurring images, such as men with bowler hats and fish with human legs. Magritte was not widely known until after the Second World War. His work became familiar through its use in advertising and graphic design; he is now one of the most popular painters of the twentieth century.

OTHER MASTERPIECES Time Transfixed; *1939; The Art Institute of Chicago, USA*
Promenades of Euclid; *1955; Mineapolis Institute of Arts, Minnesota, USA*

Malevich Kasimir

Born Kiev, Ukraine 1878; died Leningrad, USSR 1935

**Dynamic
Suprematism**
*1915; oil on canvas;
60 x 73 cm; Tate
Collection, London,
England*

Kasimir Malevich went to Moscow in 1905, where his work developed under the influence of French Post-Impressionism. He was invited to take part in Larionov's first Knave of Diamonds exhibition. Malevich visited Paris in about 1912 and returned full of enthusiasm for Cubism. Declaring that he wished to "free art from the burden of the object", he invented a new movement called Suprematism, which was a pure form of Cubism. In 1915, he exhibited thirty-six abstract works including the infamous **Black Square** – literally just that. In later Suprematist works, Malevich moved away from his stark minimalism to introduce colour, depth and, occasionally, softer forms. **Dynamic Suprematism** is an example of a cool, coloured, geometric work in which the abstract forms combine and overlap without any emotional distraction. In 1918, a painting of a white square on a white ground became the logical extension of his non-objective art. Realizing that there was nowhere further for him to go, he stopped painting and turned to writing and teaching. In the 1920s he developed three-dimensional sculptures, important to the growth of Constructivism.

OTHER MASTERPIECES Woman with Buckets; *1912; Museum of Modern Art, New York City, USA* **Suprematism: Yellow and Black**; *1916–1917; Russian Museum, Leningrad, Russia*

Mantegna Andrea

Born Isola di Cartura, Italy 1431; died Mantua, Italy 1506

The Dead ̣_urist c.1465; distemper on canvas; 68 x 81 cm; Pinacoteca di Brera, Milan

A·ıdrea Mantegna was the pupil and adopted son of archaeologist and painter, Squarcione, who ınspired his early interest in ancient artefacts and sculpture. He married into the eminent Bellini family in about 1453. In 1459, he became the court painter to Ludovico Gonzaga in Mantua, and stayed in the service of the family until his death. For the interiors of the ducal palace, he created the decorative series **The Triumph of Caesar**, which is strewn with classical ruins. **The Dead Christ** features a dramatic close-up of a cadaver. The mourners are extraneous figures in this painting; through dramatic foreshortening the viewer is placed in an unusual position at the feet of the corpse. The choice of viewpoint, the carefully planned elements such as the draped shroud, the stony colour of the skin and above all the posture of the body all emphasize the feeling of complete stillness. Mantegna worked within the tradition of Masaccio, but modelled his figures by layering washes of thin tempera. This was a Venetian technique, suiting the damp northern climate better than fresco painting.

OTHER MASTERPIECES Madonna della Vittoria; c.1495; Musée du Louvre, Paris, France
Agony in the Garden; c.1460; National Gallery, London, England

Mapplethorpe Robert

Born New York City, USA 1946; died Boston, USA 1989

Calla Lily *1988;*
photograph; Estate of
Robert Mapplethorpe

Robert Mapplethorpe is recognized as a photographer of outstanding technical ability – and
notoriety. His homoerotic imagery and representations of sexuality through portraiture have
established him as one of the most controversial artists to come to prominence during the
1970s and 1980s. From 1963 to 1970 he studied at the Pratt Institute, New York. In his earliest
work he was "playing with charged imagery"; he was also assembling sculptural pieces from
banal or found objects and collage. Experiments with Polaroid photographs followed, the
seriality of images being as important as each composition itself. Through such explorations of
the medium he developed a mastery of technique that enabled him to concentrate on his
primary interest, which was to make pornographic imagery artistically beautiful. The similarity
of approach by other gay artists, such as David Hockney and the illustrator Tom of Finland,
encouraged Mapplethorpe to realize his idealized, romanticized preoccupation with erotic
fantasy images. He specialized in stereotypical visions of male sexuality in addition to "straight"
portraits of known individuals – Lord Snowdon and Louise Bourgeois, for example. His pictures
of flowers, such as **Calla Lily** are astonishing portrayals of natural beauty, often depicted as
sexually charged as his human subjects.

OTHER MASTERPIECES Easter Lilies; *1979; Estate of Robert Mapplethorpe*
Derrick Cross; *1983; Estate of Robert Mapplethorpe*

Marc Franz

Born Munich, Germany 1880; died Verdun, France 1916

Foxes *1913; oil on canvas; 88 x 266 cm; Kunstmuseum, Düsseldorf, Germany*

Franz Marc began to develop his academic, naturalistic style after visiting Paris in 1903 and 1908. In 1910 he became friends with Macke, who introduced an Expressionist sense of strong colour into his work. Marc was a founding member of Der Blaue Reite group in Munich in 1911. A deeply religious man, his painting was a vehicle for his spiritual values. He chose to depict animals believing that, unlike human beings, they experienced nature as a whole and were in harmony with it. In a notebook of 1911 he questioned if there could be a "more mysterious idea for the artist than how nature is reflected in the eye of an animal?" **Foxes** was painted in 1913, by which time Marc's ideas about the unity and rhythm of the natural world had strengthened. In the painting there is little distinction between the foxes' bodies and the surrounding space. The geometric grid of the fragmented picture surface also reflected Marc's awareness of the recent developments in Cubism in Paris. His late work is almost entirely devoid of representational content. Franz Marc was killed in action in the First World War.

OTHER MASTERPIECES Blue Horses; *1911; Minneapolis Institute of Arts, USA*
Forest with Squirrel; *1913; Kunsthaus, Zurich, Switzerland*

Martin John

Born Haydon Bridge, England 1789; died Douglas, England 1854

Sadak in Search of the Waters of **Oblivion** *1812; oil on canvas; 76.2 x 63.5 cm; Southampton City Art Gallery, England*

John Martin's excessively dramatic and apocalyptic visions of landscape as the backdrop for cosmic or biblical happenings seem to have been designed with Hollywood epics in mind. These spectacular, melodramatic scenes made an impact on the Romantic imagination, appealing more to literary circles than being directly influential in the visual arts. From 1811 Martin exhibited at the Royal Academy and came to attention with **Joshua Commanding the Sun to Stand Still** (1816). He illustrated Milton's *Paradise Lost* in 1827 and was described as "the poet's painter". Engravings of his grandiose compositions were widely circulated across Europe, his reputation being particularly high in France where he received a gold medal from Charles X in 1829. **Sadak in Search of the Waters of Oblivion** is a typical canvas, illustrating an awesome vision of towering rocks and cathartic light effects. Martin's virtuoso handling and capacity for illustrating fantastical scenes, rendering them convincing, is extraordinary. The almost imperceptible presence of diminutive man is highly evocative and must have fired the imagination of God-fearing spectators.

OTHER MASTERPIECES Destruction of Sodom and Gomorrah; *c.1850; Laing Art Gallery, Newcastle-Upon-Tyne, England* **The Great Days of his Wrath**; *c.1853; Tate Collection, London, England*

Martini Simone

Born Siena, Italy, c.1284; died Avignon, France 1344

Christ Discovered in the Temple (detail) *1342; tempera on panel; 49 x 35.1 cm; Walker Art Gallery, Liverpool, England*

After his teacher, Duccio, Martini was the most significant Sienese master of the fourteenth century. Unlike Duccio, who gave a solid, sculptural quality to his figures, Martini developed the International Gothic Style, with its emphasis on graceful, flowing lines and two-dimensionality. He won numerous commissions, including the prestigious frescoes for the Palazzo Pubblico at Siena and a painting of St Louis of Toulouse for his patron, the King of Anjou.

With his brother-in-law, Lippo Memmi, he painted arguably his finest piece, **The Annunciation** of 1333. By 1340, he was established in the Franco-Italian enclave in Avignon – then the Papal seat – where he painted the unusual **Christ Discovered in the Temple** (detail). Mary and Joseph had spent several days frantically looking for Jesus, finally discovering him in the Temple where he had been discussing religion with the Elders. Here, Simone Martini attributes human emotion to sacred characters. Mary reasons with Jesus who, with arms folded, listens demurely but with a hint of defiance. Martini arranges the figures within this awkwardly shaped panel with the utmost ease and simplicity, creating a religious painting that is at once beautiful and moving.

OTHER MASTERPIECES The Annunciation; *c.1333; Galleria degli Uffizi, Florence, Italy*
Portrait of Guidriccio da Fogliano; *1328; Palazzo Pubblico, Siena, Italy*

Masaccio Tommaso

Born San Giovanni, Val d'Arno, Italy 1401; died Rome, Italy 1428

**Adam and Eve Banished
from Paradise** *1424—1428;
fresco; 214 x 90 cm; Brancacci
Chapel, Santa Maria del Carmine,
Florence, Italy*

In importance, Masaccio is
ranked alongside Donatello
and Brunelleschi. It is
uncertain who his teacher
was. The artist Masolino came
from the same Florentine
parish and, being twenty years
older, was in a position to
teach him. However, there is
little stylistic evidence of his
influence. This is a fragment
from the Brancacci Chapel,
which Masaccio painted with
Masolino. Because the artist
shared the same Christian
name (Thomas), nicknames
were coined and Tomasso di
Giovanni became Big Tom or
"Masaccio". **Adam and Eve
Banished from Paradise**
shows Masaccio's main
innovation. Primarily, his
figures are solid, sculptural and imbued with an extraordinary intensity – the hopeless gesture of
Adam being especially dramatic. Masaccio understood that the fall of light originating from one
source could help define volume: here it casts a shadow behind Adam and Eve. He had also
learnt the unifying device of a single-point perspective, perhaps from Brunelleschi. Furthermore,
he had no interest in charming the viewer – his work is consistently austere and direct. Had he
lived longer, his work may have mellowed, but within two months of his second trip to Rome
he was dead, aged twenty-seven. Some believe he was poisoned.

OTHER MASTERPIECES The Virgin and Child; *c.1426; National Gallery, London, England*
The Trinity with the Virgin and St John; *1425; Santa Maria Novella, Florence, Italy*

Matisse Henri

Born Le Cateau, France 1869; died Cimiez, France 1954

La Danse *1910; oil on canvas; 260 x 391 cm; Hermitage, St Petersburg, Russia*

Henri Matisse originally trained as a lawyer, turning to art while recovering from appendicitis. Initially seduced by the Impressionists and, in particular, by Cézanne, Matisse brought together a circle of like-minded artists who became known as the Fauves (the Beasts) after their sensational exhibition of 1905. These early paintings revealed an intuitive and explosive colour sense which was to become the defining feature of Matisse's long career. Believing art to be "something like a good armchair in which one rests from physical fatigue", he was dedicated to producing work that expressed a harmony close to a musical composition. There are two versions of **La Danse**, originally produced with another enormous panel entitled **Musique** for a Russian collector. Dance was a popular topic at the time as Diaghilev and the Russian Ballet had just visited Paris. Despite, or because of, the simplification of colour, form, and line, the figures appear to be full of life. Matisse made sculptures, designed sets and costumes and illustrated books. He was also an important graphic artist who, in his bed-ridden final years, evolved his own method of arranging cut-out paper shapes. He is indisputably the greatest decorative artist of the twentieth century.

OTHER MASTERPIECES The Red Studio; *1911; Museum of Modern Art, New York City, USA*
Polynesie, La Mer; *1946; Musée Matisse, Nice, France*

Matta Roberto

Born Santiago, Chile c.1912; died Civitavecchia, Italy 2002

Abstraction *c.1940; oil on canvas; 96.5 x 132 cm; Private Collection*

Roberto Sebastian Echaurren Matta trained as an architect in Santiago and under Le Corbusier in Paris. He turned to painting in 1937 and quickly became involved with the Surrealist movement in which he remained a prominent figure until he broke contact in 1947. Matta emigrated to America in 1939. The impact of his solo show at the Julien Levy Gallery in 1940 on American experimental artists was enormous. The automatism of Matta's organic Surrealism provided a radical alternative to, and its inventiveness surpassed, the achievements of the academic European Surrealism of Dali, Magritte and Tanguy. During the 1940s, along with André Breton, Matta became one of the most influential émigré artists in New York, with creative implications for the development of Abstract Expressionism. His morphological paintings, such as **Abstraction**, combine ambiguous elements from the unconscious with landscapes from a volatile, futuristic dream-world. The cataclysmic, explosive meetings between brilliant highlights and thunderous shadows suggest cosmic violence, indefinable but evocatively wrought by abstract means. Matta's work became more dynamic, developing into "transparent cubism". From the mid-1940s he reintroduced the figure into increasingly mechanistic imagery.

OTHER MASTERPIECES Invasion of the Night, *1941; Jacqueline-Marie Onslow Ford Bequest, San Francisco, USA* Disasters of Mysticism, *1942; Estate of James Thrall Soby, New Canaan, Connecticut, USA*

Memling Hans

Born Seligenstadt, Germany c.1433; died Bruges, 1494

The Mystic Marriage of St Catherine
1474–1479; tempera on oak panels; 193.5 x 194.7; Memling Museum, Bruges, Belgium

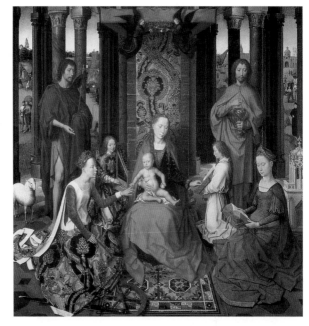

Hans Memling was a pupil of Rogier van der Weyden. He entered the painter's guild in Bruges, the great centre of the medieval corporations, in 1467. Some measure of his success can be gleaned from the fact that by 1480 he was one of the largest taxpayers in the city. He produced calm and devotional pictures full of gentle piety, characterized by their rich texture and strong hues. His paintings combined elements of work by both van der Weyden and Hugo van der Goes, and they were well liked by the rich middle class of the time. A strong Italian influence is evinced in **The Mystic Marriage of St Catherine** through the use of landscape as a backdrop to the central scene. This serves to unify the different parts of the painting, and emphasizes the contrasting formal presence of the classical columns. St Catherine of Alexandria is thought to have lived in the fourth century. The infant Christ turns toward her and places a ring on her finger, while St John the Baptist on the left, and St John the Evangelist on the right, look on.

OTHER MASTERPIECES Diptych of Martin Van Nieuwenhove; *1487; Hospital Museum, Bruges, Belgium* **The Donne Triptych**; *c.1477; National Gallery, London, England*

Mengs Anton Raphael

Born Aussig, Germany 1728; died Rome, Italy 1779

Maria Amalia of Saxony, Queen of Spain *undated; oil on canvas; 154 x 110 cm; Museo del Prado, Madrid, Spain*

Mengs established a prodigious reputation when he was taken to Rome in 1741 and made Court Painter at Dresden in 1745. However, it was not until he had met and absorbed the theories of his friend Johann Winckelmann that he achieved acclaim as the leading exponent of Neoclassicism. This attribution is now in doubt. However, the importance of his influence remains undisputed. Mengs' treatise on *Beauty in Painting* was published in 1762, only for it to be plagiarized and published in 1760 by an Englishman, Daniel Webb. He is best known for his ceiling painting **Parnassus** (1761) at the Villa Albini Rome. Breaking away from the illusionism of the Baroque, the surface is treated as in relief, with drawings after the Antique, and as if seen from the spectator's eye-level. Other frescoes include those for the Royal Palaces in Madrid, which Mengs made as Court Painter to Charles III; in this medium he was soon to be surpassed by Tiepolo. His portraits are perhaps more memorable. **Maria Amalia of Saxony** is a typical example of his eloquent, straightforward approach to the depiction of individual characters.

OTHER MASTERPIECES Maria Luisa of Parma; *Museo del Prado, Madrid, Spain*
Parnassus; *1761; Villa Albani, Rome, Italy*

Merz Mario

Born Milan, Italy 1925; died Milan, Italy 2003

Do We Turn Around Inside Houses *1977–1985; mixed media; 259 x 500 cm; Tate Collection, London, England*

Mario Merz made a radical artistic response to the social and political unease in Europe and America toward the end of the 1960s until the mid-1970s. In common with other Italian artists, such as Kounellis, Pascali, Paolini and Fabro, Merz re-examined and reinterpreted methods of sculptural construction. His use of banal, cheap or found objects and materials distinguished him as a leading exponent of Arte Povera (Poor Art). Referencing the principles of Duchamp and Beuys, his work was a gesture toward changing the status of art from marketable commodity to a means of expression that focused on society and its survival. The rejection of classical traditions freed Merz to symbolize fundamental and universal concerns via a diversity of form and content. **Do We Turn Around Inside Houses** employs a variety of unusual elements to engender a reconsideration of how we construct our lives. The beauty of the installation belies the humble nature of the materials; the construction offers associations of shelter that are symbolic rather than practical. The path to security, despite being transparent, is blocked and fraught with difficulties and inherent danger.

OTHER MASTERPIECES Fibonacci Tables; *1974–1976; Tate Collection, London, England*
Igloo Di Petra; *1982; Rijksmuseum Kröller-Müller, Otterlo, Netherlands*

Michelangelo Buonarroti

Born Caprese, Italy 1475; died Rome, Italy 1564

**Sistine Chapel :
The Last
Judgement**
*1536—1541, fresco,
14.8 x 13.30 m;
Sistine Chapel, The
Vatican, Rome, Italy*

Michelangelo was a
draughtsman,
sculptor, painter,
poet and architect
whose many talents
helped to establish
the Renaissance in
Florence. He learnt
the skill of fresco
painting from Ghirlandaio to whom he was apprenticed in 1488. His genius emerged in early
works such as the **Pietà** of St Peter's in Rome and a large marble David for the city of
Florence. Pope Julius II commissioned Michelangelo to decorate the ceiling of the Sistine
Chapel in the Vatican in 1508. It took four years to complete. For much of this time,
Michelangelo was forced to lie flat on his back, his face too close to the ceiling to facilitate a
proper overview. The fresco of **The Last Judgement** was commissioned for the altar wall of
the Sistine Chapel in 1534. This detail reveals Michelangelo's extraordinary ability to realize
the human form. The perfect muscular bodies have a sculptural weight, which is enhanced by
the depth of the surrounding space. The mood and tone of this piece is altogether darker than
the ceiling frescoes – it is a nightmarish vision of pandemonium, where the good are rewarded
and the bad are damned.

OTHER MASTERPIECES David, *1501—1504; Accademia, Florence, Italy*
The Creation of Adam, *1508—1512; Sistine Chapel Ceiling; The Vatican, Rome, Italy*

Millais Sir John Everett

Born Southampton, England 1829; died London, England 1896

The Blind Girl *1856; oil on canvas; 82 x 60.8 cm; Birmingham City Museums and Art Gallery, Birmingham, England*

John Everett Millais's prodigious talent meant that at the age of 11 he was the Royal Academy's youngest ever student. Together with Holman Hunt and Rossetti, he founded the Pre-Raphaelite Brotherhood in 1848. Until the 1850s, Millais's work, with its intensity of feeling, brilliant colour and minutely observed detail, closely followed Pre-Raphaelite principles. He painted **The Blind Girl** near Winchelsea in the summer of 1854, using models to complete the figures. This poignant painting manages to avoid sentimentality in its depiction of a blind girl unable to appreciate the intense beauty of the sky before a storm. The emotional force of the painting is reinforced by the closeness of the relationship between the girl and her younger companion, as well as by the unity of the figures with their natural surroundings. In the late 1850s Millais's style changed. Declaring that he had a family to support, he moved away from the Pre-Raphaelite principle of expressing serious moral concepts to satisfy a public demand for popular storytelling. Technically brilliant, he developed into a fashionable and prosperous Victorian painter.

OTHER MASTERPIECES Autumn Leaves; *1856; Manchester City Art Gallery, England*
Ophelia; *1852; Tate Collection, London, England*

Millet Jean François

Born Gruchy, France 1814; died Barbizon, France 1875

The Angelus *1857–1859; oil on canvas; 55.5 x 66 cm; Musée d'Orsay, Paris, France*

Jean François Millet was born into a family of peasant farmers near Cherbourg. He trained locally as a painter and then went to Paris in 1837 to study under Delaroche. His early work comprised conventional portraits and fashionable eighteenth-century pastoral scenes. However, in 1848 he chose to exhibit **The Winnower**, a painting depicting peasant life, at the Paris Salon. It was the first of many rural scenes based on memories of his own childhood. Criticized for allowing socialist concerns to infiltrate his art, Millet stated that it was "the human side" of life that he wished to portray. In 1849 he moved to Barbizon where he remained for the rest of his life, painting labourers going about their daily business. In **The Angelus**, his best-known work, Millet chose to celebrate a dignified, hard-working couple at work in the fields – their heads bowed in an expression of devotion in the face of nature. Depicting his human figures with a classically sculptural simplicity, Millet's concern was to show the pair in harmony with their peaceful and unchanging rural existence.

OTHER MASTERPIECES The Winnower; *1848; Musée d'Orsay, Paris, France*
The Gleaners; *1857; Musée du Louvre, Paris, France*

Modersohn-Becker Paula

Born Dresden, Germany 1876; died Worpswede, Germany 1907

Self Portrait with Blue Irises
1906–1907; painting on board; 38 x 24 cm; Folkwang Museum, Essen, Germany

Paula Becker learnt to draw and paint while being encouraged by relatives and friends. From 1893–1895 she attended the Association of Berlin Women Artists. In 1898, she moved to an established artist's colony in Worpswede and became a friend of the poet Rainer Maria Rilke. Her early work concentrated on landscapes and earthy representations of peasant life. In Paris in 1900, she became acquainted with the work of Cézanne, Gauguin, van Gogh and Rodin. During the following year she married widower Otto Modersohn, eleven years her senior. In her later, mainly portrait, work she was concerned to convey feeling; there is a quieter, introspective quality to her painting that separates it from the harsh colour and violent distortions of other Expressionists. **Self Portrait with Blue Irises**, with its simplified forms and restrained use of colour, is a striking image of self-possession and vulnerability. It becomes all the more poignant having the knowledge of Modersohn-Becker's tragic personal history. In 1906, she escaped from her oppressive marriage and returned to Paris; in 1907 she gave birth to her daughter Mathilde and died after childbirth of an embolism.

OTHER MASTERPIECES Old Peasant Woman Praying, *c.1905–1907; Detroit Institute of Arts, Detroit, USA* **Kneeling Girl in Front of a Blue Curtain**; *1907; Landsemuseum, Oldenburg, Germany*

Modigliani Amedeo

Born Leghorn, Italy 1884; died Paris, France 1920

Jeanne Hébuterne with White Collar
1919; oil on canvas;
139.7 X 116.8 cm;
Private Collection

After studying in Venice and Florence, Amedeo Modigliani went to Paris in 1906. He never completely aligned himself with any particular movement but his work displayed a diverse range of influences including Cézanne, the Fauves, African sculpture and Cubism. His superb skills as a draughtsman owed more to his Italian heritage, especially to Botticelli and the Mannerists. Modigliani met Brancusi between 1910 and 1913 and, fascinated by sculpture, started to carve. He was forced to abandon sculpture for painting in 1915 when stone dust damaged his lungs, which were already weakened by tuberculosis. The last few years of his life became legendary. Poverty-stricken, he lived with artist friends in Montparnasse, his dissolute life ending when his declaration "I am going to drink myself to death" became a self-fulfilling prophesy. This wistful portrait is of **Jeanne Hébuterne**, his mistress. Pregnant with their second child, she committed suicide the day after Modigliani died. It is a portrait characteristic of the Modigliani woman, displaying a pronounced oval face, a long neck and sloping shoulders. Through her dark almond eyes and small pursed mouth, he conveys the impression of a graceful and vulnerable person.

OTHER MASTERPIECES Head; *c.1911–1912; Tate Collection, London, England*
Reclining Nude; *c.1919; Museum of Modern Art, New York City, USA*

266

Moholy-Nagy László

Born Basebarsod Hungary 1895; died Chicago, USA 1946

Sil I *1933; oil on silberit; 50 x 20 cm; National Gallery, Edinburgh, Scotland*

László Moholy-Nagy was a sculptor, painter, designer and photographer. Originally a law student, he went to Berlin after the First World War. Influenced by Lissitzky and Russian Constructivism, Moholy-Nagy's paintings made use of collage and photomontage. He became interested in the pictorial possibilities of new materials, especially translucent and transparent plastics. From 1923 to 1928 he taught at the Bauhaus, where he was able to further his experiments in a number of different media, including film, theatre, photography and industrial design. In 1928 he returned to Berlin to work as a designer of film and stage sets. He spent two years in London from 1935, where he produced documentary films and designed cinematic special effects. In 1937 he settled in Chicago where he led the New Bauhuas and founded the Institute of Design. Moholy-Nagy's significance lay in his constant experimentation with

complex ideas and new materials. **Sil I** shows his concern with dynamic relationships of form in space. A delicate web of strings highlights the interaction between three geometric objects, which rotate like planets.

OTHER MASTERPIECES Compostion A II; *1924; Guggenheim Museum, New York City, USA*
Jealousy; *1930; George Eastman House, Rochester, New York State, USA*

Mondrian Piet

Born Amersfoort, Netherlands 1872; died New York City, USA 1944

Composition with Red, Yellow and Blue *c.1937–1942; oil on canvas; 73.7 x 69.2 cm; Tate Collection, London, England*

Piet Mondrian's early landscape paintings owed much to the bright, colourful work of Matisse and van Gogh. In 1909 Mondrian moved to Paris where he experienced the work of the Cubists and was influenced by the simplified geometric shapes and tight structures he discovered in their paintings. **Composition with Red, Yellow and Blue** comprises coloured rectangles intersected and divided by a flat grid of black lines. It is part of a series of geometric paintings in which Mondrian attempted to shut out all reference to the outside world, in a desire to achieve what he called "universal harmony". It is in his use of contrasting primary colours through both balanced vertical and horizontal forms, that he fulfils this aim. Mondrian's importance lies in his development of "pure" abstraction. He was a founding member of the *De Stijl* journal of 1917, which helped spread his artistic theories. However, it would be wrong to conclude that his paintings can be seen merely as a series of formal experiments. By reducing painting to its most basic elements, Piet Mondrian achieved a simple purity and spirituality that radiated throughout the twentieth century.

OTHER MASTERPIECES Still Life With Ginger Jar II; *1911; Gemeentemuseum, The Hague, Netherlands* Broadway Boogie Woogie; *1942–1943; The Museum of Modern Art, New York City, USA*

Monet Claude

Born Paris, France 1840; died Giverny, France 1926

**Blue
Waterlilies**
*c.1916—1919;
oil on canvas;
200 x 200 cm;
Musée d'Orsay,
Paris, France*

Claude Monet was born in Paris but educated at Le Havre, on the northern French coast, where
he was encouraged to turn away from portraiture to paint directly from nature. In the 1860s he
met Pissarro, Sisley, Renoir and Manet in Paris. These friendships combined to create a new
direction in art for the first Impressionist exhibition of 1874. The aim of this movement was to
produce paintings entirely faithful to reality – to make an exact analysis of tone and colour as
well as capture the reflections on the surfaces of objects. Monet was dedicated to the study of
light and its changing effect on nature. He settled at Giverny, northern-eastern France in 1883,
where he created a beautiful garden filled with elaborate arrangements of plants and flowers.
Here, in the 1890s, he began to paint subjects in series recording the varying light conditions at
different times of the day. In this painting **Blue Waterlilies**, from the most famous of all his
series the **Waterlilies**, the shimmering pools are secondary to the atmosphere that envelopes
them. Suffused in light, the painting surrounds and submerges the spectator and is all the more
astonishing with the knowledge that Monet's eyesight was failing. He was to die nearly blind.

OTHER MASTERPIECES Gare St Lazare; *1877; Musée du Louvre, Paris, France*
Rouen Cathedral; *1894; Musée du Louvre, Paris, France*

Moore Henry

Born Castleford, England 1898; died Much Hadham, England 1986

Mother Preparing Child for Bath *c.1944; pencil, white wax crayon watercolour wash, coloured crayon, pen and black ink; 41.6 x 50.2 cm; Private Collection*

Moore trained in Leeds, where he met Barbara Hepworth, and at the Royal College. He taught there between 1925 and 1932 and at Chelsea School of Art through the 1930s. Moore gradually revised his early rejection of traditional, classical sculpture as a result of travelling to Paris and Italy in 1925. He had originally been impressed by the "barbaric" vitality of African wood carvings and pre-Columbian sculpture. Intrinsically, non-Western, constructive qualities infuse his work, which combines geological and human forms. He defined "truth to material" as a primary aim, seeing the artistic contemplation of realistic beauty as a digression. From 1928 he received public commissions which alternately attracted controversy and admiration. His international reputation was established in the 1940s, by which time, after the bombing of his studio, he had moved to Hertfordshire. Moore's **Shelter** drawings, made as an official war artist, offer a unique interpretation of the search for refuge from the Blitz. Drawing was an essential and integral aspect of Moore's practice and **Mother Preparing Child for Bath** exemplifies the graphic, generic forms that inform and typify his sculptural work. Arguably, he remains the most important British sculptor of the twentieth century.

OTHER MASTERPIECES Reclining Figure; *1929; Leeds City Art Gallery, Leeds, England*
Family Group; *1950; Museum of Modern Art, New York City, USA*

Morandi Giorgio

Born Bologna, Italy 1890; died Bologna, Italy 1946

Still Life *1946; oil on canvas; 37.5 x 45.7 cm; Tate Collection, London, England*

Giorgio Morandi remained at a distance from most of the frenzied artistic developments of the twentieth century. He never left Italy. He studied in Bologna where he had a fleeting association with the Futurists, taking part in their first International Exhibition in Rome in 1914. In 1918 he was influenced by de Chirico's metaphysical work and briefly introduced a few surreal elements into his paintings. Apart from a few early landscapes, Morandi's work consisted almost entirely of still life. This contemplative **Still Life**, with its huddled collection of bottles and bowls is a quintessential Morandi. The delicate austerity of the simple composition is reinforced by a restrained use of colour. In his single-minded devotion to his subject matter, as well as his subtle, sparse and serene arrangements, Morandi's still life has echoes of both Chardin and Cézanne. The cool, classical spirit infusing his work can also be traced to the fourteenth-century artist Piero della Francesca. Held in great esteem by the younger generation of Italian artists, Morandi taught at the Bologna academy from 1930. He was also an accomplished engraver.

OTHER MASTERPIECES Metaphysical Still Life; *1919; Collection Dr Emilio Jesi, Milan, Italy*
Still Life; *c.1957; Hamburger Kunsthalle, Hamburg, Germany*

Motherwell Robert

Born Aberdeen, USA 1915; died New York City, USA 1991

Open No. 122 in Scarlet + Blue *1969; acrylic drawing on canvas; 213.4 x 254 cm; Tate Collection, London, England*

Robert Motherwell was unusual among the New York artists in that he was a true academic, possessing a rational mind that has suffused his art with an ordered, contemplative stillness. He had studied philosophy before embarking on serious artistic studies in the form of art history at Columbia University. He became a professional painter in 1941, after having become acquainted with the Surrealists and involved in their work, Roberto Matta's in particular. Motherwell is credited with being one of the initiators of the Abstract Expressionist movement. The informal art school he founded with fellow painters, Mark Rothko among them, called The Subjects of the Artist, was a significant development. The concerns of the Symbolists were of interest to Motherwell and his own work appropriates their ideology of equivalencies between colour, sound, sensation and memory. Beyond his extensive series of Elegy paintings, including **Elegy to the Spanish Republic 34**, his tranquil abstracts, such as **Open No. 122 in Scarlet + Blue**, are described by the artist as, "not hard-edge paintings, but romantic ones – essences".

OTHER MASTERPIECES Elegy to the Spanish Republic 34; *1953–1954; Albright-Knox Art Gallery, Buffalo, New York State* State USA Open No. 121 (**Bolton Landing Elegy**); *1969; Tate Collection, London, England*

274

Mucha Alphonse

Born Ivancice, Czechoslovakia 1860; died Prague, Czechoslovakia 1939

F. Champenois, France 1898 *1898; print on paper; 55.2 x 72.7 cm; Victoria and Albert Museum, London, England*

Alphonse Mucha trained and worked in Munich, Vienna and Paris. He produced a broad range of work during his career but came to international prominence through his poster designs. **F. Champenois, France 1898** is a prime example of his linear-based, decorative style. A product of Art Nouveau, the image features a beautiful woman surrounded by a swirling, circular design. Mucha's women, unusually for Art Nouveau, are not depicted as *femmes fatales*, but as the gentle, graceful, idealized version of femininity shown here. In this pale, neutrally-toned work, the figure appears entwined by tendrils against the soft background of flowers. Many of Mucha's best-known designs featured the actress Sarah Bernhardt, for whom he was also employed to design sets, costumes and jewellery. After several visits to the USA, he successfully built up a following there. In 1922, he returned to his native Czechoslovakia and continued to work there until his death in 1939. His prolific output of posters, drawings, wallpaper, furniture, stage sets, stained-glass work and jewellery featured in a major retrospective of his work at the Grand Palais in Paris in 1980.

OTHER MASTERPIECES Salon Des Cents; *1896; Mucha Foundation, Prague, Czech Republic*
Gismonda; *1894; Mucha Foundation, Prague, Czech Republic*

Munch Edvard

Born Lote, Norway 1863; died Oslo, Norway 1944

Puberty *1894; oil on canvas; 151.5 x 110 cm; Nasjonalgalleriet, Oslo, Norway*

Edvard Munch was an exponent of the Nordic spirit and possessed an artistic vision that communicated the exploration of anxiety and anguish. His work gave meaning to the notion of Expressionism for Northern European artists. He studied in Oslo and travelled across Europe until 1908 when he returned to Norway. He suffered from bouts of mental illness, which could account for the extraordinary quality of his art. Munch was impressed by the work of contemporary French artists he encountered on his travels. He felt particular empathy with the work of van Gogh and Gauguin. The emotive nature of the former and the visionary, decorative elements of the latter are evident in Munch's strange, dreamlike images. His affinity with the Symbolist movement focused his ideas accordingly into painting, etchings, lithographs and woodcuts. In these he explored the power of colour and form as effective compositional and symbolic tools. Life, love and death were recurring subjects, often focusing on women as powerful, enigmatic creatures. **Puberty** is an alluring, enigmatic picture laced with unease. The viewer becomes intruder and the naked girl, haunted by a great, sinister shadow, eyes us with trepidation, covering herself awkwardly from our gaze.

OTHER MASTERPIECES The Scream; *1893; Nasjonalgalleriet, Oslo, Norway*
Ashes; *1894; Nasjonalgalleriet, Oslo, Norway*

Murillo Bartolomé Esteban

Born Seville, Spain 1618; died Seville, Spain 1682

**Children Playing
with Dice**
c. 1670–1675; oil on
canvas; 146 x 108 cm;
Alte Pinakothek, Munich,
Germany

Bartolmé Estebán
Murillo spent nearly
all his life in Seville.
He started his career
painting pictures to be
sold at fairs. In 1648
he visited Madrid,
where he met
Velasquez. In 1660,
Murillo was one of
the founders of the
Seville Academy and
became its first
President. He made
his reputation with a
series of paintings
documenting the lives
of Franciscan saints
for the Franciscan
monastery in Seville.
His religious paintings
display a pious devotion and tenderness distinct form the harsh realism of his contemporaries,
Ribera and Velasquez. His mature work comprised genre scenes featuring saints, beggar boys
and fruit-sellers, having a softness and sweetness bordering on sentimentality. **Children Playing
with Dice** is one of his more unembroidered paintings. Nowadays it could be considered
uncomfortable as a rather provocative, sexualized image of young boys. Murillo was hugely
popular during his lifetime, working in a large studio to cater for the demand for his work. By
the nineteenth century, his work was considered cloying and his reputation declined.

OTHER MASTERPIECES The Two Trinities; c. 1675–1682; National Gallery, London, England
Self-Portait; c. 1670–1673; National Gallery, London, England

Nash Paul

Born London, England 1889; died Boscombe, England 1946

Harbour and Room
1932—1936; oil on
canvas; 91.4 x 71.1 cm;
Tate Collection, London,
England

Paul Nash studied at
the Slade School from
1910 to 1911.
Primarily a landscape
painter, his early
visionary drawings of
faces superimposed on
the landscape were
influenced by Rossetti.
Nash made his
reputation as an official
war artist during the
First World War. In the
1920s and 1930s he
was influenced by the
Surrealists. Through its confusion of interior and exterior space as well as through the
mysterious, lurking presence of the black boat, **Harbour and Room** has a distinctly surreal feel.
It clearly shows the influence of de Chirico, whose work he saw in London in 1928. Nash was
one of the founders in 1933 of Unit One, an avant-garde group of British artist that included
Ben Nicholson and Henry Moore among its members. During the Second World War, Nash
once again worked as an official war artist. In his later landscape work he evolved a complex
symbolism. Not content with recording the surface of the natural world, he wanted to penetrate
beneath to express its spiritual essence. He also worked as a photographer, writer, book
illustrator and a designer of textiles and scenery.

OTHER MASTERPIECES Dead Sea; *1940—1941; Tate Collection, London, England*
Landscape of the Vernal Equinox; *1944; Scottish National Gallery of Modern Art, Edinburgh,*
Scotland

Nauman Bruce

Born Fort Wayne, Indiana, USA 1941

Good Boy, Bad Boy *1985; colour video monitors; Tate Collection, London, England*

Bruce Nauman read mathematics and physics before studying art at the University of Wisconsin, graduating in 1964. He continued his art training at the University of California. Although he began as a painter, after 1965 he rejected the medium to work in film, performance and sculpture. He is regarded as a leading Post-Minimalist artist, concerned more with the activity of production than with the finished object. His first solo exhibition in New York, in 1968, revealed his preoccupation with the body, shown in what is typically associated with Nauman – neon sculpture. During the 1970s, these concerns were extended beyond the body and into more conceptual realism of behavioural and sociological issues. In the mid-1980s his thematic focus was on notions of power and sex. The "animated" neon sculptures take on a Pop-inspired, satirical edge. Nauman's inventiveness made him one of the most influential American artists of the 1970s and 1980s. **Good Boy, Bad Boy** is a video-piece of two actors reciting the same string of statements, unsynchronized. The force of each respective statement depends upon the gender and the tone of voice of the actor. It epitomizes Nauman's interest in the manipulation of language and experience.

OTHER MASTERPIECES Corridor with Mirror and White Lights, *1971; Tate Collection, London, England* **Human Nature/Know Doesn't Know**, *1983–1986; Froblich Collection, Stuttgart, Germany*

Newman Avis

Born London, England 1946

The Day's Residues VI
1982; drawing on paper;
101.5 x 136.8 cm; Tate
Gallery, London, England

Since 1982, Avis Newman has made drawing the central concern of her art practice. During the early 1980s, her mixed-media work, including **The Day's Residues**, drew upon a profusion of broken lines, marks and scratches to create an imaginary space that referenced the pre-linguistic world of cave paintings. Through symbolic reference to humans, animals and birds, the artist described how she wished to "suggest the mobility of the image and that ambiguity of form which one experiences in dreams". These discordant works were pieced together from fragments, the exposed areas of paper or canvas ensuring that the work was open and not closed to meaning. In her **Webs (Backlit)** series from 1994, Newman extended her metaphorical enquiry into animal and human forms, presenting a series of stretched and unstretched canvases in which the image of a spider's web is of key importance. The web is alternately revealed and obscured through layers that form the surface of the work, alluding to the problematic nature of representation and acknowledging the gap between idea and realization. Newman has also made a series of boxed works containing natural matter such as feathers, pebbles and sand.

OTHER MASTERPIECES Sculpture of Essential Movement; *1989; Tate Collection, London, England* Webs (Backlight) V; *1994; Lisson Gallery, London, England*

Newman Barnett

Born New York City, USA, 1905; died New York City, USA 1970

Moment *1946; oil on canvas; 76.2 x 40.6 cm; Tate Collection, London, England*

Barnett Newman trained in New York. He attended classes at the Art Student's League, while also studying at the City College. In the 1930s, he painted in an Abstract Expressionist style. However, although closely associated with other members of this movement, his own work gradually began to change, rejecting their characteristically loose, painterly technique in favour of a stricter, more rigorous approach to abstraction. By 1948, he was working on monochrome canvases, interrupted only by the presence of one or more bands, travelling vertically from one edge of the canvas to the other. Known as "zips", these became the trademark of Newman's large, abstract paintings, providing a contemplative focus on the vast fields of colour and effectively opening out the space. Despite their minimalist appearance, paintings like **Moment** are suffused with sublime mysticism, drawing upon vast concepts like

creation and creativity. Between 1958 and 1962 Newman painted solely in black and white. In the late 1960s he employed colours of exceptional purity and depth. His late work was prolific and, from 1965, included a small number of large, steel sculptures. Newman was a radical influence on younger American artists such as Larry Poons and Jasper Johns.

OTHER MASTERPIECES Adam; *1951—1952; Tate Collection, London, England*
Who's Afraid of Red, Yellow and Blue III; *1966—1967; Stedelijk Museum, Amsterdam, Holland*

Nicholson Ben

Born Denham, England 1894; died London, England 1982

December 1951 – St Ives – Oval and Steeple *1951; oil and pencil on board; 50 x 66.5 cm; Bristol Art Gallery, Bristol, England*

Ben Nicholson's only formal training was undertaken between 1910–1911 at the Slade School of Art, London, where he befriended Paul Nash. His visits to Paris in the 1920s and 1930s were a seminal influence on his own work, due to his contact with such significant artists as Picasso, Arp, Brancusi and Braque. His white relief pictures and later hard-edged geometrical paintings and reliefs of the early 1940s reveal an original application of his grasp of Cubist principles. The impact that Mondrian's calculated abstracts had on Nicholson was absorbed and is echoed in the simple shaped blocks of pure colour that reinforced the structural strength of his refined pictorial design. At the outbreak of the Second World War, Nicholson and his second wife, sculptor Barbara Hepworth, moved to St Ives, in Cornwall, which was becoming the centre of an artistic community. The local environment acted as a catalyst for the return of figuration to his work. By 1951, when his marriage ended and he moved to Switzerland, these elements were becoming more subtle, as in **December 1951 – St Ives – Oval and Steeple**. This elegant composition of line and colour is characteristic of Nicholson's understated sophistication and of his contribution to British abstraction.

OTHER MASTERPIECES White Relief; *1935; Ivor Braka Ltd, London, England*
A Window in Cornwall; *c.1942; Whitworth Art Gallery, Manchester, England*

Nolan Sidney

Born Melbourne, Australia 1917; died London, England 1992

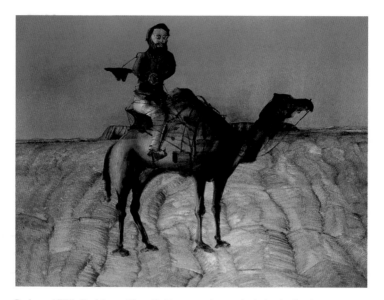

Burke and Wills Expedition "Gray Sick" *1949; ripolin enamel and oil on hardboard; 92 x 120 cm; Private Collection*

Sidney Nolan contributed significantly to the development of Pop art. His work came to prominence on the London art market shortly after the Second World War. Before the 1940s, Nolan had primarily been an abstract painter. However, his fascination with the exploits of the Australian outlaw Ned Kelly provided the inspiration for a series of paintings featuring the antics of this Antipodean anti-hero. The naive and comic style of Nolan's paintings belied a more serious concern with issues of Australian nationalism. This, and the **Burke and Wills** series of paintings, reference a culture mindful of territorial disputes between white settlers and indigenous Aborigines. The paintings that followed in the 1950s also appeared ahead of their time, being an eclectic mix of figuration and abstraction, handled in brash colours and with paint applied in the characteristic, gestural fashion of the Expressionists. Landscape remained a central concern and was interpreted as a wasteland inhabited by alien beings; strange amorphous figures, with shapes for heads and daubs for limbs, which populated spaces devoid of naturalistic elements.

OTHER MASTERPIECES Kelly, Spring; *1956; Arts Council of England Collection, London, England* **The Leda Suite**; *1961; Tate Collection, London, England*

Nolde Emil

Born Schleswig-Holstein, Germany 1867; died Seebüll, Germany 1956

The Sea B *1930; oil on canvas; 73.7 x 101 cm; Tate Collection, London, England*

Emil Nolde was born into a peasant family and originally trained as a woodcarver. After studying in Munich, Nolde was invited to become a member of Die Brücke in 1906. Although also associated with the artist's group Der Blaue Reiter, Nolde was essentially a solitary artist whose particular brand of sensual Expressionism, with its spontaneous use of colour, was very much his own. He was a prolific artist who painted figurative subjects, including theatre audiences, dancers and religious works. He also painted landscapes, seascapes, gardens and flowers. His energetic, primitive style was characterized by its use of violent colour, simplified drawing and wild brush marks. **The Sea B** depicts a windswept seascape typical of the flat coastline around the German-Danish border where Nolde lived for most of his life. The sea was an elemental force for Nolde, who saw, "…it not from the beach or from a boat but as it exists in itself, devoid of any reference to man, eternally in motion, ever changing". Nolde travelled to Russia and to the South Sea islands. After the Second World War he lived like a recluse, completing his series **Unpainted Pictures** in secret, apparently still fearing persecution by the Nazis.

OTHER MASTERPIECES Meeting on the Beach; *1921; Nolde Foundation Seebull, Germany*
Evening Landscape, North Friesland; *1920; Nolde Foundation, Seebull, Germany*

284

O'Keeffe Georgia

Born Sun Prairie, USA 1887; died Santa Fe, USA 1986

Cow's Skull with Calico Roses *1931; oil on canvas; 92.2 x 61.3 cm; Art Institute of Chicago, USA*

Georgia O'Keeffe was one of the pioneers of modernism in the USA. She was part of a group of artists associated with Alfred Stieglitz, an American photographer and art dealer, who imported avant-garde European art into the USA at the beginning of the twentieth century. She married Stieglitz in 1924. In the 1920s she made a series of precise, clearly defined paintings featuring the skyscrapers of her native New York. With its clinical interest in the rhythm of geometric structures, and the lack of any human interest or social comment, her work was defined by a new term, "Precisionist". Throughout her career, O'Keeffe moved effortlessly in and out of abstraction. Indeed, there is no real distinction between her abstract and figurative works – both feature enlarged, simplified, sculptural forms often derived from nature. From the 1930s, she spent each winter in New Mexico where she painted the desert landscape. **Cow's Skull with Calico Roses** features a surreal juxtaposition of dry, bleached bones and flowers. The clear-cut realism of the folds and crevices, swelling forms and hidden hollows allows for a powerful, sexual interpretation.

OTHER MASTERPIECES Black Iris; *1926; Metropolitan Museum of Art, New York City, USA*
The Mountain, New Mexico *1931; Whitney Museum of American Art, New York City, USA*

Oldenburg Claes

Born Stockholm, Sweden 1929

Soft Drainpipe – Blue (Cool)
Version *1967; acrylic on canvas and*
metal; 259.1 x 187.6 cm; Tate
Collection, London, England

Claes Oldenburg was a principal
American Pop artist dominating
the New York art scene in the
1960s. "Without the intention of
making art," Oldenburg claimed
to, "use naive imitation," of reality.
His work, combining elements of
painting and sculpture, is overtly
humorous. He transformed
common objects by enlarging
their scale to outlandish
proportions and altering their
familiar material state. Oldenburg
emigrated to Chicago at the age
of five. He graduated from Yale
University in 1950 and went on
to study at the Art Institute of
Chicago, before moving to New
York in 1956. Here he came into
contact with artists producing and
participating in "Happenings". By
1960, he was constructing
sculptural pieces based on
consumer items. In 1961, he
opened "The Store" in a vacant
shop, where his replicas of food and clothing were appropriately displayed. Such imitations had
developed into the "soft" sculptures by 1962 – such as **Soft Drainpipe** – for which he is best
known. For public art commissions from 1965 he realized colossal versions of everyday objects
– a lipstick and a peg to name two. Our reaction to these works is bound up with our
realization that the absurdity of Oldenburg's creations are safely locked in an art arena.

OTHER MASTERPIECES Lunchbox; *1961; Louisiana Museum of Modern Art, Humlebaek, USA*
Needle, Thread and Knot; *2000; Piazzale Cadorna, Milan, Italy*

Paik Nam June

Born Korea 193

Polaris 1990, v
142.25 X 142.
Dorothy Goldee
Santa Monica, (

Nam June died
music and l theory
in Tokyo, uating in
aesthetics. ard the en
of the 195 travelled
to Germa ere he
encounter Cage
and bega eer as a
compose erformer
of avant music. His vities achieved attention via his involvement in the early 1960s
with the p of concept artists and poets who formed the Fluxus movement. The
extravag performance p es he created were the beginning of his exploration into the visual
potenti usic. He mo l to New York in 1964 and has since become widely recognized
for his scale, often ov whelming sculptures constructed from television sets and video
monito y experimentin with this medium he fused art with modern communications
techno while resisting e elitism and ideology which attached itself to fine art production.
His int ive work appea o a wide audience. **Polaris** uses flashy, computer-driven
electro to make a state nt. The artist incorporates imagery that combines the past with
the pr and the East w the West, referring to contemporary themes confronting global
cultur civilization.

OTH AASTERPIECI Fin-De-Siecle II, 1989, *Whitney Museum of American Art, New York*
City, l **7AIS Station T** er, 1996, *Art Museum of the Americas, Washington D.C., USA*

Palmer Samuel

Born London, England 1805; died Reigate, England 1881

A Hilly Scene c.1826–1828;
tempera on paper and wood;
20.6 x 13.7 cm; Tate Collection,
London, England

Samuel Palmer was a child prodigy who first exhibited landscape drawings at the Royal Academy when he was fourteen years old. He was introduced to the great visionary artist William Blake in 1824, a meeting that significantly intensified Palmer's already mystical imagination. After a move to Shoreham, in Sussex, in 1826, Palmer produced a number of small ink and wash landscapes, as well as several oil paintings, that are now generally regarded as his best work. **A Hilly Scene** shows a nocturnal and mysterious scene that, in his own words, reveals "a mystic glimmer" behind the hills. His imaginative, lyrical landscapes relied on the Pantheistic idea of the unity in all things. Palmer's depiction of sheaves of corn and trees abundant with fruit symbolized the idea that the way to salvation was through a simple life led in harmony with nature. In Shoreham, Palmer became the central figure of a group known as the Ancients. He returned to London in 1835, after which he acquired a reputation as a conventional, academic painter. His early work was rediscovered in the 1930s and 1940s and influenced several painters, Graham Sutherland and Paul Nash in particular.

OTHER MASTERPIECES In a Shoreham Garden; c.1829; *Victoria and Albert Museum, London, England* Coming Home from Evening Church; 1830; *Tate Collection, London, England*

Paolozzi Sir Eduardo

Born Edinburgh, Scotland 1924

Wittgenstein in New York
1964; pen and ink on paper;
76.3 x 53.8 cm; Tate
Collection, London, England

Paolozzi is generally
recognized as a sculptor
belonging to the Pop Art
movement in Britain. Born
in Scotland of Italian
parents, Paolozzi graduated
from evening classes in
Edinburgh to studying in
London at St Martin's
School of Art and the
Slade School. He finished
in 1947 and for the next
two years lived in Paris
where he came into
contact with numerous
notable artists. On
returning to London he
shared a studio with
sculptor William Turnbull. From 1951 he undertook many public art commissions in Britain and
abroad and taught textile design and sculpture, as well as in the ceramics department of the
Royal College of Art. Paolozzi possesses diverse technical skills. These are reflected in his
complex sculptural constructions, reliefs developed from eclectic sources and 2D works such as
Wittgenstein in New York. In wood, plaster and on paper he continually recomposes and
reorders shapes that have been created, altered and found. Maquettes are reproduced on a large
scale, often in bronze. They comprise a conglomeration of influences from Classicism to
Constructivism, Cubism to Futurism, and are a mixture of the organic and the mechanical, the
representational and the abstract.

OTHER MASTERPIECES The Wealth of Nations; *1993; Drummond House, Edinburgh, Scotland*
Mosaics; *1980; Tottenham Court Road Tube Station, London, England*

Parmigianino Francesco

Born Parma, Italy 1503; died Casalmaggiore, Italy 1540

Madonna with Saint Zacharias
c.1530; oil on canvas; 73 x 60 cm; Galleria degli Uffizi, Florence, Italy

An artist who displayed his prodigious talent at an early age, Francesco Parmigianino took his name from Parma, his birthplace. He was a contemporary of Correggio, who also worked in Parma for much of his life. Both men separately worked on commissions for the frescoes in the chapels of St Giovanni Evangelista. Parmigianino went to Rome in 1523. Here his dramatic and intense style, with its propensity for distortion, started to reveal a softer and more graceful influence from Raphael and Michelangelo. He moved to Bologna four years later, when Rome was sacked by German troops. Returning to Parma in 1531, the last ten years of his life were spent in bitter dispute over his failure to complete frescoes for the church of Sta Maria della Steccata. **Madonna with Saint Zacharias** reveals, through its flowing robes and disproportionate group of figures, the Mannerist elongation of forms for which Parmigianino is renowned. The unusual and imaginative composition includes the remarkable portrait of the old man to the right of the painting, sitting staring into space as spectator to the scene rather than active participant.

OTHER MASTERPIECES Self-Portrarit in a Convex Mirror; *1524; Kunsthistorisches Museum, Vienna, Austria* **Madonna with the Long Neck**; *c.1535; Galleria degli Uffizi, Florence, Italy*

Pasmore Victor

Born Warlingham, Surrey, England 1908; died England 1997

Spiral Motif in Green, Violet, Blue and Gold: The Coast of the Inland Sea *1950, oil on canvas; 81.3 x 100.3 cm; Tate Collection, London, England*

While employed in clerical work during the day, Victor Pasmore studied art in the evening at St Martin's School of Art, London, "painting cubist pastiche". In 1932, he joined the London Artists' Association, run by the Bloomsbury Group, and was elected to the avant-garde London Group. Through this he made contact with artists William Coldstream and Claude Rogers. Together, they formed the Euston Road School in 1937. In 1938, Kenneth Clark became his patron. Throughout the 1940s, Pasmore worked in a naturalistic way, producing sensitive portraits and atmospheric landscapes. However, toward the end of the decade he moved to an abstract mode of expression, influenced by his contemporaries and inspired, not by Picasso's art, but by his spirit of artistic independence. Pasmore began reformulating the idea of "basic form" as used by the Bauhaus. With Richard Hamilton at Newcastle University, he developed a radical way of teaching art, known as Basic Design. Pasmore painted **Spiral Motif in Green, Violet, Blue and Gold: The Coast of the Inland Sea** around the time that he was in St Ives, Cornwall. "The Inland Sea", however, refers to, "the coast of subconscious experience", revealing Pasmore's confidence in abstraction as "a modern romanticism".

OTHER MASTERPIECES The Park; *1947; Sheffield City Art Galleries, Sheffield, England*
The Snowstorm (**Spiral Motif in Black and White**); *1950–1951; Arts Council of England Collection, London, England*

Patenier Joachim

Born Netherlands c.1485; died Antwerp, Belgium 1524

Charon Crossing the River Styx *c.1520; oil on canvas; 64 x 103 cm; Museo del Prado, Madrid, Spain*

Patenier is notable for producing some of the first Flemish paintings in which landscape takes precedence over figures. He was described by Dürer, whom he met in 1521, as a "good landscape painter" and many works have been attributed to, but few signed by him. Very little is known about his early life. He became a member of the Antwerp guild in 1515 and collaborated with a number of artists, either painting landscape backgrounds for them or having them paint figures into his work. Specific narrative made the subjects of his paintings but it is the environments in which the unfolding of respective stories take place which dominate. Scenes such as **Charon Crossing the River Styx** reveal Patenier's attention to detail, which is a mixture of imaginative fantasy and observation from nature. It has a quality which owes something to the strangeness of Bosch and offers a panoramic view that foreshadows the achievements of Claude. His precision and attention to systematic colouring in order to describe depth and recession is evidence of his importance in developing the formal elements in the depiction of landscape as a subject in its own right.

OTHER MASTERPIECES St Jerome in a Rocky Landscape; *c.1515; National Gallery, London, England* The Temptation of St Anthony; *c.1515; (With Quentin Massys), Museo del Prado, Madrid, Spain*

Picasso Pablo

Born Malaga, Spain 1881; died Mougins, France 1973

Les Demoiselles d'Avignon *1906; oil on canvas; 244 x 234 cm; Museum of Modern Art, New York City, USA*

Pablo Picasso's painting **Les Demoiselles d'Avignon** marks the beginning of Cubism, a revolutionary artistic movement initiated by Picasso and his fellow artist Georges Braque. Picasso first started work on this painting in his Parisian studio in 1906. The final composition shows clearly the influence of both Cézanne, who had famously declared that all nature was based on the sphere, the cylinder and the cone, and the simplified forms that Picasso had found in African art. The right-hand side of the painting, in particular, with its flat shapes and mask-like heads, shows what a dramatic break with tradition this was. Although Picasso is primarily associated with Cubism, his so-called Blue Period, with its melancholic depiction of lowlife, was another significant early phase in his development. From 1914 onward, his work evolved in many other directions. Paintings, drawings, collages, etchings, sculptures, stage designs and ceramics were produced at an astonishing rate with subjects as diverse as classical mythology and the horrors of war. After exhibiting with the Surrealists in 1925, he continued to experiment with characteristic energy and confidence until his death, aged ninety two, in 1973. He was indisputably a genius and the founder of modern art.

OTHER MASTERPIECES Guernica; *1937; Centro de Arte Reina Sofia, Madrid, Spain*
Weeping Woman; *1937; Tate Collection, London, England*

Piero della Francesca

Born Borgo Sansepolcro, Italy c.1419; died Borgo Sansepolcro, Italy 1492

Resurrection
c.1463; fresco; 225 x 200 cm; Pinacoteca Sansepolcro, Italy

The career of Piero della Francesca began in Florence as an assistant to Veneziano, but he spent most of his time in his home town of Borgo, where he was a town councillor. He was influenced by the achievements of his artistic predecessors and contemporaries such as Masaccio, Uccello and Donatello; his own fascination with mathematics became his unique contribution. In the 1470s, he stopped painting, dedicating his time instead to writing two treatises on geometry and perspective. There is a timeless, serene air to his paintings, and it seems fitting that he often delayed completing commissioned work. In **Resurrection** he paints Christ as a robust and muscular man, and the moment of his triumphal return to life, in a solemn and calm manner. This austere mood is increased by the use of pale, fresco colours and soft lighting. There is little to divert attention away from the direct gaze of Christ. Although well-known in his lifetime, Piero della Francesca's art was neglected until the nineteenth century, when his reputation as one of the greatest painters of the early Renaissance was established.

OTHER MASTERPIECES The Baptism; *c.1450; National Gallery, London, England*
Constantine's Dream; *c.1460; San Francesco, Arezzo, Italy*

Piero di Cosimo

Born Florence, Italy c.1462; died Florence, Italy c.1521

A Satyr Mourning Over a Nymph *c.1496; oil on poplar; 65.4 x 184.2 cm; National Gallery, London, England*

A pupil of Cosimo Rosselli, Piero di Cosimo adopted his master's Christian name. He was influenced by Leonardo da Vinci and Signorelli but painted allegories and classical myths in a singular, imaginative style consistent with contemporary accounts of him as an eccentric and a recluse. Vasari, in his fifteenth-century account of artist's lives, for example, records Piero's extreme love of nature and his unlikely diet of hard-boiled eggs as evidence of his idiosyncratic tendencies. In **A Satyr Mourning over a Nymph**, Piero di Cosimo depicts the personal tragedy of infidelity and jealousy of a young couple, believed to have been Cephalus and Procris. While his handling of their suffering is tender and convincing, the painting is equally remarkable for the artist's rendition of the effects of natural light and his keen observation of animals. The depiction of the faithful dog is particularly impressive. The painting, which is on wood, was probably designed to adorn a bench or a chest in a Florentine town house. He also painted a few religious works, and worked on designs for festivals, masques and processions.

OTHER MASTERPIECES Fight Between the Lapiths and the Centaurs; *c.1507; National Gallery, London, England* Immaculate Conception; *c.1507; Galleria degli Uffizi, Florence, Italy*

Piper John

Born Epsom, England 1903; died Fawley, England 1992

St Mary Port, Bristol
*1940; oil on canvas;
76.2 x 63.5 cm; Tate
Collection, London,
England*

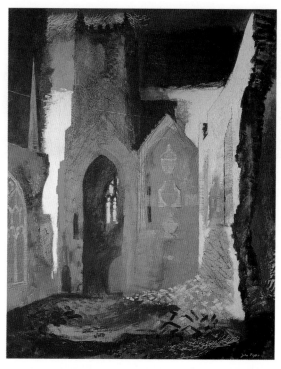

John Piper began his career as clerk in his father's firm of solicitors. After his father died in 1926, he studied at the Richmond School of Art, and then at the Royal College of Art in 1927. A member and secretary of the Seven and Five Society of artists, he exhibited abstract sculpture with the group from 1934. Piper helped to produce Axis, the review of abstract art, the editor of which, Myfanwy Evans, became Piper's second wife in 1937. This pioneering publication attracted contributions from eminent art theorists, historians and avant-garde artists of the day. It, and associated papers, contributed to the rise of landscape art in the English tradition, taking into account recent European artistic developments, most notably Surrealism. Piper incorporated romanticism and nostalgia into his work, sharing in the spirit of work by Sutherland and Nash. Via his experimentation with collage, he returned to a representational mode of working. **St Mary Port, Bristol** is moody rather than naturalistic. This "neo-picturesque", serene but sombre image of church ruins is a composite of numerous techniques and reveals Piper's versatility. It also reflects his interest in architecture and his confirmed religious beliefs.

OTHER MASTERPIECES Abstract I; *1935; Tate Collection, London, England*
Seaton Delaval; *1941; Tate Collection, London, England*

302

Pissarro Camille

Born St Thomas, West Indies 1830; died Paris, France 1903

The Vegetable Garden with Trees in Blossom, Spring, Pontoise *1877; oil on canvas; 65.5 x 81 cm; Musée d'Orsay, Paris, France*

In order to achieve his ambition of becoming an artist, Camille Pissarro moved to Paris at the age of twenty-four. Here he worked under Corot, who advised him to paint directly from nature and to, "...study light and tonal values". Despite earning praise for his early landscapes, Pissarro was poverty-stricken and made his living painting fans and blinds. From the late 1860s he was a leading Impressionist – he helped organize all eight Impressionist exhibitions and was the only one to participate in them all. He and Monet were both in London during the Franco-Prussian War, the two men admiring the work of Constable and Turner. From 1872 until 1884 Pissarro lived at Pontoise, working directly on out-of-doors paintings. In this painting, **The Vegetable Garden with Trees in Blossom, Pontoise**, he successfully evokes the atmosphere of a soft spring afternoon, achieving great luminosity through small dabs of pure colour. Pissarro influenced Cézanne, who worked with him at Pontoise between 1872–1877. Never seen as the most innovative of the Impressionists, Pissarro was nonetheless described in a pamphlet published in 1878 as, "the most naturalist of them all. He sees nature and simplifies it through its most permanent aspects". Gradually his eyesight failed; he died blind.

OTHER MASTERPIECES Lower Norwood, London; *1870; National Gallery, London, England*
Place du Theatre Francais; *1898; County Museum of Art, Los Angeles, California, USA*

Polke Sigmar

Born Olesnica, Poland 1941

Paganini *1982; acrylic on fabric; 200 x 450 cm; Thomas Ammann Collection, Zürich, Switzerland*

Sigmar Poke grew up in East Germany. After moving with his family to West Germany, settling in Willich, he studied glass painting from 1959 to 1960 at Düsseldorf-Kaiserwerth and then transferred to the Academy of Art. With fellow student Gerhard Richter he formulated a Pop-inspired "Capital Realist" anti-style of art, appropriating the pictorial short-hand of advertising. The anarchistic element of the work Polke developed was largely engendered by his mercurial approach. His irreverence for traditional painting techniques and materials and his lack of allegiance to any one mode of representation has establish his now-respected reputation as a visual revolutionary. **Paganini**, an expression of "the difficulty of purging the demons of Nazism" – witness the "hidden" swastikas – is typical of Polke's tendency to accumulate a range of different mediums within one canvas. It is not unusual for Polke to combine household materials and paint, lacquers, pigments, screen-print and transparent sheeting in one piece. A complicated "narrative" is often implicit in the multi-layered picture, giving the effect of witnessing the projection of a hallucination or dream through a series of veils.

OTHER MASTERPIECES Girlfriends; *1965; Collection Froehlich, Stuttgart, Germany*
Swimming Pool; *1988; Collection Froehlich, Stuttgart, Germany*

Pollaiuolo Antonio

Born Florence, Italy c.1432; died Rome, Italy 1498

Battle of the Ten Nudes *c.1471–1472; engraving on paper; 38.3 x 59 cm; Cleveland Museum of Art, Ohio, USA*

With his younger brother, Piero, Antonio Pollaiuolo maintained one of the most successful workshops in Florence during the second half of the fifteenth century. It produced a wide range of art forms including tapestry designs, sculpture, metalwork and paintings. Among the most prestigious commissions were a silver reliquary for the Florentine Baptistery and the bronze tombs for Pope Sixtus IV and Pope Innocent VIII in St Peter's, Rome. The high quality engraving, **Battle of the Ten Nudes**, is a good example of Antonio's abiding passion for anatomical study and his skilled draughtsmanship; this is represented by his depiction of figures in vigorous action. According to the treatise of humanist and architect Alberti, painting should be divided into contour, composition and light – contour being the clear delineation between figures, and composition the way individual elements fit together. When the latter was applied to anatomy, Alberti allegedly advised artists to draw the skeleton first, add the muscles next and then pad out with flesh and skin. This engraving epitomizes Alberti's theories and, along with other works, gained Antonio the reputation of being the precursor to Leonardo.

OTHER MASTERPIECES Martydom of Saint Sebastian; *1475; National Gallery, London, England* Tombs of Popes Sixtus IV and Innocent VIII; *1493 and 1492–1498; St Peter's Church, Vatican City, Rome, Italy*

Pollock Jackson

Born Cody, USA 1912; died Long Island, USA 1956

Yellow Island *1952; oil on canvas; 143.5 x 185.4 cm; Tate Collection, London, England*

Jackson Pollock's early landscapes were characteristic of the American romantic realism of the 1930s. By the end of the 1940s, he was painting in a completely abstract manner, producing canvases covered with dripped paint. The central figure in a movement known as Abstract Expressionism, Pollock saw painting as a spontaneous activity, believing that the canvas should express directly the artist's emotions. The picture was not painted: it "happened". To quote Pollock, "The painting has a life of its own. I only let it come through". Typically, Pollock would let the paint fall from the brush or vessel on to a huge canvas laid on the floor. The result was a network of coloured lines of extraordinary delicacy and complexity. **Yellow Island** reveals a darker, more melancholic side to the artist. Executed on the floor, using black paint on raw, unprimed canvas, this particular picture is from a series that was thought by critics to indicate Pollock's dependence on alcohol. Pollock's concept of "action painting" as something into which one threw one's whole body contributed hugely to the rise of modern American painting. His early death, in a road accident in 1956, has added to his legendary reputation.

OTHER MASTERPIECES Summertime Number 9A, *1948; Tate Collection, London, England*
Pasiphae; *1943; Museum of Modern Art, New York City, USA*

Pontormo Jacopo Carucci

Born Pontormo, Italy 1494; died Florence, Italy 1557

Joseph in Egypt *1518; oil on wood; 96.5 x 109.5 cm; National Gallery, London, England*

Pontormo's master was Andrea del Sarto whom he surpassed in his vigorous and original treatment of religious subjects. Pontormo transformed late Classicist style into dramatic Mannerist art. Reverential themes become vehicles for transporting vibrant colouring and theatrical compositions almost to the realm of fantasy. An accumulation of incongruous elements form **Joseph in Egypt**. Witness the unreal and unbelievable mixture of architectural styles, strange depiction of space and the almost living statues. Pontormo's compositions tend to overwhelm the spectator by the amount of activity and complicated rhythms set by figure groups. Each portion within the frame is busy, with no respite from colours and gestures jostling for attention. In contrast, his portraits have strength and clearly defined focus. The robust modelling of his figures and clearly cut folds of his drapery owes something to Michelangelo, seen most clearly in Potormo's last and greatest commission, the decoration of the choir of San Lorenzo in Florence. The high-key, nervously energetic quality of Pontormo's painting compensates for his reputedly introspective, melancholic personality. His work provides an antidote to the comparatively stilted, formal quality characterizing the Classical art which preceded his.

OTHER MASTERPIECES *Visitation; 1530–1532; Pieve di San Michele, Carmignano, Italy*
Deposition; 1526–1528; Capponi Chapel, Church of Sta Felicita, Florence, Italy

Poussin Nicholas

Born Les Andelys, France c.1593; died Rome, Italy 1665

The Rape of the Sabines c.1638; oil on canvas; 96.5 x 109.5 cm; Musée du Louvre, Paris, France

Poussin is considered as the leading exponent of French Classicist painting. He settled in Paris in 1612. Rather than being influenced by artists still working in a sixteenth-century Mannerist vein, he focused instead on emulating the Antique and studying Classical works of the Renaissance. He paid particular attention to Raphael and to Roman statuary and reliefs. In 1623 Poussin travelled, via Venice, to Rome. Through his contact with the poet Marino, he began working under the patronage of Cardinal Barberini. Poussin avoided current Baroque tendencies and after 1630 concentrated on mythological subjects, developing to maturity the Classical style for which he is best known. The Venetian painters, particularly Titian, influenced his colouring, injecting verve and vibrancy into sublime, pastoral scenes. In a different mood, works made from the late 1630s, such as **Bacchanal** and **The Rape of the Sabines**, illustrate a predilection for more complicated pageantry and austerity. Formal compositional construction identifies Poussin's growing preference for imbuing his vision with the Classicist spirit. In the late 1640s he applied these academic design principles to landscape paintings which mark an achievement that became an entire genre for his counterpart, Claude Lorraine.

OTHER MASTERPIECES The Worship of the Golden Calf; c.1635; National Gallery, London, England **Orpheus and Eurydice**; c.1650; Musée du Louvre, Paris, France

Puvis de Chavannes Pierre

Born Lyons, France 1824; died Paris, France 1898

Poor Fisherman *1881; oil on canvas; 155 x 192.5 cm; Musée d'Orsay, Paris, France*

Puvis de Chavannes was a leading decorative muralist. He produced his images on canvases, in flat fresco pigments, which were then affixed to the walls. His subjects tended to be abstracted from the Antique or allegorical themes, devoid of literary references. Simpler, poetic works, **Poor Fisherman**, for example, are more evocative than his monumental frieze projects. The theme of fishing and fishermen recurs in his work. The mood dictating the message of **Poor Fisherman** is difficult to interpret and a melancholic atmosphere pervades the consciously non-naturalistic scene. This is enhanced by anaemic colours which are typical of works from 1880s onward, dominated by a single tone. This two-dimensionality and high horizon-line is a precursor of Picasso's calm Blue Period. Puvis de Chavannes justified his methods by stating that "Painting is not merely an imitation of reality, but a parallel with nature". In spite of being critically underrated and described as a thinker, not a painter, he won the respect of numerous artists with a variety of aims and ideologies from Seurat to Toulouse-Lautrec. The expressive qualities of his work were of particular interest to Synthetist and Symbolist artists.

OTHER MASTERPIECES Le Bois Sacré Cher Aux Arts et Aux Muses; *1883–1884; Palais des Arts, Lyons, France* **The Inspiring Muses**; *1893–1895; Boston Public Library, Boston, USA*

Raphael (Raffaello Sanzio)

Born Urbino, Italy 1483; died Rome, Italy 1520

La Belle Jardinière *1508;*
wood panel; 122 x 80 cm;
Musée du Louvre, Paris, France

The son of a painter,
Raphael worked with the
successful Umbrian painter
Perugino at an early age.
Raphael's feeling for colour
and his ability to convey a
sense of emotional
tranquillity through his
work led to his talent being
quickly recognized.
Younger than Leonardo and
Michelangelo, Raphael
identified the enormous
contribution these artists
were making in Florence
and, in 1504, went there to
study. From Leonardo he
absorbed a sense of
composition and drawing
skills, and further
strengthened his work through a close examination of Michelangelo's dynamic figures. By 1508,
Raphael was much in demand and received his most prestigious commission to date, namely the
decoration of the papal apartments of Pope Julius II in the Vatican. Over the next twelve years
– until his premature death from fever caused the entire papal court to plunge into grief –
Raphael's great achievements were much celebrated and admired. **La Belle Jardinière** is one of
his many depictions of the **Madonna and Child**. In his harmonious composition the figures
unite, combining grandeur, grace and a sense of calm. The relaxed serenity of this work typifies
Raphael's many evocations of the classical "Golden Age".

OTHER MASTERPIECES Saint Catherine of Alexandria; *c.1507–1508; National Gallery,*
London, England Baldassare Castiglione; *c.1515; Musée du Louvre, Paris, France*

310

Rauschenberg Robert

Born Port Arthur, USA 1925

The Red Painting *1943;
oil, fabric and paper on canvas;
179.5 x 122 cm; Private
Collection*

Robert (born Milton)
Rauschenberg's art has
more to do with leaping
the boundaries of art in
the spirit of Dada than it
has to do with the
Abstract Expressionist
movement in America with
which he is associated.
More significant than his
attendance at the Art
Institute in Kansas City
from 1946–1947, and at
the Academie Julian in
Paris in 1948, were the
periods spent studying
under the "hard edge"
abstract painter Josef
Albers at Black Mountain
College. His contact here
with the experimental
composer John Cage proved influential; Rauschenberg collaborated on "Happenings" and
sought to expand the possibilities of his visual art beyond traditional painting or assemblage.
The all-white and the all-black series of paintings that were included in his first exhibitions at
the beginning of the 1950s were the minimal antithesis of work that was shortly to follow. All
manner of ephemera were combined with three-dimensional objects and painting to produce
unsettling, controversial works, the significance of which was formulated largely by the
spectator. In **The Red Painting**, for example, the dripping paint, sodden material and awkward
juxtaposition of the various elements has a more resounding impact than the overrriding colour.

OTHER MASTERPIECES Canyon; *1959; Sonnabend Collection, New York City, USA*
Bed; *1955; Collection of Mr and Mrs Leo Castelli, New York City, USA*

Redon Odilon

Born Bordeaux, France 1840; died Paris, France 1916

The Red Sphinx
c.1910; oil on canvas;
100 x 80 cm; Private
Collection, Switzerland

Odilon Redon
experienced an
unhappy childhood
after an early illness led
to his being brought up
by his uncle. His
attempt to train as an
architect was thwarted
and his artistic
development was slow,
largely the result of
time spent in the studio
of Bresdin, a printmaker
based in Bordeaux.
From the 1870s until
the 1890s Redon worked almost exclusively in black and white. His early efforts consisted of
charcoal drawings and etchings that looked to the landscape for inspiration to express his
intense and mournful vision. He developed a distinctive, spiritual and symbolic art drawing
upon a broad range of sources, including the unconscious, philosophy, literature and Charles
Darwin's theories of evolution. After the publication of the Symbolist Manifesto in 1886 he
became, with the writer Mallarmé, one of the leading Symbolists. During the 1890s Redon
began to explore new media such as oils and pastels and introduced colour to his work. By the
turn of the century the work of this hitherto little known artist, in particular his decorative,
colourful flower-pieces, was much in demand. **The Red Sphinx** is a bizarre hybrid, typical of
his poetic style that proved especially influential to the Surrealists.

OTHER MASTERPIECES Sita; *c.1893; The Art Institute of Chicago, USA*
Flower Clouds; *c.1903; The Art Institute of Chicago, USA*

Rego Paula

Born Lisbon, Portugal 1935

The Dance *1988; acrylic on paper; 212.6 x 274 cm; Tate Collection, London, England*

Paula Rego came to London in the early 1950s and began studying, "unofficially" as an art student at The Slade School in London. Here she met and fell in love with painter Victor Willing whom she later married. Under his influence, Rego learned to draw whatever came into her head. Such spontaneous activity became directed to the production of Expressionist pictures and collages. The death of her father in 1966 and the progressive illness of Willing delayed her own artistic development. In 1976 Rego received a grant to illustrate a series of Portuguese fairy-tales. At the same time Jungian therapy had encouraged her thoughts back to childhood themes. Stories became her art. Compositions of the early 1980s are like overloaded cartoons, colourfully packed with the energy of animals and creatures engaged in frenetic activity. Her work has become a more formal interpretation of the complications inherent in human relationships and associated symbols and metaphors. The vivid imagery of **The Dance**, for example, is inspired by Portuguese folk art and the caricatured figures and compositional format have their roots in classicism. The traditions of nineteenth-century illustrations inform her bold paintings which have a disquieting atmosphere and subversive narrative.

OTHER MASTERPIECES Red Monkey Beats his Wife; *1981; The Artist's Collection*
After Hogarth: Betrothal; Lessons; Wreck; *1999, Tate Collection, London, England*

Rembrandt (Harmensz van Rijn)

Born Leyden, Netherlands 1606; died Amsterdam, Netherlands 1669

The Anatomy Lesson of Dr Tulp *1632; oil on canvas; 169.5 x 216 cm; Mauritshaus, The Hague, Netherlands*

One of the greatest artists of all time, Rembrandt van Rijn trained principally in Amsterdam before working as an independent master in Leyden. His early paintings were of figures depicted in a biblical or philosophical context. He moved to Amsterdam in 1631–1932, where he received his first portrait commission. He made his name with this group portrait, **The Anatomy Lesson of Dr Tulp**. Unsparing in its depiction of the dissection of a human corpse, the boldly-lit composition is given added potency through the enrapt group of notables, each one a fully realized individual. The culmination of this lucrative phase of his career was **The Night Watch**, a group portrait of the militia's defence of Amsterdam. Rembrandt's fortune declined after 1642. He received no significant portrait commissions and experienced great financial difficulties, which led to bankruptcy in 1656. In later years he reverted to biblical subjects. His many self-portraits produced at every stage of his career provide an analytical account of his life. He had the incomparable ability to capture the outward appearance of his subjects, while laying bare the inner truth of their character. It is this understanding of humanity that makes his work unique.

OTHER MASTERPIECES Portrait of the Artist; *c.1665; Kenwood House, London, England*
A Woman Bathing in a Stream; *1654; National Gallery, London, England*

Reni Guido

Born Bologna, Italy 1572; died Bologna, Italy 1642

Massacre of the Innocents
undated; oil on canvas; 268 x 170 cm;
Pinacoteca Nazionale, Bologna, Italy

Guido Reni trained at the Carracci Academy in Bologna, Italy. Here his work benefited from the special emphasis that was placed on drawing from life. He visited Rome in 1600, where Raphael exerted a significant influence. Reni painted graceful reworkings of ancient and classical themes, distinguished mainly by the refined beauty of his colouring. He reputedly remarked that, "the only paintings that were beautiful and perfect were those that continued to grow on one as one viewed them day after day". He could well have been referring to his own work, **Massacre of the Innocents**. The melodramatic nature of this powerful composition has – due to the studied concentration of upturned faces and the folds of draperies – a static, almost frozen, beauty. Reni was an eccentric whose allegedly modest character did not temper his penchant for expensive clothes or gambling. He became the most important painter in Bologna after Ludovico Carraci's death in 1619 and managed a large and busy studio. Reni enjoyed a great reputation in the eighteenth and early nineteenth centuries, which only declined after Ruskin launched an attack on the pious sentimentality of his religious works.

OTHER MASTERPIECES Crucifixion of St Peter; *1603; Vatican, Rome, Italy*
Aurora; *1613–1614; Casino Rospigliosi, Rome, Italy*

Renoir Pierre Auguste

Born Limoges, France 1841; died Cagnes, France 1919

Les Parapluies *1881–1886;*
oil on canvas; 180.3 x 14.9 cm;
National Gallery, London, England

Renoir is often criticized and dismissed as a "chocolate-box" painter of frivolous themes, using the techniques of the Impressionists to depict the light-hearted scenes of contemporary life. However, his importance lies in his skilful, innovatory use of a rainbow palette, which discounted the inclusion of black, to interpret his subjects. This he does with a fresh, sincere feeling for beauty, light and sparkling colours, often portrayed under the effects of dappled sunlight. At the age of thirteen Renoir was a porcelain painter, an occupation which, no doubt, influenced the decorative, charming qualities of his canvases. These underwent considerable stylistic change during his life-time. By 1870 he was a leading member of the Impressionists, unusually focusing on figure compositions. The gaiety of crowds at social gatherings was his forte. **Les Parapluies** took a number of years to realize, comprising a range of handling and fashions dating from slightly different periods. The movement set by the rhythm of the umbrellas is grounded by the little girl's gaze meeting ours. The composition is further balanced by the rather pensive young woman with the band-box.

OTHER MASTERPIECES At the Moulin De La Galette; *1876; John Hay Whitney Collection, New York, USA* The Bathers; *c.1918; Musée du Louvre, Paris, France*

Reynolds Sir Joshua

Born Plympton, England 1732; died London, England 1792

Nelly O'Brien
c.1762—64; oil on canvas;
126.3 x 110 cm; Wallace
Collection, London, England

Joshua Reynolds was
the first president of the
Royal Academy,
founded in 1768. His
greatness resides less in
his abilities as a painter
than in the subsequent
impact of his artistic
ideology – via his
famous *Discourses* – and
in his success in raising the status of the artist. Reynolds was brought up in an atmosphere of
learning, establishing himself as a portraitist in Devon after a period of training in London.
From 1750–2 his studies in Italy of great Renaissance masters set the tone for his future artistic
practice and theoretical concerns. His aim was to express the rational ideal as the basis of
aesthetic judgement, rather than perpetuate the Romantic movement in painting. The classical
dignity that permeated his portraits complements the Grand Manner doctrine, which became
his war cry of "reason and philosophy". His academic considerations pronounced the supremacy
of noble and sublime interpretation as opposed to the depiction of the natural and the
particular – as Hogarth had done. **Nelly O'Brien** is a generous painting, full of character and
sensitivity. Such portraits of women and of children show Reynolds at his most responsive.

OTHER MASTERPIECES Portrait of Miss Bowles with her Dog; *1775; Wallace Collection,*
London, England **Captain Robert Orme**; *1756; National Gallery, London, England*

Richier Germaine

Born Grans, France 1904; died Montpelier, France 1959

Water *1953–1954; sculpture on bronze; 144.1 x 62.3 cm; Tate Collection, London, England*

Germaine Richier was primarily a sculptor, although she also made engravings, book illustrations and ceramics. From 1925–1929, Richier trained as a carver under Bourdelle in Paris. Briefly influenced by Surrealism, she began to make bronze figurative sculptures that, with their spindly limbs, were not entirely dissimilar to those by Giacometti, also a pupil of Bourdelle. However, Richier developed an increasingly idiosyncratic style, using sculpture to represent ambivalent, amorphous, asexual beings whose bodies at once suggested human, animal, plant and insect life. Through battered and lacerated surfaces, Richier suggested a morbid concern with decay and decomposition. In **Water** she has created a metaphor to express her deep fears and anxieties. The human figure alone seems incapable of containing her charged emotions – a woman depicted as a water carrier becomes a vessel of both emptiness and retention. Richier's feeling for sculpture as an emotional site, as well as her emphasis on the space between and around the solid forms, have contributed significantly to a reputation that has grown steadily since the Second World War.

OTHER MASTERPIECES The Ant; *1953; Private Collection, Scotland* **The Bullfight**; *1953; Peggy Guggenheim Collection, Venice, Italy*

Richter Gerhard

Born Dresden, Germany 1932

Abstraktes Bild
*1990; oil on canvas;
250 x 350 cm; Private
Collection*

Gerhard Richter
first worked as a
painter of stage sets
and then as an
advertising designer,
among other jobs.
He studied as a
painter in Dresden
and Dusseldorf until
the early 1960s,
when his paintings
were mainly
figurative. In 1962,
he produced a series of blurred, indistinct paintings based on photographic images from
newspapers and magazines. Always concerned with the narrow distinction between
photography and painting, Richter's work constantly operates on the borderline – whether
between abstraction and figuration or between colour and monochrome. Tending to produce
work in a series, Richter's oeuvre includes minimalist abstractions of great emotional weight,
such as **Colour Streaks**, 1968, and aerial photographs of cities transformed by expressionistic
brushstrokes into abstract paintings such as the **Townscape** series, 1968–1973. Since the late
1970s, he has produced a number of huge canvases such as **Abstraktes Bild** that, through their
virtuoso technique and distanced subject matter, explore the role of the artist. A versatile and
surprising painter, Richter's consistent ability to reinvent the medium poses important questions
about the nature and value of painting in our time.

OTHER MASTERPIECES Stag, *1963; Staatliche Museum Preussischer Kulturbesitz, Nationalgalerie,
Berlin, Germany* **Lesende (Reader)**; *1994; San Francisco Museum of Modern Art, USA*

319

Riley Bridget

Born London, England 1931

In Attendance *1994; oil on linen; 165.5 x 22.7 cm; Collection of the Artist*

Bridget Riley is the most important exponent of Op art in Britain. The term "Op art", short for "Optical art", came into use around 1965 following the exhibition "The Responsive Eye" in New York. It describes a type of abstract art that works directly on visual perception, producing an optical illusion that allows the work to vibrate. Riley studied at Goldsmiths' College of Art (1949–52) and the Royal College of Art (1952–5), where her contemporaries were Peter Blake and Joe Tilson. Influenced by the Futurists Boccioni and Balla, and the American colour-field painters, she began to develop her optical work in the early 1960s. Initially she worked in black and white, but started to use colour in 1966. Her contribution to the Museum of Modern Art's exhibition of Op art "The Responsive Eye" (one of her paintings was used on the catalogue cover) attracted international attention. Three years later, in 1968, she won the International Prize for Painting at the Venice Biennale. **In Attendance** is a dazzling piece that appears to pulsate. It uses repeated bands of singing colour that subtly vary in tone and measure to enhance the overall pattern.

OTHER MASTERPIECES Cataract 3; *1967; British Council, London, England*
Fission; *1963; Museum of Modern Art, New York City, USA*

Rivera Diego

Born Guanajuato, Mexico 1886; died Mexico City, Mexico 1957

Court of the
Inquisition
(detail)
*1929–1930;
fresco; Palacio
Nacional, Mexico
City, Mexico*

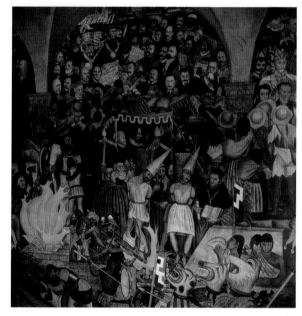

After studying art in Mexico and Madrid, Diego Rivera travelled to Europe and settled in Paris in 1911. Here he made contact with Picasso and contributed to Cubism, producing paintings inspired by Braque and Gris. He returned to his native country via Italy where he studied fresco paintings of the early Renaissance and ancient murals at Pompeii. In Mexico in 1921 he became an active participant in the revolutionary movement. As a member of an artist's commune, Rivera produced mural art for the walls of ministries, hospitals, colleges and schools. After the overthrow of the regime, in between bouts of falling out of favour with the left-wing – and his wife, artist Frida Khalo – Rivera continued to receive ministry commissions to celebrate the achievements of the revolution. The mural, **Court of the Inquisition**, represents the Madero revolution of 1910 and the Holy Inquisition trials, which made Mexican history between 1571 and 1820. Rivera rejected the advanced techniques he had assimilated in Europe to create simple forms and bold colours that contributed to the vitality of the national spirit, being popularly regarded as art for the people.

OTHER MASTERPIECES Workers of the Revolution; *1929; Palacio Nacional, Mexico City, Mexico* **Zapatista Landscape – The Guerrilla**; *1915; Museo Nacional de Arts (INBA), Mexico City, Mexico*

Rodin Auguste

Born Paris, France 1840; died Meudon, France 1917

Eternal Spring *1898;*
bronze sculpture; 4.64 cm;
Musée Rodin, Paris, France

Rodin studied under the Classicist master Horace Lecoq de Boisbaudran from 1854–1857. He then worked as an ornamental mason having failed to gain entry to the Ecole des Beaux-Arts. Drawing from sculpture in the basements of the Louvre confirmed his allegiance to the art which led to his becoming the most celebrated sculptor of the French Romantic School. He underwent a religious crisis in 1862, which caused him to work solely within a secular context. He encountered the work of Michelangelo on a visit to Italy in 1875, whose work, he claimed, freed him from academicism. His control of the effect of light and shade, his love of expressive movement and character and awareness of the bony structures beneath skin enabled Rodin to model figures of startling realism; pieces such as **Eternal Spring** caused a sensation. In addition to free-standing sculpture he completed numerous commissions of statues, portraits, gates and monuments and made designs for other works. His prolific graphic work was also extraordinary. By 1900 the reputation of his exemplary skill and craftsmanship was internationally established but still subject to controversy. He exerted a powerful and lasting influence on successive generations of sculptors.

OTHER MASTERPIECES The Kiss; *1886; Tate Collection, London, England*
The Hand of God; *c.1898; Musée Rodin, Paris, France*

Romney George

Born Dalton-le-Furness, England 1734; died Kendal, England 1802

Lady Isabella Hamilton *1777;*
oil on canvas; 213.4 x 137.2 cm;
Private Collection

After a brief apprenticeship to a cabinet-maker, George Romney trained as a painter in Kendal. His early education in the mixture of pigment was important to his established reputation as a colourist. He moved to London from the north of England in 1762. Romney's intention was to become a historical painter in the Grand Manner and he visited Italy between 1773 and 1775, where he became familiar with the work of Raphael, Titian and Correggio. On his return to England, he developed the style of portraiture for which he is best known. His success ranked him alongside Reynolds and Gainsborough, although Romney never enjoyed the distinction of being admitted to the Royal Academy. Around 1781, he became infatuated with Emma Hart, later Lady Hamilton, Admiral Nelson's mistress and went on to paint over fifty sensitive and delicate paintings of her. This painting, **Lady Isabella Hamilton** is one of his only full-length portraits. Romney's reputation rests on his portraits of fashionable society. His aspiration to paint grandiloquent historical and literary subjects was never realized. Illness and an ever decreasing number of commissions forced his return to Kendal in 1798, where he died four years later.

OTHER MASTERPIECES Mrs Mark Currie; *1789; Tate Collection, London, England*
Richard Cumberland; *c.1776; National Portrait Gallery, London, England*

Rosa Salvator

Born Naples, Italy 1615; died Rome, Italy 1673

Landscape with Mercury and the Dishonest Woodman *c.1649; oil on canvas; 125.7 x 202.1 cm; National Gallery, London, England*

Salvator Rosa was a larger-than-life character whose versatility led to a number of occupations, including those of poet, musician, actor, etcher and painter. He trained in Naples, where he produced small-scale battle scenes and landscapes of his native countryside. He worked for a while in Rome, as well as at the Medici court in Florence between 1640 and 1649. Rosa became best-known for his turbulent, dramatic and, at times, highly theatrical landscapes. **Landscape with Mercury and the Dishonest Woodman**, with its depiction of twisted tree stumps and a stormy sky, reveals Rosa's rejection of ideal beauty, an eighteenth-century pursuit, in favour of the picturesque. The sublime, savage beauty of this essentially Romantic landscape contrasts with the cool, harmonious Classicism exemplified by such contemporaries as Poussin and Claude. Rosa also became known for his depictions of the macabre and, in particular, of witchcraft. His successful etching career was launched in the 1660s. Horace Walpole unwittingly provided a memorable epitaph for Rosa when, in describing an Alpine journey in 1739, he wrote, "Precipices, mountains, torrents, wolves, rumblings – Salvator Rosa".

OTHER MASTERPIECES Self Portrait; *c.1645; National Gallery, London, England*
The Baptist in the Wilderness; *c.1650; Glasgow Art Gallery, Glasgow, Scotland*

Rosenquist James

Born Grand Forks, USA 1933

**Homage to Kiesler's
Endless House** *1962;
oil on canvas with
hardboard; 96 x 92 cm;
Private Collection*

James Rosenquist is a
leading American
Pop artist, taking as
his cue advertising
and consumerism on
a mass scale. After
winning a scholarship
to attend the
Minneapolis School
of Art, he studied at
the University of
Minnesota,
graduating in 1954.
Further training at
the Art Students League in New York brought him into contact with, among others, Jasper
Johns and Robert Rauschenberg. With like minds, these artists drew upon the culture of their
everyday lives. Rosenquist's work as a commercial artist, painting billboards and signs, informed
his art, particularly the large-scale landscape format that was a feature of the advertisement
hoardings that dominated Times Square in New York. Although essentially a formalist, in that
he constructed his pictures from "traditional" drawing and painting techniques, the dynamism of
his imagery, as seen in **Homage to Kiesler's Endless House** set him apart from easel painters.
Working from collages comprising a conglomeration of photographs, adverts and pictures,
Rosenquist enlarges and emphasizes details, significant words and images, approximating and
subverting the notion of the American Dream.

OTHER MASTERPIECES The Swimmer in the Econo-mist; *1998; Deutsche Guggenheim,
Berlin, Germany* **F-111;** *1965; Private Collection, New York City, USA*

Rossetti Dante Gabriel

Born London, England 1828; died Birchington-on-sea, England 1882

Beata Beatrix
*c. 1864—1870; oil on
canvas; 86.4 x 66 cm; Tate
Collection, London, England*

Dante Gabriel Rossetti
was the son of a Dante
scholar and the brother
of poet Christina
Rossetti. Prodigiously
talented as a poet and
painter, Rossetti received
tuition from John Sell
Cotman, before studying
under Holman Hunt
from 1848. In the same
year, Rossetti, with
Millais and Holman
Hunt, founded the Pre-
Raphaelite Brotherhood.
However, Rossetti's
essentially romantic imagination set him apart from the earnest and more literal endeavours of
the other two and their mutual association was short-lived. Between 1850 and 1860 he worked
mainly in watercolour, and pen and ink, choosing to depict medieval subjects. **Beata Beatrix** is
an idealized, spiritual and symbolic portrait of Rossetti's beautiful wife, Elizabeth Siddal. The
couple married in 1860 but she died tragically two years later of narcotic abuse. Rossetti's
haunting memorial to his dead wife is expressed through a parallel with the story of Dante and
Beatrice. His later paintings on Arthurian and Dantesque themes used Jane Morris, wife of
William Morris, as his model. With their pale, intense faces and luxurious hair, both Elizabeth
and Jane represented, for Rossetti, an ideal of feminine beauty that came to define the notion of
an archetypal Pre-Raphaelite woman.

OTHER MASTERPIECES Girlhood of Mary Virgin; *1849; Tate Collection, London, England*
Found; *1853; Birmingham Museums and Art Gallery, Birmingham, England*

Rothenberg Susan

Born Buffalo, USA 1945

Vertical Spin
1986–1987;
oil on canvas;
360.7 x 285.7 cm;
Tate Collection, London,
England

Susan Rothenberg's
paintings and prints
occupy the space
between abstraction
and figuration. In
the 1970s, she
became known for
her mostly
monochrome series
of horses. Through
flattened forms and simplified outlines, she revealed an interest in the mythic power of the
equine form. In the 1980s, her archetypal images of horses gave way to various representations
of the human figure. However, the introduction of the body, or its fragmented parts, was again
symbolic, rather than specific or personal. There is an open-ended, unconscious element to
much of Rothenberg's work, which accords perfectly with her own statement that, "most of my
work is not run through a rational part of my brain". **Vertical Spin** is from a series of twelve
paintings Rothenberg made over a period of two and a half years. It features the upward flight
of a dancer and attempts to pinpoint the actual positions of the body in time and space. In
reference to this painting, the artist acknowledged the difficulties of depicting movement. Her
later paintings, with their loose, painterly marks, reveal a Neo-Expressionist influence.

OTHER MASTERPIECES Butterfly, *1976; National Gallery of Art, Washington D.C., USA*
Beggar, *1982; Willard Gallery, New York, USA*

Rothko Mark

Born Dvinsk, Russia 1903; died New York City, USA 1970

Red on Maroon
1959; oil on canvas
266.5 x 239 cm;
Tate Collection,
London, England

Mark Rothko
went to the USA
from Russia when
he was ten years
old. During the
1950s and 1960s
he became one
of the leading
figures of
Abstract
Expressionism. Principally self-taught, he was initially inspired by Expressionism and Surrealism.
His mature work dates from 1948. A characteristic Rothko painting features a series of mainly
rectangular shapes built up from the successive applications of washes. The edges of the shapes
are deliberately blurred, which gives the image a gentle, oscillatory quality. He utilized a
restricted palette, focusing on colours close together in the range, such as brown and red, or
grey and blue. **Red on Maroon** is one of nine canvases that currently occupy a designated
space within the Tate. Originally designed for the Seagram Building's restaurant in New York,
Rothko presented the series to the Tate shortly before his death. The simplified shapes, like
dark clouds, are suspended in shallow space, providing the viewer with a focus for meditation as
well as a screen on to which to project experience. The sombre colour was believed to be a
reflection of his depressed state of mind. He committed suicide in 1970.

OTHER MASTERPIECES Red, White and Brown; *1957; Kunstmuseum, Basel, Switzerland*
Orange, Yellow Orange; *1969; Malborough-Gerson Gallery, New York City, USA*

Roualt Georges

Born Paris, France 1871; died Paris, France 1958

**Bust of a Woman
Wearing a Necklace**
*1930; gouache on paper;
28.5 x 22 cm; Private
Collection*

Georges Roualt
trained in a stained-
glass workshop, where
he developed a feeling
for strong colours and
bold outlines. In 1892,
he studied under
Gustave Moreau at
the Ecole des Beaux-
Arts where he met
Matisse. This led to a
brief association with
the Fauves, but
Roualt's dark, sombre
art was very different
from the colours and
decorative paintings
produced by the circle
of artists around

Matisse. Initially an ardent Catholic, Roualt experienced a crisis of artistic and religious
confidence in 1902. Surveying the world around him, he looked to people existing on the
margins of society, such as clowns and prostitutes, to express his Old Testament vision of a
world fallen from grace. His harsh, violent style, with its dark outlines and distorted forms,
revealed an admiration for Goya. The expressionistic **Bust of a Woman Wearing a Necklace** is
a typical Roualt portrait, the black outlines helping to give structure to the woman's head and
shoulders. Dramatic intensity is given to the composition through the touches of red on the
lips, in the hair and around the throat. From 1940, Roualt painted exclusively religious themes.
His prodigious output included book illustrations, ceramics, tapestry and stage-set designs.

OTHER MASTERPIECES Circus Performer; *1905–1906; Musée de Grenoble, France*
The Three Judges; *1913; Tate Collection, London, England*

Rousseau Henri (Le Douanier)

Born Laval, France 1844; died Paris, France 1910

The Snake Charmer

1907; oil on canvas; 169 x 189.5 cm; Musée National d'Art Moderne, Paris, France

Henri Rousseau gained his nickname "Le Douanier" because he began to paint while working for the Paris customs office. He retired from the service in 1885 and devoted his life to his art, producing naive and direct paintings of great sophistication. Although untrained, Rousseau had great faith in his own abilities. From 1886, he exhibited almost every year at the Salon des Indépendants, a place where artists could show their work without being subjected to a selection procedure. Picasso was particularly impressed by his talent, holding a banquet in his honour in 1908. Rousseau's paintings use flat, clear colours, which he sharply defined with a simplified outline. He is best known for his jungle scenes, which he claimed were the product of a trip to Mexico, but were more likely derived from studying animal and plant life at the zoo and the botanical gardens in Paris. **The Snake Charmer** is a late and accomplished work that, through its exotic mystery, reveals a more conscious side to his primitive art. The furtive atmosphere is created through the presence of the unlikely inhabitant and the haunting stillness of the darkened mass of vegetation.

OTHER MASTERPIECES Surprised! (Tropical Storm with a Tiger); *1891; National Gallery, London, England* The Sleeping Gipsy; *1897; Museum of Modern Art, New York City, USA*

Rubens Sir Peter Paul

Born Siegen, Germany 1577; died Antwerp, Belgium 1640

**Samson and
Delilah** *c.1609;
oil on wood;
185 x 205 cm;
National Gallery,
London, England*

Although Rubens studied art under mediocre masters he had sound knowledge of Latin, the classics and major European languages. His letters reveal him to have been an antiquarian, businessman and diplomat; as the latter his artistic career gained a momentum which established him as one of the greatest painters of his age. He entered the Antwerp Guild of St Luke in 1598 and went to Italy in 1600. His work as Court Painter put him in a privileged position to admire Titian's and Raphael's paintings in royal collections. While in Italy his studies of the Antique and of the High Renaissance inspired his own work on his return to Flanders in 1608. **Samson and Delilah** reveals these sources in the observation of contrast between youth and age, between Delilah's pale and soft body and Samson's dark and muscular back. The impression made upon him by Caravaggio is evident in the dramatic lighting effects and theatrical staging within the composition. It is a more powerful and poignant image than his familiar, fleshy Bacchanalian paintings. Rubens continued to charm various European monarchs, collecting major commissions until his death. His achievements mark a high point in Baroque painting.

OTHER MASTERPIECES Life of Maria de Medici; *1622; Musée du Louvre, Paris, France*
An Autumn Landscape with a View of Het Steen; *c.1636; National Gallery, London, England*

Ruisdael Jacob van

Born Haarlem, Netherlands 1628; died Amsterdam, Netherlands 1682

An Extensive Landscape with a Ruined Castle and a Church c.1665–1670; oil on canvas; 109 x 146 cm; National Gallery, London, England

Regarded as the greatest of all Dutch landscape painters, Jacob van Ruisdael is believed to have been taught by his father and by his uncle Salomon van Ruisdael. He became known in the late 1640s for his panoramic views of the flat fields of his native countryside. However, in the course of a prolific career, he chose to paint a wide range of landscapes, including beaches, seascapes, forests, hills and rivers. He travelled to Germany in the early 1650s, where he was inspired to depict the more rugged terrain. By 1657, he had settled in Amsterdam, where he lived for the rest of his life. **Landscape with a Ruined Castle and a Church** probably depicts a view in an area to the east of Amsterdam. Ruisdael is less concerned with topographical accuracy than with depicting the subtle atmospheric effects. The sky dominates this painting and, through his mastery of perspective, the blustery clouds seem to sweep over our heads. He exercised a major influence both on his Dutch contemporaries and later English landscape artists such as Gainsborough and Constable.

OTHER MASTERPIECES The Jewish Cemetery; c.1660; Detroit Institute of Arts, Detroit, USA **A Waterfall**; late 1660s; Dulwich Picture Gallery, London, England

Ryman Robert

Born Nashville, USA 1930

Ledger *1982;*
enamel, acrylic and
metal; 76.2 x
71.1 mm;
Tate Collection,
London, England

Robert Ryman is credited with having bridged the gap between Abstract Expressionism and Minimalism. A leading figure in American abstract painting, with his "white" canvases he has pushed out the boundaries of picture-making by focusing on light, material and surface as his subjects. He reduces the painting's content to a specific enquiry, in which the medium and the meaning of painting itself become the act of intellectual and physical creativity. He studied at Tennessee Polytechnic from 1948–1949 and at the George Peabody College for Teachers, in Nashville, until 1950. In 1952 he moved to New York City, making a living as a gallery attendant at the Museum of Modern Art. The process of painting has been, from the start of his career, a central concern. Ryman's exploration of the variety of visual effects made possible by combining different materials is seemingly inexhaustible. The numerous ways in which he applies his concoctions and displays them continues to be a preoccupation. The square format, shown in **Ledger**, painted in pigmented shellac (or enamelac), became fixed in the late 1950s and the whiteness dominated by the mid-1960s. According to Ryman, "White enables other things to become visible".

OTHER MASTERPIECES Delta III; *1966; Hallen für Neue Kunst, Schaffhausen, Germany*
Surface Veil III; *1971; Solomon R. Guggenheim Museum, New York City, USA*

Sargent John Singer

Born Florence, Italy 1856; died London, England 1925

Luxembourg Gardens at Twilight *1879; oil on canvas; 64.7 x 91.4 cm; Philadelphia Museum of Art, Philadelphia, USA*

John Singer Sargent was born in Italy to American parents, studied in Paris and eventually settled in England. His cosmopolitan background encouraged an urbane style most commonly revealed in his numerous portraits of fashionable society. In 1880, he visited Spain where Hals and Velasquez were important to the development of his considerable technical facility. He studied in Paris for ten years, leaving in 1884 after his Salon portrait of **Madame Gautreau** was criticized for its sexually provocative nature. The following year, Sargent founded the new English Art Club in London. **Luxembourg Gardens at Twilight**, with its soft, atmospheric haze, is an example of a style of painting in which Sargent emulated the light effects of the French Impressionists. While admired for its technical mastery, his work is often seen only as superficially impressive. However, aside from his portraits, he painted some remarkable watercolour landscapes, as well as murals for public buildings in Boston and, in 1918, a huge, tragic painting entitled **Gassed** as part of his role as an official war artist.

OTHER MASTERPIECES Ena and Betty, Daughters of Asher and Mrs Wertheimer; *1901, Tate Collection, London, England* Gassed; *1918; Imperial War Museum, London, England*

Schiele Egon

Born Vienna, Austria 1890; died Vienna, Austria 1918

The Embrace *1917; oil on canvas; 100 x 170.2 cm; Osterreichsches Galerie, Vienna, Austria*

Egon Schiele was a chief exponent of the ideology of the Vienna Secession which took hold c.1908. Founded in 1897 by Gustave Klimt, this avant-garde artists' organization and exhibiting society introduced Modernism into Austrian art. It focused on using traditional painting subjects as vehicles for the expression of mood and emotion. Schiele applied this and the influence of Freudian psychology to his portraits. His complex personality, imbued with sexual anxiety and fear of death, informs often explicit images of young women and of himself. Haunted eyes and emaciated limbs and torsos of semi-clad or naked figures are rendered in memorable watercolour drawings. Schiele treated the medium unconventionally. Natural colour is dramatized, pigments bleed together and are mottled, barely contained by expressive outlines. Sexual tension is ever-present as is the suggestion of abuse, self-inflicted or otherwise. In **The Embrace**, the lovers appear loveless and lifeless, bound up in resignation to mortality. Schiele married in 1915 and his painting seemed to respond to this stability by becoming brighter and more sensuous. It is tantalizing to speculate how his work would have developed had he survived the influenza epidemic of 1918.

OTHER MASTERPIECES **Nude Self-Portait**; *1910; Graphische Sammlung Albertina, Vienna, Austria* **Reclining Woman**; *1917; Private Collection*

Schmidt-Rotluff Karl

Rottluff, Germany 1884; died Berlin, Germany 1976

Lofthus
1911; oil
on canvas;
87.2 x
95.8 cm;
Kunsthalle,
Hamburg,
Germany

Karl Schmidt-Rottluff studied architecture in Dresden, where he met painters Heckel and Kirchner. With these two artists he founded Die Brücke (the Bridge) group in 1905. They were joined later by Nolde and Pechstein, and shared a common studio but failed to produce a clear declaration of intent. Committed to nature as the main source of inspiration, their paintings were distinguished by a simplification of form and colour, revealing an admiration for Cézanne, Gauguin, van Gogh, Munch and African art. Schmidt-Rottluff stayed with the group until it dissolved in 1913. Uninhabited landscapes were his most common theme, although his work includes figure pictures, portraits and still life. **Loftus** reveals his Expressionistic style, using flat planes of contrasting, raw colour. In 1906, he stayed with Nolde on the island of Alstein in Norway in order to experience the inhospitable and forbidding side of nature. He moved to Berlin in 1911, where he was influenced by African sculpture, producing several carvings and woodcuts. Declared degenerate by the Nazis in 1941, he was barred from painting until 1945.

OTHER MASTERPIECES Portrait of Rosa Schapire; *1911; Brücke Museum, Berlin, Germany*
Bursting Dam; *1910; Brücke Museum, Berlin, Germany*

Schnabel Julian

Born 1951; New York City, USA

Humanity Asleep *1982; collage on wood; 274 x 366 x 28 cm; Tate Collection, London, England*

Julian Schnabel trained at the University of Texas between 1969 to 1972 and started exhibiting in 1976. He is best known for working on a monumental scale, with an inventive, bravura approach to painting and skill for self-promotion and marketing. A celebrity on the New York gallery scene in the late 1980s, his work is appropriately theatrical. In a bid to challenge previous limits set on painting he redefined the term Action Painting, stretching it to incorporate an essentially physical approach to creating an image. He moved away from gesture to concentrate on surface, treating the thick support of the painting without reverence. In 1979 he began plastering broken crockery over tactile paint, making the surface appear fragmented and restless. These works, such as **Humanity Asleep**, are literally volatile, and are already causes for concern to the conservators of collections where they are held. As a complement to these he also made large-scale paintings on velvet. Schanbel created monolithic, isolated imagery bearing disparate references to Classicism, mythology and history, in addition to association with love, romance and optimism. Ultimately, his work exudes his love for the act of painting itself.

OTHER MASTERPIECES Owl; *1980; Museum of Contemporary Art, Los Angeles, USA*
Self Portrait in Andy's Shadow; *1987; Broad Art Foundation, Santa Monica, USA*

Schwitters Kurt

Born Hanover, Germany 1887; died Ambleside, England 1948

Chocolate *1947;*
collage and oil on
canvas; 44 x 39 cm;
Private Collection

Kurt Schwitters
worked as an artist,
writer, architect,
typographer and
publisher. These
various interest were
reflected in a multi-
media approach to
his art. His early
interest in Cubism
was quickly
superseded by an
association with the
leading Dadaists Hausmann, Hoch and Arp. In 1918, Schwitters was one of the founders of the
Dada group in Hanover. As part of a Dadaist anti-art statement, he made collages and montages
out of a combination of unrelated discarded elements, objects and materials. His aim was to
disrupt the acceptance of bourgeois values while producing a new construction from the
disparate, disordered fragments. His random assortments utilized bits of torn-up paper, bus
tickets, chicken wire and even the wheels of a pram. **Chocolate** makes use of a chocolate
wrapping and the postmark torn from a letter. Schwitters referred to his assemblages as "Merz".
This was also the title of a Dadaist magazine he ran from 1923 to 1932. Around 1920, he
started to build his first "Merzbau", a huge construction of refuse designed to fill a whole
building. Exile in Norway was followed in 1940 by flight to England after the German invasion.

OTHER MASTERPIECES Spring Picture; *1920; Kunstmuseum, Basel, Switzerland*
Le Point Sur Le I; *1939; Musée Nationale d'Art Moderne, Paris, France*

Scully Sean

Born Dublin, Ireland 1945

Paul *1984; relief and oil on canvas; 259 x 320 cm; Tate Collection, London, England*

Sean Scully grew up in London, attended Croydon College of Art from 1965–1968 and then Newcastle University until 1972. He studied at Harvard University from 1972–1973, moving to America in 1975. His work charts a complex mix of British and American influences. On the one hand his art is related to the cool, Conceptual and Minimal experiments of the 1970s, combined with the achievements of British artists such as Noel Forster and Joe Tilson. On the other hand, it carries romantic, symbolic essences of the American Abstract Expressionists, particularly Barnett Newman and Mark Rothko. In spite of **Paul** having the hallmarks of the minimal approach, the tangibility of the painting's relief construction would suggest that modernist, traditional forces are at work. The triptych format, one Scully uses often, is evocative of devotional art from the beginnings of art history. However, the slightly awkward joining of the three canvases brings our attention back to the material reality of the piece. **Paul**, dedicated to the artist's son who died in 1983, is an economically conceived, grounded composition, painted with gestural marks. It complies with Scully's view of abstraction that "It's the spiritual art of our time".

OTHER MASTERPIECES The Fall; *1983; Tate Collection, London, England*
White Window; *1988; Tate Collection, London, England*

Serra Richard

Born San Francisco, USA 1939

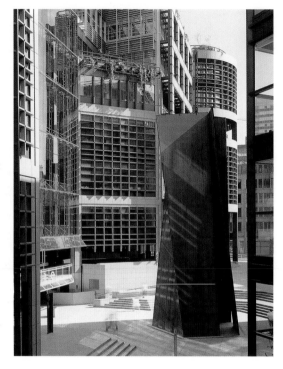

Fulcrum *1987; steel,
18 metres high; Broadgate
Complex, London, England*

Richard Serra trained at
the Universities of
California, Berkley,
Santa Monica and Yale,
paid for by funds made
while he was working
in steel factories. He
spent 1965–1966 in
Europe, producing an
exhibition in Rome.
The abstract sculpture
he was making was
fashioned from unlikely
materials – rubber and
neon tubing. He then
made the transition to
molten lead as the substance of his "process art". In 1969, lead was also the basis for Serra's **One
Ton Prop (House of Cards)**. This is the earliest piece that is recognizable as quintessentially
his. The four plates balance precariously against one another, held in place by the force of
gravity. By 1970, Serra was employing steel as his material to create so-called "anti-
environments". His sculptural pieces of "engineering" have since grown in scale and these, such
as **Fulcrum**, the sculpture at Broadgate, London, have found their metier in public spaces. The
siting and contextual specificity of Serra's monstrous and yet graceful work has been a major
preoccupation. However, his sited pieces, intended to be "a field force" by which "space is
discerned physically", have been controversial, due to popular scepticism about their safety
because of their lack of conventional construction.

OTHER MASTERPIECES Belts; *1966–1967; Solomon R. Guggenheim Museum, New York City,
USA* **Torqued Ellipse IV;** *1998; Museum of Modern Art, New York City, USA*

Seurat Georges

Born Paris, France 1859; died Paris, France 1891

Bathers at Asnières *1884; oil on canvas; 201 c 300 cm; National Gallery, London, England*

Georges Seurat studied at the Ecole des Beaux-Arts where he was a disciplined and academic student. A master draughtsman, he studied Ingres's drawings and familiarized himself with Chevreul's book on colour. Dedicated to the pursuit of order in painting, he evolved his own colour theory known as Divisionism. This involved applying a multitude of tiny dots of pure colour directly on to the canvas, to be mixed by the eye rather than on the palette. It was a method that also became known as Pointillism. In his first major work, **Bathers at Ansières**, there was initially little evidence of his new technique. However, Seurat reworked parts of it three years later, modifying details such as the bather's orange hat and areas of water. The painting is the result of careful planning – he made over twenty preparatory studies in pastel and in oil. His observation of ordinary people relaxing was considered subversive in its day and the canvas was rejected by the Salon. Unlike the Impressionists, who aimed to capture the flickering movement of light, Seurat aimed for a static, almost frozen quality, which has prompted comparisons with great masters such as Poussin and Piero della Francesca.

OTHER MASTERPIECES Sunday Afternoon on the Island of Grande Jatte; *1884–1886; Art Institute of Chicago, USA* The Can-Can; *1889–1890; Rijksmuseum Kröller-Müller, Otterlo, Netherlands*

Sherman Cindy

Born Glen Ridge, USA 1954

Untitled 22 *1983; colour photograph; 221 x 147 cm; Saatchi Collection, London, England*

Cindy Sherman graduated from the State University College at Buffalo, New York State in 1976. She moved to New York City in 1977. Sherman's significance lies in her capacity to reinvent herself as both subject, object and artist. As a photographer, she has elevated the photographic medium to fine art status. Her black and white **Untitled Film Stills** from the late 1970s are the works that established her reputation and with which she is most commonly associated. These are generic movie stills, of a recognizable style – Hitchcock or Scorcese – scrupulously detailed but not identifiable as a film with a particular title. Each is a carefully reconstructed scene with herself as actor, director and cameraman. Subsequent series of works develop this theme of fantasy and disguise with the camera as voyeur. Sherman's technical skills are flawless, making the unrealities she constructs completely believable. **Untitled 22** comes from the fashion series of 1983–1984 and still retains the spirit of cinematic heroism from early work. Since the late 1980s, Sherman has also used food, vomit, prostheses and other materials to create evocative fairytale, disaster, horror and sex pictures in which neither she nor other humans feature.

OTHER MASTERPIECES Untitled Film Still 4; *1980; Metro Pictures, New York City, USA*
Untitled 25 *1990; Metro Pictures, New York City, USA*

Sickert Walter Richard

Born Munich, Germany 1860; died Bath, England 1942

**Minnie Cunningham
at the Old Bedford**
c.1889; oil on canvas;
75.5 x 63.8 cm;
Tate Collection,
London, England

In 1868 Walter Sickert's family moved permanently to London. After a brief career as an actor, Sickert studied at the Slade School of Art from 1881–1882. He was a pupil and studio assistant of Whistler, whose limited tonal range later influenced Sickert's palette. In 1883 he met Degas in Paris. This lifelong friendship reinforced his earlier interest in the theatre and it became a staple theme of his work. Sickert joined and exhibited with the New English Art Club in 1888. Between 1895 and 1905 he divided his time between working in Dieppe and Venice. Back in London, he linked the artistic activities in London and developments in France, proving influential to the Camden Town Group and The London Group. The strength of his views and his importance as a teacher were considerable and sustained. His scenes of intimacy within domestic interiors were often misinterpreted as sordid and the low-key, naturalistic colours in dim light seen as dull. In tonal contrast his painting, **Minnie Cunningham at the Old Bedford** is typical of numerous works that focused on stars of the music hall. In late works his touch and palette became lighter and his composition more reliant on photographs.

OTHER MASTERPIECES La Hollandaise Nude; c.1906; Tate Collection, London, England
Ennui; c.1914; Tate Collection, London, England

Sisley Alfred

Born Paris, France 1839; died Moret-sur-Loing, France 1899

The Bark During the Flood at Port-Marly *1876; oil on canvas; 50.5 x 61 cm; Musée d'Orsay, Paris, France*

Alfred Sisley was born in Paris to English parents. His early work showed the influence of Corot in its feeling for tonal values expressed through a sober palette of browns, greys and greens. From 1862, he studied under Gleyre in whose studio he met Monet and Renoir and painted with them near Fontainebleau. Under their influence, his palette lightened and his brushstrokes became freer. He showed with the Impressionists from 1874 and is regarded by many as the most consistent member of the group. He was almost exclusively a landscape painter, his best work displaying a subtle evocation of atmosphere. He visited Britain several times between 1871 and 1897, where he painted at Hampton Court, in the London suburbs and in Wales. **The Bark During the Flood at Port-Marly** is one of three pictures on the same subject that Sisley painted in 1876. These are now regarded as his masterpieces. Revealing a typical Impressionistic awareness of light, Sisley is concerned with capturing transient reflections in the limpid water. After his father's death, Sisley spent much of his life in poverty. He never quite achieved the success or renown of many of his Impressionist colleagues.

OTHER MASTERPIECES Wooden Bridge at Argenteuil; *1872; Musée du Louvre, Paris, France*
Snow at Veneux-Nadon; *1879–1882; Musée du Louvre, Paris, France*

Soulages Pierre

Born Aveyron, France 1919

Painting 23 May 1953 *1953;*
oil on canvas; 194.9 x 130.2 cm;
Tate Collection, London, England

Pierre Soulages was mainly
self-taught. His diverse,
seminal influences included
prehistoric and medieval art,
Romanticism and van Gogh.
His mature style developed
on his return to Paris after
military service in the Second
World War. His innovatory,
abstract work established him
as one of the leading
members of the post-war
School of Paris. Soulages
worked in the direction of
what has become known as
"physic improvisation". His
expressive, intense and
dynamic paintings are
disciplined through the intersection of dark, heavy bars or bands. On to this monumental
scaffolding Soulages applies contrasting strokes from an unchanging, almost monochromatic,
palette of black, grey, ochre and white. As a result, his sculptural paintings, such as **Painting 23
May 1953**, have a depth and illumination that is enhanced by the freedom and vitality of his
brushstrokes. He was one of a number of European painters whose work was defined in 1952
by the term Art Informal. This was as an acknowledgement of the movement toward
spontaneous abstract painting that took place in the 1940s and 1950s. Soulages also worked as
a theatrical designer. In 1959, he travelled to Japan. He continues to live and work in Paris.

OTHER MASTERPIECES Painting; *1953; Guggenheim Museum, New York City, USA*
Painting; *1956; Museum of Modern Art, New York City, USA*

Soutine Chaim

Born Smilovitch, Lithuania 1893; died Paris, France 1943

Flayed Ox *1926; oil on canvas;*
72.5 x 50 cm; Kunstmuseum,
Bern, Switzerland

Chaim Soutine came to Paris
in 1913 after studying at
Vilno. Alongside other
expatriate painters, Chagall
and Modigliani, who became
his friend, he injected a
different mood into the art of
the School of Paris. Soutine's
Expressionist work is akin to
the bravura of the Fauves, led
by Matisse and the German
Expressionism of Nolde.
However, he admired the
old, rather than the modern,
masters. More emotional
than intellectual, Soutine's art
was a passionate expression
of his sincere response to life
as he saw it. Intense and gruesome, fervently wrought through lurid colour and wild, convulsive
brushmarks of impasto, **Flayed Ox** is typical of Soutine's painting. It was inspired by
Rembrandt's treatment of the same subject, worked from life. The artist was somewhat of a
recluse, whose driving passion was the act of creativity. Contemporary accounts of him describe
his uncleanliness and lack of discipline. The dead birds and fleshy carcasses he loved to recreate
in oils often rotted in his studio, much to his neighbour's distress. Although he was reluctant to
promote and exhibit his work, the support of his patrons secured the reputation of his art,
which proved influential during the 1930s, particularly in America.

OTHER MASTERPIECES Pageboy at Maxim's; *1927; Albright-Knox Art Gallery, Buffalo, New
York State, USA* **Portrait of Modigliani;** *1917; National Gallery, Washington DC, USA*

Spencer Sir Stanley

Born Cookham, England 1891; died Cookham, England 1959

The Resurrection, Cookham *1923–1927; oil on canvas; 274.3 x 548.6 cm; Tate Collection, London, England*

Although Stanley Spencer trained at the Slade School of Art in London, from 1909–1912, his art reveals him to be an individual spirit, untouched by avant-garde developments of the time. If he looked to the art of the past it was, perhaps, to the Pre-Raphaelite Brotherhood. Not only did he share a stylistic affinity, but the religious concerns of the Brotherhood are reflected in Spencer's idiosyncratic painting. He spent his life in Cookham, devoting his art to describing the village and his personal experiences of the characters who populated it. His paintings translated sacred incidents and biblical stories into happenings within his local environment. The Resurrection, Cookham is a good example of his artistic inclinations and a monumental work. Characteristically, it was painted piecemeal over a complete drawing. Spencer himself is depicted several times, as is his first wife, Hilda Carline. His relationship with her lingered long after he entered into a second marriage with Patricia Preece; Spencer's communications even continued beyond Hilda's death via love letters. His controversial personal life and his experiences of the war fuelled passionate, memorable pictures that are heightened by distortion.

OTHER MASTERPIECES Double Nude Portrait: The Artist and his Second Wife; *1936; Tate Collection, London, England* Decorative Murals; *1926–1934; War Memorial Chapel, Burghclere, Hampshire, England*

Spero Nancy

Born Cleveland, USA 1926

Codex Artaud
*1970; painting and
collage on paper; 61 x
48 cm; Galerie Rudolf
Zwirner, Cologne,
Germany*

Nancy Spero
trained at the Art
Institute of
Chicago before
attending the Ecole
des Beaux-Arts in
Paris from
1949–50. After
living in the USA,
Greece and Italy
she moved to Paris,
France in 1959,
where she had her
first solo exhibition
in 1962. Spero
returned to the

Cette chair qui ne se
touche plus dans la
vie
Artaud

USA in 1964. Actively opposed to the Vietnam War, her work began increasingly to document
her social and political concerns. From 1969 to 1972 she worked on the **Codex Artaud** series, a
cycle of thirty-four drawings on paper scrolls. The preoccupation of this and other key works is
the abuse and torture of women in domestic life as well as in the wider political sphere, such as
in work and war. Spero uses cut-and-pasted scraps of paper, fragments of typewritten script and
disembodied parts of the female figure to reference women throughout history. Her obsessive
documentary style leaves space for viewers to draw their own conclusions. In 1971 she helped
to found AIR, the first co-operative gallery for women in New York. In 1978, Spero introduced
a stamping technique into her drawings and she has made extensive use of this in her work
since then. She lives and works in New York.

OTHER MASTERPIECES The Torture of Women*, 1976; Josh Baer Gallery, New York City,
USA* **Marlene, Lilith, Sky, Goddess***; 1989; Anthony Reynolds Gallery, London, England*

Staël Nicholas de

Born St Petersburg, Russia 1914; died Antibes, France 1955

Rectangles, Jaunes et Verts *1951; oil on canvas; 30 x 97 cm; Fukuoka Museum, Japan*

Nicholas de Staël studied in Brussels, from where he travelled to Italy, Holland, Spain and North Africa. He went to Paris in 1932 from where he joined the Foreign Legion at the outbreak of war. Resettled in Paris in 1943, de Staël renewed contact with Braque and studied under Léger. By the end of the decade, he had established himself as a leading abstract painter. Although his works were considered non-representational they had a tangible sense of form, indicative of their closeness to the natural world. Through the introduction of simplified images from nature – such as the sun and the sea – he attained a near-perfect balance between abstraction and figuration. De Staël's dense and richly worked surfaces were built up through layers of paint: sensuous, impasto canvases revealed his enjoyment of the act of painting itself. **Rectangles, Jaunes et Verts** is constructed with simple blocks of colour on a monochrome ground. Unexpectedly, spatial qualities and an atmospheric depth emerge through the abstract ensemble. De Staël's later paintings returned to a more recognizable form of presentation. He committed suicide at the age of 41.

OTHER MASTERPIECES The Roofs; *1952; Musée National d'Art Moderne, Paris, France* **Marathon;** *1948; Tate Collection, London, England*

Steen Jan

Born Leyden, Netherlands c.1625; died Leyden, Netherlands 1679

Skittle Players
c.1660—1663; oil on oakwood; 33.5 x 27 cm; National Gallery, London, England

Jan Steen worked in various Dutch towns including Leyden, The Hague, Delft and Haarlem. He painted humorous subjects drawn from the life of the peasant and middle classes, subjecting his biblical paintings to the same everyday treatment. Unsurprisingly, given that he leased a brewery in Delft and kept an inn in Leyden, he most represented tavern scenes. However, many of these provided him with the opportunity to depict a large, festive, social gathering rather than celebrate bucolic revelry. Indeed, he sometimes used these works to moralize, relying on humour to leaven his essentially serious message. Steen was the son-in-law of Jan van Goyen and painted a few landscapes in his style. He also painted some portraits and featured some delightful collections of still life within his larger genre paintings. **Skittle Players** does not appear to have any didactic purpose. It is a cheerful scene of people taking advantage of a sunny day to relax and enjoy themselves. The harmonious composition reveals Steen's remarkable skills as a colourist.

OTHER MASTERPIECES The Effects of Intemperance; *c.1663—1665; National Gallery, London, England* **The Morning Toilet**; *1663; Rijsmuseum, Amsterdam, Netherlands*

Steer Philip Wilson

Born Birkenhead, England 1860; died London, England 1942

Beach at Etaples *1887; oil on canvas; 36.8 x 54.6 cm; Private Collection*

Philip Wilson Steer studied at Gloucester School of Art in 1882, leaving for Paris later in the same year. Like his close friend, Sickert, he was an English artist who looked to the French for inspiration. In Paris he discovered Impressionism, in particular the works of Degas and Monet. He returned to England in 1884 and, with Sargent and Sickert, helped found the New English Art Club in 1886. In 1889, Steer was one of the members who exhibited separately under the title "The London Impressionist". **Beach at Etaples** is one of a number of beach scenes and seascapes that are generally regarded as his most accomplished work. This painting, with its poetic and melancholic atmosphere, helped Steer gain his reputation as the best of the English Impressionists. He taught at the Slade for thirty-one years. His later work was more conventional, revealing the influence of Constable and Gainsborough. He also made increasing use of watercolour, his lyrical style derived in part from Turner. Steer went blind in the last few years of his life.

OTHER MASTERPIECES Girls Running: Walberswick Pier; *1894; Tate Collection, London, England* **The Horseshoe Bend of the Severn;** *1909; City Art Gallery, Manchester, England*

Stella Frank

Born Malden, USA 1936

Agbatana II *1968, acrylic, 305 x 458 cm, Musée d'Art et d'Industre, St Etienne, France*

Frank Stella studied at the Phillips Academy in Andover from 1950–1954 and went on to Princeton University. He graduated in 1958 and settled in New York, working as a house painter. His artistic path led straight to abstraction, admiring as he did the work of European art, particularly that of the Bauhaus and specifically the "hard-edge" abstract painter, Josef Albers. His approach to the abstract image was initially systematic and largely monochromatic, influenced to an extent by the **Flags** and **Targets** series of Jasper Johns. Stella's **Striped** and then **Black Paintings**, first shown in 1959, were the antithesis of gestural Abstract Expressionism; they heralded the arrival of Minimalism. Although **Agbatana II** seems to follow this ordered pattern in a multicoloured way, it was in fact painted at a time when Stella was developing the decorative potential of abstraction. Aping the swirls and accidental marks of freehand painting, he cut out shapes and constructed them into reliefs of day-glo and metallic colours. Since the mid-1970s, Stella's work has exaggerated the effusive pigment – see the **Exotic Birds** series – and has explored the dissolution of the distinction between sculpture and painting. He has also produced large-scale works such as the 1997 murals for the Princess of Wales Theater, Toronto.

OTHER MASTERPIECES Tuxedo Park Junction; *1960, Stedlijk Van Abbemuseum, Eindhoven, Netherlands* Harewa; *1978, Gabriele Henkel Collection (Courtesy of Hans Strelow), Dusseldorf, Germany*

Still Clyfford

Born Grandia, North Dakota, USA 1904; died New Windsor, USA 1980

Untitled 1953 *1953; oil on canvas; 235.9 x 174 cm; Tate Collection, London, England*

Clyfford Still studied in Washington before moving to San Francisco in 1941. He was an influential teacher at the California School of Fine Arts from 1946 to 1950, and became a leading Abstract Expressionist. Within this disparate movement, his work was most closely associated with the large monochromatic canvases produced by Rothko and Newman. He shared their interest in the single unified shape and the expressive potential of colour. Where Still differed from these artists was in the thick application of his paint. **Untitled 1953** has this tactile and sensuous quality. The sheer physicality of the work is overwhelming. A yellow gash and a small smudge of red are the only disturbances to the evenly coloured but richly wrought surface. Having gained a reputation as an artist somewhat prone to pretension and mystification, Still himself wrote of this work that, "the yellow wedge at the top is a reassertion of the human context – a gesture of rejection of any authoritarian rationale or system of politico-dialectical dogma." Still spent the last twenty years of his life as a virtual recluse in Maryland.

OTHER MASTERPIECES No 1; *1941; Collection EJ Power, London, England*
Jamais; *1944; Peggy Guggenheim Collection, Venice, Italy*

Stubbs George

Born Liverpool, England 1724; died London, England 1806

Lion Devouring a Horse *1763; oil on canvas; 69.2 x 103.5 cm; Tate Collection, London, England*

George Stubbs was the most celebrated animal painter of his day. However, it would be more accurate to say that he was a painter of nature, as landscape and environmental details were scrutinized with as much attention as the animal subjects that proliferate in his canvases. Largely self-taught, he was renowned for his observational skills, imagination and sensitivity. He had established himself as a portrait painter in Leeds while studying anatomy at York. A visit to Italy in 1754 enabled him to absorb the influence of Renaissance and antique art, which was to inform his own work. He settled in London in 1759 and in addition to experimenting with enamel paint on earthenware, proceeded to produce the "animal history" paintings for which he is best known. Perhaps the most famous of these is **Lion Devouring a Horse**, reputedly based on a dramatic scene he witnessed while in Italy. It could be, however, that this is an exaggerated account of Stubb's study of a classical sculpture of the same subject in the Palazzo dei Conservatori in Rome. In spite of the somewhat contrived, artificial proportions and expressions of the creatures, the painting must have been startling to contemporary eyes.

OTHER MASTERPIECES Mares and Foals in a River Landscape; *c. 1763–1768; Tate Collection, London, England* **Portrait of a Young Gentleman Out Shooting**; *1781; Tate Collection, London, England*

354

Sutherland Graham

Born London, England 1903; died London, England 1980

Devastation: House in Wales *1940; gouache, ink and watercolour on paper; 80 x 54.6 cm; Tate Collection, London, England*

Graham Sutherland abandoned a career in railway engineering to study at Goldsmith's College of Art in London, specializing in etching. By the late 1920s, he had developed an enthusiasm for the visionary artist Samuel Palmer. In response Sutherland's own work reflected the dreamlike, pastoral qualities of the earlier romantic. The print market collapsed due to the Wall Street Crash in 1929 and, fortuitously for Sutherland, this inadvertently influenced his decision to become a painter. His first visit to Pembrokeshire in 1934 marked the beginning of a love affair with the country's landscape. His compositions are bold perceptions of the natural world, abstracting forms and colours to startling effect. His admiration for Picasso who, he claimed, possessed the "true idea of metamorphosis", guided his own concept of emphasizing nature's personality. He was employed during the war years as an official war artist and responded to dramatic scenes of human endeavour and devastation as in **Devastation: House in Wales**. Sutherland's work retains references to the strangeness of Surrealism but it is to his beginnings as a printmaker that his painting owes its most enduring influence.

OTHER MASTERPIECES Tapestry Design, **Christ the Redeemer**; *1952; Coventry Cathedral, Coventry, England* **Red Landscape**; *1942; Southampton Art Gallery, Southampton, England*

Tanguy Yves

Born Paris, France 1900; died Woodbury, Connecticut, USA 1955

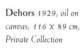

Dehors *1929; oil on canvas; 116 x 89 cm; Private Collection*

Yves Tanguy spent his late teens and early twenties as both an officer at sea and in military service. Despite such an unprepossessing start, on his return to Paris in 1922, he taught himself to sketch and paint. His enthusiasm gathered momentum in part due to the impact made upon him by the work of de Chirico. He came into contact with André Breton in 1925 and joined the Surrealist circle of artists. His own painting developed the biomorphic style of the movement, recalling the landscapes of his childhood vacations and suggesting the marine imagery and oceanic depths that featured in his past. In **Dehors**, amorphous forms rather than abstract shapes float in a subconscious sea; an imaginary space becomes a place within a dream, at once beautiful and disconcerting. Tanguy emigrated to America in 1939. He married painter Kay Sage in 1940 and they settled in Woodbury in 1942. A darker tonality pervades his later works; bony forms and pseudo-rock formations proliferate, seen in Daliesque, illusionistic perspective.

OTHER MASTERPIECES The Rapidity of Sleep; *1945; The Art Institute of Chicago, Chicago, USA* **The Invisibles;** *1951; Tate Collection, London, England*

Tanning Dorothea

Born Galesburgh, Illinois, USA 1912

A Little Night Music *1946; oil on canvas; 41 x 61 cm; Private Collection*

Dorothea Tanning worked as a librarian before briefly studying art at Knox College, Illinois. Desperate to escape the narrow confines of her home town, twenty-year-old Tanning left for Chicago, where she took evening classes at art school. In 1936 she moved to New York, where she found work as a commercial artist. Her meticulous and detailed canvases, with their elaborate depictions of childhood fantasies and nightmares brought her into contact with the Surrealists; she married Max Ernst in 1946. As a female Surrealist, Tanning used her reconstruction of the dream world to explore her own sexuality. **A Little Night Music** is an image resonant with nubile sexuality. Two girls are featured on an upstairs landing, their dresses cut to ribbons and their long hair streaming. A giant sunflower blocks the staircase, its petals discarded. The image is static, as if frozen in time, recalling, perhaps, memories of a distant childhood. Later work, from the mid-1950s onward, focuses on roundly modelled parts of the body – limbs, heads and torsos – which merge with the picture space, appealing to a sense of touch as well as to sight.

OTHER MASTERPIECES A Very Happy Picture; *1948; Musée Nationale d'Art Moderne, Paris, France* **A Family Portrait**; *1957; Musée Nationale d'Art Moderne, Paris, France*

Tapies Antonio

Born Barcelona, Spain 1923

Violet Grey with Wrinkles *1961;
mixed media; 200 x
176 cm; Scottish
National Gallery,
Scotland*

Antonio Tapies
was a self-taught
Catalan artist
who abandoned
his law studies
and began to
paint in 1946.
Coming from
Barcelona, the
left-wing
Catalonian
capital, it was
significant that
he produced a radical abstract art that lacked overtly political implications, apart from his own
liberalism. Tapies reacted against the academic legacy of Dali's Surrealism and of geometrical
abstraction in Europe and America. However, Surrealism's philosophical depth was of
importance, as were the free, lyrical aspects of art by Joan Miro, Mark Tobey and Robert
Motherwell. **Violet Grey with Wrinkles** typically reveals the influence of the French "matter
painters", most importantly Fautrier. In the employment of unusual, tactile substances – marble
dust, pigment and varnish – Tapies' informal, abstract canvases are reminiscent of Dubuffet and
are similar in spirit to those of the Italian artist, Alberto Burri. The inscribed and marked
surfaces are richly layered, often incorporating objects, cloth, signs and symbols – the cross, the
foot, hands and doors, for example. Such inclusions satisfy Tapies's concern that for him, "a
work of art must contain a vision of the world…having a philosophy is not enough".

OTHER MASTERPIECES Perforated Body; *1956–1958; Panza Collection, Milan, Italy*
Peintre Grise Et Verte; *1957; Tate Collection, London, England*

Tatlin Vladimir

Born Kharkovsk, Russia 1885; died Novodevichye, USSR 1953

The Sailor
1911–1912;
tempera on canvas;
71.5 x 71.5 cm;
State Russian
Museum,
St Petersburg, Russia

Vladimir Tatlin was a painter, designer and maker of abstract constructions. He was the founder of Constructivism, a movement concerned with sculpture developed from collage as practised by the Cubists. From 1909–1911 Tatlin attended painting classes in Moscow and combined painting with his life as a merchant sailor, which undoubtedly provided the inspiration for **The Sailor**. In 1913–1914 he earned enough money as a folk musician to go to Paris where he worked in Picasso's studio and was heavily influenced by the latter's experiments in analytical Cubism. From these he derived his first abstract Constructions using diverse media and non-art materials. Moving out of an arena of suggestion and illusion and into the world of real objects, time and space, he worked in close contact with other visual and literary artists. The political ideas resulting from the war in 1914 and the Revolution in 1917 had their effect on the artistic community. Many of them adopted the Bolshevik, Communist cause and Vladimir Tatlin's **Monument To The Third International** was an elaborate, architectural sculpture which appropriated this as its theme. It remains a potent motif for the Constructivist movement which crystallized in 1922.

OTHER MASTERPIECES Counter Relief; *1915; reconstruction 1966–1970; Annely Juda Fine Art, London, England* **Letatlin**; *1929–1931; reconstruction, 1969; Moderna Museet, Stockholm, Sweden*

Tiepolo Giovanni Battista

Born Venice, Italy 1696; died Madrid, Spain 1770

America (detail) *1751; fresco; Residenz, Würzburg, Germany*

Tiepolo was the sparkling star of eighteenth-century decorative painting in Italy. He was a virtuoso master of the fresco medium, sought-after not only in Italy but also in Germany and Spain. Tiepolo brought imagination and Baroque grandeur to the frivolous Rococo spirit and infused it with sound pictorial composure, gleaned from his knowledge of Rubens, Rembrandt and Dürer. The influence of the Venetian masters Veronese and Tintoretto is also prevalent in the eloquence and drama with which Tiepolo imbues his large-scale compositions. As a colourist, Tiepolo is unsurpassed, progressing from the rather dark tonality of his early works to his characteristically sunny palette from the early 1730s. At the peak of his career, in 1750, Tiepolo was commissioned to decorate the Würzburg Palace, the Prince Archbishop's residence. **America** is one of Tiepolo's allegorical interpretations of the four continents, decorating the grand staircase of the palace. This exotic scheme is a tour-de-force, full of vigour and creative originality and is considered the masterpiece of Tiepolo's maturity. In the last years of his life the rising popularity of Neo-Classicism caused the decline of Tiepolo's career but did not affect its lasting impact.

OTHER MASTERPIECES Cleopatra's Banquet; *c.1750; Palazzo Labia, Venice, Italy*
Marriage of Frederick Barbarossa and Beatrice of Burgundy; *c.1750; Residenz, Wurzburg, Germany*

Tintoretto Jacopo

Born Venice, Italy 1518; died Venice, Italy 1594

The Last Supper *c.1592; 365.8 x 569 cm; San Giorgio Maggiore, Venice, Italy*

Jacopo Tintoretto is thought to have studied briefly under Titian, the great Venetian master. In Venice in 1548, a year when Titian was out of the city, Tintoretto made his name with **Miracle of Saint Mark Freeing the Slave**, a fine example of a Mannerist painting with its vivid colouring, distorted figures and foreshortening. After this success, he began decorating the interiors of churches and scuole – that of Saint Rocco being his greatest achievement. His work was invariably completed with great speed, in part due to his large workshops in which he employed Marietta, his highly talented daughter. In order to construct his compositions he would set up a miniature stage in a box. Into this he would position maquettes, and experiment with artificial light to observe the play of shadow on form. In **The Last Supper**, a late painting, the central drama is almost perpendicular to the picture plane. There are numerous light sources, incidental characters and dramatic gestures, presenting an intense, chaotic and lively scene. In his desire to capture the thrill and excitement of this spiritual occasion he has used dark tones punctuated by the odd patch of bright colour.

OTHER MASTERPIECES Miracle of Saint Mark Freeing the Slave; *1548; Galleria della Accademia, Venice, Italy* The Ascension; *c.1576—81; Scuola di San Rocco, Venice, Italy*

Titian Tiziano Vecellio

Born Pieve di Cadore, Italy c.1487; died Venice, Italy 1576

Danae Receiving the Shower of Gold *1545–1546; oil on canvas; 210 x 172 cm; Museo e Gallerie Nazionali di Capodimonte, Naples, Italy*

After an early training in a mosaicist's workshop, Titian came under the strong influence of Giorgione. After Giovanni Bellini's death, he was appointed Painter to the Venetian Republic and was revered as highly as his southern contemporary, Michelangelo. Titian twice refused invitations to Rome, but at the age of sixty he agreed to spend eight months as a guest of the Vatican. In Rome he made the first version of **Danae Receiving the Shower of Gold** for the Pope's grandson and eight years later he made this, the second version, for King Philip of Spain. That two powerful patrons had no qualms about an artist replicating the same subject matter and composition suggests that painting was now being judged on aesthetic grounds, not for its narrative content or interpretation. Ostensibly there is little difference between the two, but his painting technique is dramatically different – sharp outlines are replaced by softer brushstrokes. This picture epitomizes the Venetian High Renaissance style, characterized not just by draughtsmanship but by the free handling of paint. Titian's overriding contribution was his innovatory approach to subject matter and the oil medium. He extended the emotional range of his work through his warm, rich palette.

OTHER MASTERPIECES The Rape of Europa; *c.1562; Gardner Museum, Boston, USA*
Presentation of the Virgin; *c.1538; Galleria della Accademia, Venice, Italy*

Toulouse-Lautrec
Henri Marie Raymond de

Born Albi, France 1864; died Gironde, France 1901

Woman at her Toilet
*1896; oil on cardboard;
67 x 54 cm; Musée
d'Orsay, Paris, France*

Toulouse-Lautrec was born into an aristocratic family. He began to study art in Paris in 1882 and was working in a studio in Montmartre by 1885. He became part of an artistic circle which included Impressionists and Post-Impressionists. The local theatres, café-cabaret bars, the circus and low-life scenes of prostitution provided subject matter which he translated into paintings and lithographs. From 1888 he was critically acclaimed and exhibited regularly at the Salon des Indépendants from 1889, working under the influence of Degas, and of alcohol, which was to cause his death. From 1890, the Moulin Rouge informed the work for which he is most popularly known. His paintings and particularly his posters advertising the Moulin's dancers and performers, confirmed his reputation as an artist of wit, movement and energy. He was a master of characterization and a major influence on upgrading the poster to an art-form. **Woman at her Toilet** is an unusually tender painting, probably of a prostitute as he disliked posed models. It shows his draughtsmanship and rapid brushwork at its best, the chalkiness of the paint on cardboard being reminiscent of pastel.

OTHER MASTERPIECES At Rue Des Moulins; *1894; Musée Toulouse-Lautrec, Albi, France*
At the Moulin Rouge; *1892; Art Institute of Chicago, USA*

Turner Joseph Mallord William

Born London, England 1775; died London, England 1851

Norham Castle: Sunrise *1845; oil on canvas; 90.8 x 121.9 cm; Tate Collection, London, England*

Joseph Mallord William Turner was, with Constable, one of two outstanding geniuses of British painting in the nineteenth century. He started drawing as a child and was admitted into the Royal Academy School in 1789. A master of topographical drawing, he began to make sketching tours from 1792, filling his sketchbooks with reminders of places that would later feature in his large-scale landscape compositions. He travelled around Britain and then to Paris, Switzerland and Venice. Turner's oil and watercolour landscapes referred to mainly historical and seascape scenes; he rarely featured human figures, preferring to focus on the natural elements. These romantic landscapes showed the influence of Claude and Dutch seventeenth-century marine painters. Works from 1830 onward are almost exclusively concerned with light. Turner visited Norham Castle in Northumberland several times and first exhibited a watercolour of the same composition in 1798. **Norham Castle: Sunrise** is one of the most spare of all his oil paintings – it presents an infinity of space in which the cool grey-blue castle appears like a chimera. Constable's description, "he seems to paint with tinted steam," seems especially apt for a work that comes close to abstraction. Turner greatly influenced the Impressionists, Monet and Pissarro both encountering his work for the first time in London.

OTHER MASTERPIECES The Fighting Temeraire; *1838; National Gallery, London, England*
Sunrise with Sea Monsters; *c.1845; Tate Collection, London, England*

364

Twombly Cy

Born Lexington, Virginia, USA 1928

Nini's Painting *1971; oil-based house paint, wax crayon and lead pencil on canvas; 250.3 x 300.4 cm; Private Collection*

Cy Twombly is an original talent whose independent spirit and vision has formulated an art that is definable neither by style nor artistic movement. He spent from 1948 to 1952 training at the Boston Museum of Fine Arts, the Art Students League in New York and finally, at the invitation of his peer and friend Robert Rauschenberg, at Black Mountain College. Here he was taught by Robert Motherwell and Franz Kline. He travelled with Rauschenberg and moved to Rome in 1957, leaving only for short periods to work in New York. His early work reflected the influence of those around him. The open, expansive gestures of the Abstract Expressionists appealed to him, particularly the graphic elements in the work of Kline. However, unlike his contemporaries, popular culture did not interest him as a subject worthy of artistic exploration. He looked instead to the classical art of the Renaissance, Greek mythology and Roman antiquity. His mature paintings reflected these interests without offering descriptive references to form or narrative. As **Nini's Painting** shows, his artistic language is formulated from a wide vocabulary of pencil lines, paint marks and chalk scribbles to create a rich, multi-layered image, full of vital energy and cryptic symbols.

OTHER MASTERPIECES Empire of Flora; *1961; Marx Collection, Berlin, Germany*
Untitled; *1968; Museum of Art, Rhode Island School of Design, Providence, Rhode island, USA*

Uccello Paolo

Born Florence Italy c.1396; died Florence Italy 1475

Battle of San Romano *c.1450–1460; tempera on panel; 182 x 323 cm; Galleria degli Uffizi, Florence, Italy*

Uccello was the son of a barber-surgeon called Paolo di Dono, but may have taken his name from his love of birds – uccello means bird in Italian. He was an apprentice to the sculptor, Ghiberti, from c.1407 to 1414 and then left to join the guild of the Medici e Speciali. The **Battle of San Romano** is one of three panels commissioned by the Medicis. It depicts the rout of San Romano on June 1, 1432. For the year prior to this date, the Sienese had been ravaging Florentine territory and finally at this battle, the Florentines were victorious. Uccello's works, interpreting the hostilities, are an unusual marriage of old and new. The strong decorative element, with the patchwork of hills in the background, the flora and fauna and the frieze-like battle scene itself are all reminiscent of medieval tapestries. However, our overriding impression is of an artist who revelled in exploiting the novel rules of perspective and who was particularly preoccupied with foreshortening. Ultimately, it is for this that we remember Uccello. According to Vasari, Uccello ended his days, "solitary, eccentric, melanchol[ic] and poor". It was a sad demise for a master of hitherto unknown pictorial liveliness.

OTHER MASTERPIECES St George and the Dragon; *c.1450; National Gallery, London, England* **The Deluge**; *c.1445; Chiostro Verde of Santa Maria Novella, Florence, Italy*

Utrillo Maurice

Born Paris, France 1883; died Dax, France 1955

L'Impasse, Cottin *c.1910;*
oil on canvas; 540 x 730 cm;
Tate Collection, London,
England

Maurice Utrillo was the
illegitimate son of the
painter Suzanne Valadon.
An alcoholic and a drug
addict, he was reputedly
encouraged to paint by
his mother during one of
his several admissions to
a sanatorium. He had his
first exhibition at the
Paris Salon in 1909. His
early work was affected
by the Impressionists, in
particular Pissarro, but
was characterized, in
Utrillo's own words, by
"a wild thirst for reality".
His intense vision,
paradoxically, was largely the result of copying Parisian street views from postcards. Mainly
concentrated on the area around Montmarte, he did much to establish the area's romantic
image. The paintings produced between 1909 to 1916 are known as his "white period" because
of their distinctive pale tones. L'impasse, Cottin is almost monochromatic. The darkened
windows and empty doorways give the picture a haunting atmosphere and emotional flatness.
By the 1920s, Utrillo was introducing richer colours into his work. Highly popular, his
paintings were the subject of numerous forgeries and imitations. Utrillo turned to religion in
his later years.

OTHER MASTERPIECES La Place du Tetre; *c.1910; Tate Collection, London, England*
Street in a Paris Suburb with Trees; *c.1920–1923; Wallraf-Richartz-Museum, Cologne, Germany*

Valadon Suzanne

Born Bessines near Limoges, France 1865; died Paris, France 1938

Self Portrait *1883; pastel on paper; 45 x 32 cm; Musée Nationale d'Art Moderne, Paris, France*

Suzanne Valadon moved to Paris as a child and from an early age made her living as an acrobat, dressmaker and artist's model. She posed for Puvis de Chavannes, Renoir, Toulouse-Lautrec and Degas, who encouraged her to draw. Valadon started to paint in 1909. Her work, featuring still life and figure subjects, retained a strong linear quality. Her primitive, decorative style was later influenced by both Matisse and Derain. She was keenly aware of the dichotomy involved in being both an artist and a model. In 1927, she produced a poster for a Parisian benefit dance. As the back view of a naked woman holding up a palette, the image called into question the role of the female nude as object for the male artist. In the assertive **Self Portrait** (1883) seen here, Valadon centres on her determined facial expression. A renowned beauty, she depicts her own heavy jawline and dark feature with unerring realism. Her treatment of herself is in stark contrast to the idealized version of femininity presented in the many paintings for which she posed.

OTHER MASTERPIECES Nu à la Couverture Rayée; *1922; Petit Palias, Paris, France*
Nu à la Palette; *1927; Musée National d'Art Moderne, Paris, France*

Vaughan Keith

Born Selsey Bill, England 1912; died London, England 1977

Small Assembly of Figures *1951; oil on canvas; 55.9 x 61 cm; Tate Collection, London, England*

Keith Vaughan received no formal art training and struggled throughout his artistic life to find his own visual language. He had an interest in visual art theorists and the artistic and the literary achievements of the French. This was qualified by the challenge to resolve the conflict between the formal and the humanistic, expressive elements of painting. He sought to arrange non-precise forms, focusing almost exclusively on the depiction of male nudes. From the 1950s this preoccupation is realised via classical compositions orchestrated by Vaughan's talent as a colourist. His paintings of bathers, such as **Small Assembly of Figures**, acknowledge Cézanne as a lifelong source of admiration. Vaughan produced his most striking pictures during the 1960s. In other figure compositions, each group becomes a solidly wrought moonlight of flesh; a palette of warm blues, lilacs and pinks supersedes the brown and olive tones dominating earlier works. His dalliance with photography materialized on canvas in cropped figures, profiles and silhouettes. His works do not narrate the trauma of his personal life but are transmutations of the sexual tensions which dictated it and which undoubtedly culminated in his suicide in 1977.

OTHER MASTERPIECES Landscape with Figures; *1971; Private Collection*
Landscape with Figure; *1957; Arts Council Collection, England*

369

Velasquez Diego Rodriguez de Silva y

Born Seville, Spain 1599; died Madrid, Spain 1660

An Old Woman Cooking Eggs *1618; oil on canvas; 99 x 169 cm; National Gallery of Scotland, Edinburgh, Scotland*

The son of Portuguese parents, Diego Velasquez trained in the academy of Francisco Pacheo, and married his daughter. By 1617 he had set up as an independent master. Velasquez became court painter to Philip IV in Madrid at the age of 24, and retained the position for the rest of his career. He was granted permission from the king to travel and went to Italy twice. On his second visit, in 1650, he painted the celebrated portrait of **Pope Innocent X**. His grand and graceful paintings of the Spanish royal family and the life of the court are distinguished by their profound feeling for humanity. Drawn toward human suffering, his portraits of court jesters and dwarves are, in particular, notable for both their compassion and absence of sentiment. **An Old Woman Cooking Eggs** is a detailed, realistic, early genre painting that was completed before his court appointment. The impassive stare of an elderly woman and her young companion contribute to perceptive character studies, which Velasquez has treated in a dignified and sympathetic manner. The realism of the dramatically lit composition is further heightened through the finely observed accoutrements – from the heavy pots and jugs to the eggs frying in the pan.

OTHER MASTERPIECES The Rokeby Venus; *c.1648; National Gallery, London, England* **Las Meninas**; *c.1656; Museo del Prado, Madrid, Spain*

Vermeer Johannes

Born Delft, Netherlands 1632; died Delft, Netherlands 1675

The Painter in his Studio *1666; oil on canvas; 120 x 100 cm; Kunsthistorisches Museum, Vienna, Austria*

Jan Vermeer is regarded as one of the greatest seventeenth-century Dutch artists – second only in importance to Rembrandt. Little is known of his early life; it seems unlikely that he left his native city of Delft. His early work typically focused on domestic interiors featuring women engaged in a number of everyday tasks, such as writing letters, pouring milk and playing music. An unusual aspect of his compositions is the degree to which the protagonists in his scenes are self-absorbed. Vermeer married into a wealthy Catholic family and had eleven children. He worked in a large room in the house, and produced a small number of exquisitely rendered paintings. He resisted selling them whenever he could, which suggests he had, for a time at least, a private income; however, when he died suddenly, aged 43, he was in great debt. In **The Painter in his Studio**, the brocade curtain is pulled back to reveal a painter in his studio – this may even be a self portrait. It records a timeless but intimate moment; the objects, furnishings and people are rendered with clarity and sensitivity, all enveloped in the clarity of cool, pearlized light.

OTHER MASTERPIECES View of Delft; *c.1660; Maurutshuis, The Hague, Netherlands* Woman Reading A Letter; *1662–1663; Rijksmuseum, Amsterdam, Netherlands*

Veronese Paolo Caliari

Born Verona, Italy 1528; died Venice, Italy 1588

Family of Darius before Alexander the Great *1565–1570; oil on canvas; 236 x 474 cm; National Gallery, London, England*

Veronese was brought up in Verona on the mainland territory of Venice, where he would first have experienced the Mannerist style, which had spread north through central Italy. He was particularly influenced by Titian, Raphael, Michelangelo and Parmigianino. At the age of twenty-five he painted the ceiling for the Doge's Palace in Venice, and by 1560 had made his first visit to Rome. In 1573, he produced his infamous and hedonistic **Feast in the House of Levi**, which he was forced to defend in front of the Inquisition. In Veronese's assured historical, religious and allegorical paintings he seems to relish depicting large masses of people. In **Family of Darius before Alexander the Great**, the incident – in which Darius's mother begs Alexander for mercy – is witnessed by figures peering over the balcony. Veronese's real interest appears to be in the production of a splendidly coloured theatrical scene with a Palladian backdrop, rather than the dramatic nature of his heroic subject matter. Veronese was noted for his command of pagentry and drama and his brilliance as a colourist and here the remarkable warmth of his palette helps to convey the sense of a clear, bright day.

OTHER MASTERPIECES Feast in the House of Levi; *1573; Galleria dell'Accademia, Venice, Italy* The Marriage of Cana; *c.1563; Musée du Louvre, Paris, France*

Vigée-Lebrun Marie-Elizabeth-Louise

Born Paris, France 1755; died Paris, France 1842

Portrait of the Artist and her Daughter *1789; oil on canvas; 130 x 94 cm; Musée du Louvre, Paris, France*

Elizabeth Vigée-Lebrun was taught by Louis Vigée, her father, a Parisian portraitist working in pastels. He died when she was fifteen, by which time her growing reputation allowed her to support her family. In 1776, she married picture dealer Jean-Baptiste Lebrun. Her highly successful career led to a friendship with Queen Marie-Antoinette, whom she portrayed many times. Vigée-Lebrun fled the French Revolution in 1789 and travelled across Europe before finally settling back in Paris in 1814. Her many charming and delicately executed portraits were produced during the Rococo period. **Portrait of the Artist and her Daughter** should be seen in the context of new eighteenth-century ideas centring on the notion of the family, encouraging women to place greater emphasis on the emotional bond between mother and child. In this informal portrait the artist depicts the loving embrace between mother and child. A dedicated artist, Vigée-Lebrun's memoirs revealed that she continued working, "in the intervals between labour pains," during the birth of her daughter.

OTHER MASTERPIECES Self Portrait in a Straw Hat; *after 1782; National Gallery, London, England* **Hubert Robert**; *1788; Musée du Louvre, Paris, France*

Viola Bill

Born New York City, USA 1951

Nantes Triptych *1992; video and mixed media; Tate Collection, London, England*

Bill Viola graduated from Syracuse University's Experimental Studios of the Department of Visual and Performing Arts in 1973. His first experiments with Super-8 film and with black and white video date back to 1970. Proceeding from single-screen video and video and sound-based installations he has become known for his monumental pieces incorporating computer-controlled discs and state-of-the-art techniques. These resulted partly from studying new developments in video technology in Japan in 1980–1981. His works are completely absorbing, often literally encapsulating the viewer in an experience that controls the visual and aural senses. In the **Nantes Triptych**, three large screens almost fill the viewer's field of vision with the crucial human concerns and actual moments of birth (the artist's son) and death (the artist's mother). Between the two is an enigmatic, dreamlike sequence of a clothed figure plunging into watery depths. It is a moving and disturbing meditation on states of consciousness and being and illustrates Viola's contemplation on the "philosophical mind-body problem coming to a crescendo as an ecological drama…."

OTHER MASTERPIECES Going Forth by Day; 2002; *Guggenheim Museum, New York City, USA* Room for St John Of The Cross; *1983; Museum of Contemporary Art, Los Angeles, USA*

Vlaminck Maurice de

Born Paris, France 1876; died La Tourillière, France 1958

Landscape with Red Trees c.1906; oil on canvas; 48 x 56 cm; Musée Nationale d'Art Moderne, Paris, France

The son of Flemish parents, Maurice de Vlaminck was an athlete and enthusiastic individual who took part in cycle races and earned his living mainly as a musician. He taught himself to draw and paint and was proud of the fact that he had never set foot in the Louvre. His friendship with André Derain dates from about 1900. They shared a studio together at Chatou, near Paris. Vlaminck was very impressed by the 1901 van Gogh retrospective in Paris and adopted the Dutch-born artist's use of strong colours and turbulent brushstrokes. He took part in the Fauves exhibition of 1905 at the Salon d'Automne. Painting was, for Vlaminck, a spontaneous, passionate and physical act. His belief that, "instinct is the foundation of art", meant that intense colour, often applied direct from the tube, predominates in his mainly landscape compositions. **Landscape with Red Trees** distorts basic perspective, the vertical trunks of the trees adding excitement and expression to the overall composition. His later works, showing the influence of Cézanne, are more subdued in colour. After serving in the First World War, he lived and worked in virtual isolation in rural France.

OTHER MASTERPIECES The River; 1910; National Gallery, Washington DC, USA
Summer Landscape; 1905–1906; Collection Dr A. Wilhelm Betteningen, Basel, Switzerland

Vuillard Edouard

Born Cuiseaux, France 1868; died La Baule, France 1940

Femme Lisant, le Soir
*c.1895; oil on canvas; 50.8
x 60.9 cm; Private Collection*

Edouard Vuillard studied
in Paris, completing his
training at the Académie
Julian where he met
Pierre Bonnard with
whom he shared a studio.
Both artists were enthused
by Sérusier's exposition of
a new theory based on
Gauguin's expressive use
of colour and, in 1889,
joined the Nabis artists'
group. Vuillard painted
intimate introspective,
domestic scenes,
revealing through his
small brushstrokes and
broken surfaces a feeling
for textures and patterning. His mother was a dressmaker and he grew up surrounded by rolls of
patterned material. He made use of bold colours but his close tonal range meant that the overall
effect was often muted. **Femme Lisant, le Soir** is a small work – both in terms of its actual size
and in its portrayal of an everyday subject. A corner of the room is further enclosed by the
walls, furniture and a clutter of objects. In this indistinct scene, a woman sits reading in the
lamplight and there is a subtle tension due to the ambiguity associated with her mysterious
identity. Vuillard's later works were more naturalistic, due in part to the impromptu photographs
he took to capture spontaneous impressions of his family and home life.

OTHER MASTERPIECES Mother and Child; *c.1899; Glasgow Museum and Art Gallery,
Glasgow, Scotland* **Artist's Mother and Sister in Studio;** *c.1900; Museum of Modern Art, New York
City, USA*

Watteau Jean-Antoine

Born Valenciennes, France 1684; died Paris, France 1721

The Music Party c.1718; oil on canvas; 67.3 x 92.5 cm; Wallace Collection, London, England

The work of Antoine Watteau provides a singularly distinctive precedent to the visual and decorative art known as Rococo. He is credited with creating a Parisian style and is classed alongside Chardin as a key figure among pre-Revolutionary French artists of the period. Watteau settled in Paris in 1702, and until 1708 studied under decorative painter Claude Gillot. Watteau adopted Gillot's predilection for painting scenes for the commedia dell'arte. Theatrical costume and poetic characters recur in Watteau's paintings, leading to his title of "peintre de fêtes galantes". He gained access to Rubens's decorations in the Luxembourg Palace and studied collections of work by Flemish and Italian masters. Rubens, Veronese and the Venetians had notable influence on his style, particularly in his use of colour. This incorporated a systemic method of mixing pigment optically on the canvas, which was to be developed later by Seurat into Divisionism. **The Music Party** is a typical example from Watteau's oeuvre. He renders an imaginative, ideal scene of life exquisitely, tinged with sadness. It is believable rather than superficial, full of the gravity and grace of serious skill, rather than the frivolous spirit of true Rococo which was to follow.

OTHER MASTERPIECES The Embarkation for Cythera; 1717; Musée du Louvre, Paris, France
Enseigne De Gersaint; 1719; Staatliche Museen, Berlin, Germany

Weyden Rogier van der

Born Tournai, Belgium 1400; died Bruges, Belgium 1464

Portrait of Antoine de Bourgogne *c.1460; oil on canvas; 37 x 27 cm; Musée Royaux des Beaux-Arts, Brussels, Belgium*

The pre-eminent artist of mid-fifteenth-century Flanders, Rogier van der Weyden is believed to have begun his career as an apprentice to Robert Campin. He later became Town Painter of Brussels from 1433 to 1464. As such, he would have been in charge of a workshop with at least four or five apprentices producing numerous designs for altarpieces and sculpture. He was the originator of a style of portraiture in which individual complexities were reduced to standard types, easily recognizable by the contemporary viewer. This technique, evident here in the plainness and flatness of the portrait, culminated in the work of Hugo van der Goes. Van der Weyden used slightly tinted layers of primer to soften the intensity of his colours. His simple, emotional style was popular in Italy, where many artists, such as Cosima Tura, were influenced by him. **Antoine de Bourgogne**, the illegitimate son of Philip the Good, was born in 1421; in this portrait he is in his mid-30s. Here, van der Weyden emphasizes the characteristics thought to signify good breeding – fine bone structure and sensitive features.

OTHER MASTERPIECES Deposition; *c.1435; Museo del Prado, Madrid, Spain*
Braque Triptych; *c.1452; Musée du Louvre, Paris, France*

Whistler James Abbott McNeill

Born Lowell, USA 1834; died London, England 1903

Nocturne in Blue and Gold *c. 1872–1875; oil on canvas; 67.9 x 50.8 cm; Tate Collection, London, England*

From 1851 to 1854 Whistler studied at West Point Military Academy in New York State and worked as a Navy cartographer before going to study painting in Paris in 1855. He became one of a circle of Realist artists after meeting with Fantin-Latour and Courbet in 1858. He made copies in the Louvre and developed an enthusiasm for Oriental art and decoration, being particularly impressed by Japanese prints. He brought these interests with him when he settled in London in 1859. Rather than perpetuate an English tradition of narrative painting he concentrated on the aesthetic formulation of pictorial composition itself as the subject of his work. Such arrangements came out of the harmonious juxtaposition of tones and colours; the comparison with music was intentional and made clear in the titles of his paintings. **Nocturne in Blue and Gold** is described in subtle tones and simple, flat forms in an unmistakably Japanese manner. Ruskin was appalled by Whistler's work accusing him of "flinging a pot of paint in the public's face". However, Whistler's belief in "art for art's sake", expounded in his Ten O'Clock Lecture, first delivered in 1855, was taken seriously and his painting was emulated by successive generations.

OTHER MASTERPIECES Arrangement in Grey and Black, *1871; Musée du Louvre, Paris, France* **Symphony in White No II**, *1864; Tate Collection, London, England*

Whiteread Rachel

Born London, England 1963

Untitled (House) *1993,*
London, England, demolished

Rachel Whiteread studied at Brighton Polytechnic from 1982–1985 and then at the Slade School of Art in London until 1987. **Untitled (House)** is a concrete cast of the complete interior of a terraced dwelling, doomed to demolition. It is a ghostly, yet tangible manifestation of the air that was once breath and the silence that was the stuff of its rooms. The sculpture, in Bow, London, was itself demolished in 1993. The memory of Whiteread's achievement lives on as an immovable monument in art history. The artist casts the interior spaces that were once occupied by human domestic activity or emotional emptiness. These negative areas – the hiding place under the bed, the secret, musty atmosphere inside a wardrobe, the seductive, vacant bath – are transformed into positive, inert lumps of past lives. Whiteread sculpts the intangible; she reveals the gaps in which memories are hidden as solid testimonies to life's events. Rubber casts of mattresses proliferate in Whiteread's earlier work, as do plaster casts of her own body. More recently she has received several major public commissions, creating the **Judenplatz Holocaust Memorial** in Vienna, Austria, completed in 2000, and **Monument**, a controversial clear resin plinth installed in London's Trafalgar Square in 2004.

OTHER MASTERPIECES Ghost, *1990, Saatchi Collection, London, England*
Untitled (Stairs), *2001, Tate Collection, London, England*

Wilding Alison

Born Blackburn, Lancashire, England 1948

Receiver *1988; oak and galvanized steel,*
beeswax and pigment; 195.5 x 139.7 x 99 cm;
Tate Collection, London, England

Alison Wilding trained at Ravensbourne College of Art from 1967 to 1970 and the Royal
College of Art, London, 1970–1973. Her sculpture work has gradually gained appreciation
since the early 1980s. At this time she began concentrating on the production of objects for
exhibition rather than her environmental installation pieces of the 1970s. However, the
contextual element of displaying her large and small scale sculpture has remained a concern;
this is integral to her exploration of relationships between forms and their occupation of space.
Like her contemporary, Richard Deacon, she employs a wide variety of materials – stone, metal,
wood, polypropylene, paint, rubber, cloth and wax – in a precise and measured way. More
stylish than organic, Wilding's work often incorporates two interdependent forms in each piece.
Receiver is an example of this. The soft femininity of the carved oak vessel sits at the foot of
the harsh, galvanized steel tower. The incongruous juxtaposition of such contrasting pieces
brings into focus their respectively different command of space. Their "marriage" extends this
inquiry in an understated way that is both eloquent and beautiful.

OTHER MASTERPIECES Blue Skies; *1987; Private Collection on loan to Southampton Art Gallery,*
Southampton, England **Stain**; *1991; Karsten Schubert Gallery, London, England*

Wilkie Sir David

Born Fife, Scotland 1785; died at sea off Malta 1841

The Bride at her Toilet *1838; oil on canvas; 97.2 x 122.6 cm; National Gallery of Scotland , Edinburgh, Scotland*

David Wilkie first studied in Edinburgh. In 1805, he entered the Royal Academy school in London and the following year exhibited **Village Politicians** at the Academy. This work set his style for the next twenty years, establishing him as a popular genre painter whose narrative paintings were crammed full of lively and often humorous incident. His pictures of Victorian life generally expressed a moral lesson and were strongly influenced by scenes of peasant life in the Dutch genre paintings of David Tenier and Adriaen van Ostade. **The Bride at her Toilet** is a typically moralizing domestic scene, contrasting the innocent, virginal figure in white with her huddle of fussing, female attendants. From 1825 Wilkie travelled to Italy and Spain, where his style and subject matter broadened under the influence of Velasquez and Murillo. Back in England, he became painter to the King in 1830 and was knighted in 1836. He died at sea on his return from a Middle East visit. Turner commemorated him in **Peace: Burial at Sea.**

OTHER MASTERPIECES The Blind Fiddler; *1806; Tate Collection, London, England*
The Letter of Introduction; *1813; National Gallery of Scotland, Edinburgh, Scotland*

Wilson Richard

Born London, England 1953

20:50 *1987; used sump oil and steel; dimensions variable; Saatchi Collection, London, England*

Richard Wilson studied at the London College of Printing from 1970–1971. He then went on to Hornsey College of Art. Since graduating with an MA from Reading University in 1976, he has exhibited his sculpture/installation art with Matt's Gallery in London. As a work that has a strong and lasting impact, Wilson's **20:50** is unsurpassed. Not only does it physically completely occupy one of the spaces of the Saatchi Gallery where it is now installed, but it also disorientates the senses and has a strong odour. The layer of 2,500 gallons of used, black sump oil gives the illusion of great depth, not of viscous fluid but of emptiness falling away from beneath the feet. Edging gingerly along the walkway leading into the work one feels as if one is stepping into the void; it is almost a leap of faith. The notion of the paradox is a thematic element of Wilson's work. The tenuous ways in which we live and manage our lives and the structures we create to house ourselves and our possessions – caravans, conservatories and greenhouses – and the importance we attach to them, are seen by Wilson as inventions worthy of exploration and transformation.

OTHER MASTERPIECES High Rise; *1989; Saatchi Collection, London, England*
Over Easy; *1996–99; The Arc, Stockton-on-Tees, England*

Witz Konrad

Born Constance, Germany c.1400; died Basel, Switzerland c.1444

Miraculous Draught of Fishes *c.1444; oil on canvas; 123 x 154 cm; Musée d'Art et d'Histoire, Geneva, Switzerland*

Witz was brought up in Constance but from 1434 spent most of his working life in Basel. Very little is known about his life and only one painting, **Miraculous Draught of Fishes**, is signed and dated. It was one of four painted for two wings of a Redemption altarpiece for St Peter's Cathedral in Geneva, most probably commissioned by a cardinal. This is an extraordinarily inventive interpretation of the well-known biblical story. Christ dispassionately surveys the disciples as they struggle to haul in their catch. The most significant aspect of the painting is Witz's clear observation of the surface beneath the shallow water; this was the first identified attempt at such an optical illusion. Art historians also believe it to be one of the first paintings of a recognizable landscape, that of Lake Leman in Switzerland. Witz's naturalistic treatment of this subject was advanced for its time. His revolutionary, realist way of seeing gave solidity and human substance to revered religious characters. Such an approach evinces Witz's knowledge of the achievements of other artists, van Eyck being one.

OTHER MASTERPIECES Saint Bartholomew; *c.1435; Museum of Fine Arts, Basel, Switzerland*
Saint Magdalen and Saint Catherine; *c.1480; Strasbourg Museum, France*

Wols Alfred Otto Wolfgang Schulze

Born Berlin, Germany 1913; died Paris, France 1951

Don Juan *1944–1945;*
watercolour and chalk on
paper; 12.6 x 10 cm;
Private Collection

Wols was born in
Germany but lived in
France from the mid-
1930s onward. His artistic
potential was recognized
by Moholy-Nagy, who
encouraged him to study
at the Bauhaus. From
1932 he earned his living
as a photographer in
Paris. After the Second
World War, he produced
illustrations for Jean-Paul
Sartre and Simone de
Beauvoir, who recognized his talent for producing detailed and obsessive images of the
unconscious. His mature work, especially drawings and watercolours from the early 1940s,
assimilate Surrealist notions of automatism, a process exploiting the subconscious, and
biomorphism, using forms derived from organic shapes. **Don Juan** is a delicate work from this
period. The pinkish colour and spidery lines combine in a small, evocative image that is both
fluid and exact. A work rich in associations, the title suggests that we are witness to the mating
ritual of tiny creatures observed through a microscope. Wols died aged thirty-eight, the result
of a dissolute and poverty-stricken life. Posthumously, his reputation grew and his work
influenced the development of French abstract art in the 1950s.

OTHER MASTERPIECES Untitled; *1944–1945; Tate Collection, London, England*
Composition; *1947; Museum of Modern Art, New York City, USA*

Woodrow Bill

Born Henley-on-Thames, England 1948

Self-Portrait in the Nuclear Age *1986; shelving unit, wall map, coat, globe, acrylic paint; 205 x 145 x 265 cm; Saatchi Collection, London, England*

Bill Woodrow's work is a combination of wit and technical skill. Like Tony Cragg and David Mach, other sculptors who came to prominence in the 1980s, Woodrow's art is his appropriation of banal objects, domestic appliances and materials and their subsequent metamorphosis. His work possesses a sardonic humour in the way that outmoded items, electric fires and washing machines, for example, are magically fashioned into something else, as if metal and wire become origami paper. The combined spirits of Arte Povera and of Pop Art are resurrected to comic effect in Woodrow's work. However, a more serious interpretation could be implied in the ingenious way that Woodrow makes a moral point. He seems to suggest that the greed with which we cram consumer products into our lives outweighs notions of recycling and the harm we do to the environment. The transformation of materials in **Self-Portrait in the Nuclear Age** hints at destruction and mutation. The jack-in-a-box is a surprise laced with black humour and a warning that literally balances over our world. Woodrow's more recent, larger scale works – such as **Regardless of History**, shown in London's Trafalgar Square in 2000–2001 – point to more universal themes concerning, for example, wealth and the pursuit of power.

OTHER MASTERPIECES Twin-Tub with Guitar; *1981; Tate Collection, London, England*
Life on Earth; *1983; National Gallery of Canada, Ottawa, Canada*

Wright Joseph

Born Derby, England 1734; died Derby, England 1797

Experiment with an Air Pump *1768; oil on canvas; 182.9 x 243.9 cm; National Gallery, London, England*

As Joseph Wright lived and worked in the Midlands town of Derby he became known as "Wright of Derby". He was the first British painter of significance from outside London, although his training in the 1760s took place in the capital. He first came to prominence as a portrait painter. In Derby he found admirers among industrialists and inventors, Arkwright and Wedgwood became his patrons and, from the 1760s, his paintings commented upon the scientific advances made by the emerging Industrial Revolution. He specialized in extraordinary light effects, his candlelit scenes recalled the work of Dutch artists such as Honthorst. **Experiment with an Air Pump** is generally regarded as his finest work. In the painting, the lamplight dramatically highlights a domestic interior, revealing a mixture of awe, fascination and fear in the faces of the assembled group. Wright visited Italy between 1773–1775, where he witnessed an eruption of Vesuvius, as well as a grand, theatrical firework display. Toward the end of his career, he became increasingly interested in painting the English landscape.

OTHER MASTERPIECES A Philosopher Giving a Lecture on the Orrery; *c.1763–65; Derby Museum and Art Gallery, Derbyshire, England* **The Academy by Candlelight;** *1769; Royal College of Surgeons, London, England*

Wyeth Andrew

Born Chadds Ford, USA 1917

Up in the Studio *1965; Watercolour; 43 x 60.6 cm; Museum of Modern Art, New York City, USA*

Andrew Wyeth was tutored solely by his father, N. C. Wyeth, a well-known illustrator, who taught his son to draw from casts, skeletons, still life and the life model. Andrew did not develop his own inimitable style until after his father's death in a level crossing accident. The emotional impact of this personal tragedy precipitated the change in his work. He had always been especially drawn to landscape, particularly the Brandywine Valley around his home, but his range broadened to include the study of people and their emotions. His work has a compelling, highly-detailed realism, which can be traced back to Winslow Homer and Thomas Eakins, but conveys a distinct sense of lugubrious wistfulness. In **Up in the Studio**, a drybrush watercolour, Wyeth uses the frame of his panel as a compositional device. The cropping of the lower edge, combined with the lines of the floor and window, draw the viewer into this private, isolated space. The subdued colours are characterstic of Wyeth's work and were achieved by grinding his own pigments from a range of earth and mineral colours. He paints in one of two media – drybrush or tempera – both methods being painstaking and slow.

OTHER MASTERPIECES Christina's World; *1948; Museum of Modern Art, New York City, USA*
That Gentleman; *1960; Dallas Museum of Fine Art, Texas, USA*

Yeats Jack Butler

Born London, England 1871; died Dublin, Ireland, 1957

The Rogue's March *1950; oil on canvas; 61 x 91.5 cm; Private Collection*

Brother of the poet W B Yeats, Jack Yeats is recognized as the foremost Irish painter of the twentieth century. From 1879–1887 he lived with his grandparents near Sligo on the West Coast of Ireland. He studied in London but settled permanently in Ireland in 1910. His mature pictures of the early 1920s describe the activities and characters of the ordinary people there. Although he claimed that Goya and Sickert were the only painters he admired, his painting is fluid and Expressionistic, boldly handled and courageously coloured. The outlines around his figures serve to reinforce form and character, almost to the point of caricature. By 1925 his manner had changed. Colours were lighter and shapes more loose. In the 1930s his technique became increasingly dynamic and fragmentary, charged with the energy of his subjects – sometimes imaginary from Irish history, at other times describing real life. The misfits, gypsies, tramps and musicians who populated the bars, pantomimes, beaches and circuses provided the vitality on which Yeats thrived. **The Rogue's March** demonstrates his gift for balancing figures within the landscape of their environment, affected by atmosphere and the elements. Samuel Beckett accordingly acclaimed him as a "supreme master".

OTHER MASTERPIECES The Two Travellers; *1942; Tate Collection, London, England*
A Storm; *1936; Waddingtons Gallery, London, England*

Zoffany Johann

Born Frankfurt, Germany 1733; died London, England 1810

The Bradshaw Family *1769; oil on canvas; 162.1 x 175.3 cm; Tate Collection, London, England*

German-born Johann Zoffany studied in Rome before settling in England in 1761. His work found favour with King George III and he painted numerous elegant and flattering portraits of the royal family. He was one of the original members of the Royal Academy and, in 1771, painted a group portrait of the Academy's leading artists. In addition to portraits, he painted conversation pieces, an eighteenth-century group portrait, often of a family, engaging in conversation within a domestic or landscape setting, and theatrical scenes depicting a dramatic moment in a play. Zoffany was encouraged in these stage representations by his patron, the actor David Garrick. **The Bradshaw Family** is a conversation piece in which various members of the family are shown relaxing on their land. Painted with grace, fluency and vigour, it has a sense of characterization inspired by the work of Hogarth, but lacking the latter's satirical edge. In 1772, he went to Italy and spent some years in Florence. He also increased his income considerably by painting portraits of the aristocratic members of Indian society between 1783–1789.

OTHER MASTERPIECES Queen Charlotte and Her Two Eldest Children; *1766–1767; Royal Collection, Windsor, England* The Academicians of the Royal Academy; *1772; Royal Collection, Windsor, England*

Zurbarán Francisco de

Born Fuente de Cantos, Spain 1598; died Madrid, Spain 1664

Still Life *c.1658; oil on canvas; 46 x 84 cm; Museo del Prado, Madrid, Spain*

Francisco de Zurbarán's apprenticeship was undertaken in Seville, where he met Velasquez and became one of the city's official painters. His commission to decorate the king's palace in Madrid was most probably the result of his continuing friendship with the older, and more successful, Spanish artist. Zurbarán was chiefly a portrait painter and his religious subjects, depicting meditating saints, found favour in southern Spain's many monastic and church institutions. From 1628, he worked on a number of paintings to be sent to monasteries in the Spanish colony of Guadalupe. After 1640 his austere, harsh, hard-edged style was unfavourably compared to the sentimental religiosity of Murillo and Zurbarán's reputation declined. In 1658, he moved to Madrid in search of work and renewed his contact with Velasquez. Zurbarán died in poverty and obscurity. **Still Life** is one of the few masterly compositions that he produced of the subject. Four simple pots and bowls – strangely arranged along a line in the foreground – glow, backed by deep shadow. With the composition stripped to the bare minimum, this still life remains a meditative and mystical work of great beauty.

OTHER MASTERPIECES Saint Margaret of Antoich; *c.1630–1634; National Gallery, London, England* St Serapion; *1928; Wadsworth Athenaeum, Hartford, USA*

Gallery Guide

ANTWERP
Koninklijk Museum
voor Schone Kunsten
Leopold de Waelplein
B-2000 Antwerp
Belgium

AMSTERDAM
Stedelijk Museum
Paulus Potterstraat 13
1071 CX Amsterdam
Netherlands

BALTIMORE
Baltimore Museum of
Art
Art Museum Drive
Baltimore
MD 21218
USA

BASEL
Kunstmuseum
St-Alban-Graben 16
4010 Basel
Switzerland

BEDFORD
Cecil Higgins Art
Gallery and Museum
Bedford
MK40 3NY
England

BERLIN
Staatliche Museen zu
Berlin
Preussischer
Kulturbesitz
Arnimallee 23/27
14195 Berlin
Germany

BIRMINGHAM
City of Birmingham
Museum & Art Gallery
Chamberlain Square
Birmingham
B3 3DH
England

BOLOGNA
Pinacoteca Nazionale
Via Belle Arti 56
40126 Bologna
Italy

BONN
Städtisches
Kunstmuseum
Bonn
Fredrich-Ebert-Allee 2
53113 Bon
Germany

BRISTOL
City Museum and Art
Gallery
Queens Road
Bristol
BS8 1RL
England

BRUGES
Memlingmuseum
Mariastraat 38
8000 Bruges
Belgium

BRUSSELS
Musées Royaux des
Beaux-Arts de
Belgique
Rue de la Reference, 3
1000 Brussels
Belgium

CAMBRIDGE, UK
Kettle's Yard
Cambridge
Cambridgeshire
CB3 0AQ
England

CAMBRIDGE, USA
Fogg Art Museum
Harvard University
32 Quincy Street
Cambridge
MA 02138
USA

CHANTILLY
Musée Condé
Château
60631 Chantilly
France

CHICAGO
Art Institute of
Chicago
111 S. Michigan Avenue
Chicago
IL 60603-6110
USA

CLEVELAND
Cleveland Museum of
Art
11150 East Boulevard
Cleveland
OH 44106
USA

COLOGNE
Michael Werner
Gallerie
Gertruden Strasse 24–28
Cologne 50667
Germany

Gallerie Rudolf
Zwirner
Albertusstr. 18
Cologne 50667
Germany

DRESDEN
Staatliche
Kunstsammlungen
Dresden
Theaterplatz 1
01067 Dresden
Germany

DÜSSELDORF
Kunstmuseum
Ehrenhof 5
40479 Düsseldorf
Germany

EDINBURGH
National Gallery of
Scotland
The Mound
Edinburgh
EH2 2EL
Scotland

ESSEN
Museum Folkwang
Goethestrasse 41
45128 Essen
Germany

FLORENCE
Gallerie degli Uffizi
Piazzale degli Uffizi
50122
Florence
Italy

Museo di San Marco
dell'Angelico
Piazza San Marco 1
50121 Florence
Italy

Museo dell'Opera di
Santa Maria del Fiore
Piazza Duomo 9
50122 Florence
Italy

Museo Nazional del
Bargello
Via del Pronconsolo 4
50122 Florence
Italy

Museo di Brancacci
Chapel
Santa Maria del
Carmine
Piazza del Carmine
50124 Florence
Italy

FONTAINEBLEAU
Musée National de
Château
77300 Fontainebleau
France

FUKUOKA
Fukuoka Prefectural
Museum of Arts
5-2-1 Tenjin
Chuo-ku
Fukuoka
Japan

GENEVA
Musée d'Art et
d'Histoire
2 rue Charles Galland
1211 Genevre 3
Switzerland

GLASGOW
Hunterian Art Gallery
University of Glasgow
Glasgow
G12 8QQ
Scotland

THE HAGUE
Mauritshuis
Korte Vijverberg 8
2513 AB
The Hague
Netherlands

HAMBURG
Hamburger Kunst
Halle
Glockengiesserwall
20095 Hamburg
Germany

LEEDS
City Art Gallery
The Headrow
Leeds
LS1 3AA
England

LEIPZIG
Museum Der
Bildenden Künste
Beethovenstr. 4
04107 Leipzig
Germany

LEUVEN
Museum Voor
Religieuzs Kunst
Sint-Pieterskert Grote
Markt
3000 Leuven
Belgium

LIÈGE
Musée d'Art Modern
et d'Art Contemporain
Parc de la Bouverie 3
4020 Liège
Belgium

LIVERPOOL
Tate Liverpool
Albert Dock
Liverpool
L3 4BB
England

Walker Art Gallery
William Brown Street
Liverpool L3 8EL
England

LONDON
Arts Council
Collection
14 Great Peter Street
London SW1P 3NQ
England

Courtauld Institute
Galleries
Somerset House
Strand
London WC2R 0RN
England

Harold Samuel
Collection,
Corporation of
London
Guildhall Library and
Art Gallery
Guildhall
Aldermanbury
London EC2P 2EJ
England

Imperial War Museum
Lambeth Road
London SE1 6HZ
England

Kenwood House
Hampstead Lane
London NW3 7JR
England

National Gallery
Trafalgar Square
London WC2N 5DN
England

Royal Academy of Arts
Burlington House
Piccadilly
London W1V 0DS
England

Tate Britain
Millbank
London SW1P 4RG
England

Tate Modern
Bankside
London SE1 9TG
England

Victoria & Albert
Museum
South Kensington
London SW7 2RL
England

Wallace Collection
Hertford House
Manchester Square
London W1M 6BN
England

MADRID
Museo Nacional del
Prado
Paseo del Prado 28014
Madrid
Spain

MANCHESTER
Manchester City Art
Gallery
Mosley Street
Manchester M2 3JL
England

Whitworth Gallery
University of
Manchester College
Oxford Road
Manchester M15 6ER
England

MELBOURNE
National Gallery of
Victoria
180 St Kilda Road
Melbourne
Australia

MEUDON
Musée Rodin
Villa Des Brillants
19 Avenue August-
Rodin
92190 Meudon
France

MEXICO CITY
Museo del Placio de
Bellas Aries
Av Juarez y Angela
Peralta
Colonia Centro
06050 Mexico, D. F.
Mexico

MILAN
Civica Galleria D'Arte
Moderna
Villa Reale
Via Palestro 16
20121
Milan
Italy

Pinacoteca di Brera
Via Brera 28
20121
Milan
Italy

MOSCOW
Pushkin Museum
Izobrazitelnych
Iskusstv
Ul Volchonka 12
121019 Moscow
Russia

**MÜLHEIM-AN-
DER-RUHR**
Städtsches Museum
Viktoriarl 1
45468 Mülheim-an-
der-Ruhr
Germany

MUNICH
Alte Pinakothek
Bayerische
Staatsgemäldesammlungen
Barerstr. 27
80333
Munich
Germany

NAPLES
Museo Nazionale di
Capodimonte
Palazzo Reale di
Capodimonte
80136 Naples
Italy

NEW YORK CITY
Metropolitan Museum
of Art
100 Fifth Avenue
NY 10028
USA

Museum of Modern
Art
11 West 53rd St
New York 10019
New York
USA

OSLO
Nasjonalgealleriet
Universitetsgata 13
0033 Oslo
Norway

PARIS
Musée National d'Art
Moderne
Centre Georges
Pompidou
75191 Paris
France

Musée du Louvre
Place du Carousel
75041 Paris
France

Musée d'Orsay
62 Rue de Lille
75007 Paris
France

Musée du Petit Palais
1 Avenue Dutuit
75008 Paris
France

PHILADELPHIA
Philadelphia Museum
of Art
26th St & Benjamin
Franklin
Parkway
PA 19130
USA

PORT SUNLIGHT
Lady Lever Art
Gallery
Port Sunlight L62 5EQ
England

POZNAN
Museum Narodowe
Al. Marcinkowskiego 9
61–745 Poznan
Poland

ROME
Monumenti Musei e
Gallerie Pontificie
1-00120 Vatican City
Rome
Italy

ST IVES
Tate Gallery
St Ives
Cornwall
TR26 1TG
England

ST LOUIS
St Louis Art Museum
Forest Park
MO 63110
USA

ST PETERSBURG
State Russian
Museum
Ul Inzenernaja 4
St Petersburg
Russia

Hermitage
Dworzowaja
Nabereshnaja
St Petersburg
Russia

SAN DIEGO
San Diego Museum of
Art
Balboa park
1450 El Prado
CA 92101
USA

SHEFFIELD
Sheffield City Art
Galleries
Surrey Street
Sheffield
S1 1XZ
England

SIENA
Museo dell'Opera del
Duomo
Pinacoteca Nazionale
Via San Pietro 29
53100 Siena
Italy

Museo Civico
Piazza del Campo
Palazzo
53100 Siena
Italy

SOUTHAMPTON
Southampton City Art
Gallery
North Guild
Civic Centre
Southampton
SO14 7LP
England

STUTTGART
Galerie der Stadt
Schlosspl 2
70173 Stuttgart
Germany

VALENCIA
I.V.A.M. Centre Julid
Gozalez Coll.
c/o Guillem de Castro
118
Valencia 46003
Spain

VENICE
Galleria
dell'Accademia
Campo della Carita
30121
Venice
Italy

Museo d'Arte
Moderna Ca Pesaro
S. Stae
Canale Grande
Venice
Italy

VIENNA
Albertina
Graphische Sammlung
Augustinerstr 1
1010 Vienna
Austria

Kunsthistorisches
Museum Wien
Burgring 5
1010 Vienna
Austria

Osterreichische
Galerie
Schloss Belevederf
Prinz-Eugen-Str 27
1037 Vienna
Austria

WASHINGTON DC
Hirshhorn Museum
Smithsonian Inst.
Seventh St &
Independence Avenue
S.W.
Washington D.C.
20560
USA

WIESBADEN
Museum Wiesbaden
Friedrich-Elbert-Allee 2
65185
Wiesbaden
Germany

WÜRZBURG
Residenz Würzburg
c/o Sailobund
Gartenverwaltung
Würzburg
Residenzpl 2
97070 Würzburg
Germany

ZÜRICH
Ammann Coll.
Restelbergstrasse 97
CH-8044 Zürich
Switzerland

Index

See contents (pp. 4–5) for main artist entries. Entries in **bold** indicate primary works included in this book.

Acknowledgements

Photographic Acknowledgements

AKG London 12, 63, 115, 130, 143, 151, 212, 260, 265, 277, 299, 312, 322, 359, 361, 366; Annely Juda, London 71,86; Acquavella Contemporary Art.Inc. 113; Arcaid/David Churchill 340; Arts Council Collection/South Bank Centre, London 22, 184, 209; Terry Atkinson 21; Gillian Ayres 24; Beaux Art Gallery, London 35; Bridgeman Art Library, London 10, 14, 16, 17, 23, 26, 27, 28, 30, 31, 32, 33, 36, 38, 40, 41, 43, 46, 47, 48, 49, 50, 53, 58, 59, 60, 61, 62, 64, 66 (Phillips, The Fine Art Auctioners), 67, 68, 69, 70, 72, 73, 74, 76, 77, 78, 81, 85, 87, 88, 89, 91, 95, 96, 97, 98, 99, 101, 103, 105, 108, 110, 111, 112, 116, 118, 119, 120, 121, 122, 125, 127, 129, 132, 133, 134, 136, 137, 138, 140, 144, 147, 150, 152, 154, 155, 160, 161 (Fratelli Fabbri, Milan), 162, 165, 166, 169, 174, 175, 176, 181, 185, 188, 190, 192, 194, 195, 198, 201, 202, 226, 229, 230, 231, 233, 236, 237, 238, 239, 240, 243, 244, 245, 248, 249, 251, 252, 253, 254, 255, 257, 258, 261, 262, 267, 270, 271, 272, 275, 276 (Index) 2787, 282, 283, 285, 292, 293, 294, 300, 301, 302, 304, 305, 306, 307, 309, 310, 311, 314, 315, 316, 317, 321, 323, 324, 325, 326, 328, 329, 330, 332, 334, 335, 336, 338, 344, 349, 350, 351, 352, 353, 355, 356, 357, 358, 360, 364, 370, 371, 372, 376, 378, 379, 380, 381, 384, 386, 387, 389, 391, 392, 393; Bridgeman Art Library/Christie's, London 51, 191, 256, 266; Bridgeman Art Library/Giraudon 94, 106, 109, 142, 145, 146, 200, 228, 273, 303, 308, 363, 367; Helen Chadwick 79; Courtesy Jim Dine and Alan Cristea Gallery, London 114; flowers East, London 197; courtesy Andy Goldsworthy and Michael Hue Williams Gallery, London 156; Estate of Keith Haring 172; Susan Hiller 180; Jay Jopling/Edward Woodman 173; Lisson Gallery, London 100, 107, 207; Marlborough Fine Art, London 211, 290, 313; Estate of Robert Mapplethorpe 250; Anthony d'Offay, London 242, 319; Jules Olitski 287; Saatchi Collection, London 157, 183, 342, 385, 383; Through The Flower, Albuquerque 83; Waddington Galleries, London 320;l Gallerie Michael Werner, Koln 199, 297.

Nicola Hodge and Libby Anson would like to thank the following people who have assisted in the preparation of The A–Z of Art. Thanks are due to Georgia Treacher for preparing entries for Renaissance artists, and to Pauline Hodge for her research into nineteenth-century American art. We would also like to thank Tessa Rose for her editorial judgement, Sarah Larter and other members of the production team. Finally our thanks are due to Bob Jardine and Tony Chandler for their advice and support.